CHARISMS FOR MINISTRY:

An Exploration of how the Manifest Charisms in the Early Church can be Recovered and Restored for Ministry in the Catholic Church Today.

AYO EMMANUEL EFODIGBUE, Ph.D.

Xulon PRESS

Charisms For Ministry:
An Exploration of how the Manifest Charisms in the Early Church can be Recovered and Restored for Ministry in the Catholic Church Today.
by Ayo Emmanuel Efodigbue, Ph.D.

Printed in the United States of America.

ISBN 9781498498098

www.xulonpress.com

Aeja,

Blessings with oceans of love,

Author ACC[illegible]

12/14/2017

Dedication

To my dear mother, Helen Efodigbue,
who nursed me as a sickly child, and taught me how to talk and read.
To Sharron and Mike Buchart, for their unwavering love and concern.

CONTENTS

CHAPTER ONE

The Trails of the Spirit in the Old Testament

CHAPTER TWO

The Spirit in the New Testament

CHAPTER THREE

The Manifestations and Use of Charisms in the First Eight Centuries of the Church

CHAPTER FOUR
Charisms can Be Retrieved

CHAPTER FIVE
Work Yet to Be Done

Resources and Bibliography

Abstract

G od gave chosen persons in the Old Testament special graces to fulfill their assigned tasks. Correspondingly, I believe every Catholic Christian receives *charisms* from God for ministry in the Church. I use *charisms* here, unambiguously, as gifts of the Holy Spirit that were evident in the early Church and Charismatic Churches today. The use of charismatic gifts was common in the early Church. However, manifestations and practice gradually disappeared. What happened? Were the *charisms* meant only for the early Church? Can the use of charismatic gifts be recovered? *Charisms* are the Church's heritage. This book explores how the early Christians' experience of the Holy Spirit established *charisms* for ministry and made Christianity spread all over the world. It examines why the use of charismatic gifts disappeared and shows how *charisms* were part of the early Church's liturgical life with the evidence of manifestations and utilization in the first eight centuries of the Church. It unravels how *charisms* can be retrieved and revived for ministry in the Catholic Church today.

Scope and Purpose of this Book

This book examines *charisms* as manifested in the early Church. It engages a biblical exegetical method to consider 1 Corinthians 12:8–11 and through a critical historical-theological method approach, study the following: (a) the trails of the Spirit in the Old Testament, which entails the evolutionary and conceptual understanding of the Spirit, (b) the footprints of Holy Spirit in the New Testament writings and particularly focus on Luke's Gospel and Acts of the Apostles, (c) the manifestations and use of *charisms* in the first eight centuries of the Church, (d) the reasons for the disappearance of the use of *charisms*, (e) and establish that *charisms* are not foreign but the Church's inheritance, they can, therefore, be recovered and restored for ministry in the Catholic Church today.

Methodology

This book adopts a theological-historical recovery approach that seeks to trace and retrieve a practice that evolved due to an experiential encounter with the Holy Spirit by the early Christians. It also applies a scriptural-theological-exegetical method for its investigations.

Biographical Data

Ayo Emmanuel Efodigbue is a priest of the Missionary Society of Saint Paul of Nigeria and currently the pastor of Our Mother of Mercy Catholic Church, Ames, Texas, and Sacred Heart Catholic Church in Raywood, Texas. He had two years of Ignatian Spirituality formation with philosophical and theological studies at the National Missionary Seminary of Saint Paul, Abuja, Nigeria, where he earned his Bachelor of Philosophy in 1990, and Master of Divinity in 1994.

Ayo Efodigbue is the son of Matthew and Helen Efodigbue. He grew up in a traditional, polygamous Nigerian home. His mother was the second of his deceased father's five wives. His parents were not Christians. He did not grow up going to church. However, his half-brother's education at a Catholic School drew him to the Catholic faith, where he was baptized and confirmed at 16 years of age in 1979. He attended Awori College, where he obtained his West African Examination Council Certificate. After his graduation from High School in 1982, he worked in Anne Marie Cosmetics Nig. Limited Lagos Nigerian for two years as a sales representative. Captivated by the great works of the Irish Missionaries in Nigeria, he entered the Missionary Seminary of Saint Paul in November 1985 and was ordained a missionary priest on July 2, 1994. In addition to being a full-time pastor, in May 2012, Efodigbue completed his second master's degree (Magna Cum Laude) in Pastoral Studies at Loyola University, New Orleans, Louisiana.

So far, Ayo has had the rewarding privilege and challenges of ministering in four countries, eight dioceses, and 10 Catholic Church parishes. In his faith journey through his different missions, he has witnessed the great hunger that has always plagued the human heart throughout history. He believes every Christian has the tools or *charisms* as manifested in 1 Corinthians 12:8–11. These are, wisdom, knowledge, faith, healing, miracles, prophecy, discernment, tongues, and the interpretation of tongues to be a blessing in the world. The Church only needs to empower her members in using their *charisms* to make the world a better place.

Ayo developed a passion for the *charisms* as manifested in the early Church when he did not understand and could not find an explanation to people resting in the Spirit in prayer services. Since he was still new to the experience of the workings of the Spirit and wanted to learn more about it, he started searching the scriptures and charismatic magazines for educational help.

His search led him to visit and spend three days in Pretoria with Fr. Eugene Clarkson, M.S.C., who was at that time the chaplain of the Charismatic Renewal in South Africa. He explained his experiences and bewilderment to Clarkson who was delighted to give him the following books to read: *The Power to Heal* by Francis MacNutt, *Deliverance Prayer* by Mathew and Dennis Linn, and *Resting in the Spirit* by Robert DeGrandis. These books enlightened and armed him with a better understanding of the manifestations of the gifts of the Holy Spirit.

He returned to Botswana prepared to give some explanation to whoever needed to know more about the marvels in the prayer events. He was not aware that when the news reached the Bishop, he would not have an opportunity to explain what had happened at the prayer sessions in his parish. He was withdrawn from Botswana. Contrary to the views of some that he was destroying the Catholic faith, his parish was packed each Sunday; even with people from other Church denominations. He gave retreats and revivals all over Botswana. Ayo had the privilege of attending the 10th International Leadership Conference of the Charismatic Catholic Renewal at Fiuggi, Italy between October 26 and 31, 1998. During the Congress, he met Linda Schubert, Ralph Martin, and some other leaders from other parts of the world. The conference affirmed his experiences as regular occurrences at Pentecostal and charismatic gatherings. He wanted to know more about the Holy Spirit and the *charisms* in the Church, and if those manifestations were at odds with the spirituality of the Catholic Church

After many years of searching, he discovered that the *charisms* are the Church's heritage. He is of the opinion that baptism in the Holy Spirit should be part of the Church's faith formation and parish life. He also thinks that the Church leadership should incorporate charismatic spirituality into the academic curriculum of the seminaries. It will help ministers in the Church enrich and give historical and theological understanding to their experience of baptism in the Holy Spirit if they have had one. Furthermore, a grounded study in charismatic spirituality will help priests to discern well the different manifestations of the *charisms* among their parishioners. It will also assist them to have a doctrinal appreciation of what is operative in the lives of those who readily use their gifts. In conclusion, Ayo believes that the Church that explores and uses her *charisms* through her children is a Church with a life for the future. He holds a Ph.D. in Theological Studies from the Graduate Theological Foundation.

Acknowledgments

I want to give all praise and adoration to God, whose abiding presence has continually inspired and empowered me with *charisms* to be God's embodied presence to be a blessing to all who meet with me each moment of my life.

Without the immeasurable assistance of my supervisor (Rev. Dr. Jorge R. Colón León), this work would not have seen the light of day. I would like to express my deep appreciation to him for his patience, motivation, careful supervision, and guidance through my Ph.D. studies.

I am grateful to Rev. Prof. George Montague, whose counsel in our telephone conversation helped to shape my thoughts on *Charisms* for Ministry in the Church Today. I am appreciative for the resources he recommended for my Independent studies and research. I am indebted to Rev. Dr. Cletus Obijiaku, MSP and Rev. Dr. Kenneth Adesina whose scriptural interpretive guidance and criticisms helped to polish chapter two of this work.

I am delighted to all who have read my text and offered valuable suggestions and words of support. I am especially thankful for the following: Dr. Aje-Ori Agbese, Rev. Augustine Inwang, MSP, Rev. Dr. Emmanuel Agbor, MSP, Rev. Dr. Anthony Anike, MSP, Sharron and Mike Buchart, Teresa Buoninfante, Gail and A.J. Gomez, Gloria and Deacon Ed Gauthreaux, Dr. Donna Gauthreaux, Pat and Leo Brooks, Gail Sandles, Effie Sharp, Patricia Chargois, Alma Hodge, Jerry LaChapelle, Brenda Trahan, and Rev. Dr. Samuel Paintsil.

I am beholden to my mother, Helen Efodigbue, who nursed me as a sickly child, and taught me how to talk and read; my sister, a Poor Clare nun, Mary Julie Efodigbue; Anthonia Chinyeaka Okolie; parishioners of St Catherine of Siena, Donaldsonville, LA, Our Mother of Mercy, Ames, TX, and Sacred Heart, Raywood, TX, for their continued prayers, understanding, and words of encouragement.

Foreword

————— ⚜ —————

The title of our author's research work on "charism" is very apt and relevant in today's contemporary world where secularism, emotivism, pragmatism, and nihilism have not only redefined human life and existence, but have systematically elevated man to the position of a deity. The natural consequences of this are confused and conflicting values expressed in despair and auto-destruction. The place of God and the Holy Spirit in the human day-to-day living is often doubted and called to question. With this research on "manifest charisms," our author makes a passionate appeal to the consciences of his readers to pause and call to mind the historical religious truth regarding the place and importance of the Holy Spirit both in individual personal lives and in the lives of the Church. From the theological perspective, "charism" is understood, as that supernatural gift bestowed by the Holy Spirit for the building up and maintenance of the body of Christ, the Church, conceived both as the people of God[1] and as the concrete place of worship. This gift has its source in the *charis*, i.e. grace or unmerited favor, which comes from God and is destined for "the common good" (1 Cor. 12:7), the well-being of the people of God.[2]

Our author shares in this understanding of "*charism*" and through this research; he uses the biblical exegetical tools to explore this noble theme from the perspectives of the Old and New Testaments. Practical lived experience of faith in God within an ecclesial ambience, a living church community, is an indication of the divine presence, which enables the coming together of believers through the Holy Spirit. Cognizant of this fact, our author makes recourse to the early church experience of "charism" to trace its origin and connectivity to

---

[1] SECOND VATICAN COUNCIL, Dogmatic Constitution on the Church, *Lumen Gentium*, 9, in A. FLANNERY (ed), *Vatican Council II: The Conciliar and Post Conciliar Documents,* vol. I, New York 1998⁴, pp. 359–360.

[2] WILFRID HARRINGTON, "Charism" in JOSEPH A. KOMONCHAK, MARY COLLINS, DERMOT A. LANE (eds), *The New Dictionary of Theology,* Theological publications, Bangalore 1996, p. 180.

the contemporary church experience of "charisms." History has a natural way of setting the pace, correcting anomalies, and enabling a researcher to see points of variance and convergence in its developments. From the historical perspective, our author notes that the prevalent influence and affinity of the early church to charisms seems to have been reduced or have been lost over the years due to ideological and structural ecclesiastical factors. God is one and unchangeable. The Holy Spirit remains the Truth and the Advocate, the one who leads us to the complete truth and who is ever with us all through to eternity. From his experience of God and the Holy Spirit in his pastoral ministry, our author is convinced that there is a serious need for a rebirth in the Holy Spirit, a forceful re-enactment of the role, the place and importance of the Holy Spirit in the pastoral ministries of clerics and lay faithful. This conviction is what has inspired him to make this clarion call for the recovery and restoration of "charisms" in pastoral ministry in the Catholic Church today.

Having had the privilege of reading through this beautiful piece of writing, I dare to say that it is inspiring and enriching. It brings to simple minds the truth of the love of God for man in giving us His only son and how we, as God's children, can benefit from the rich reservoir of divine wisdom through a personal encounter with God in the Holy Spirit. It is through this encounter that we experience the divine outburst of "charisms," unmerited favors, destined for the common good for the glory of God and the sanctification of the church community and the individual self. I, therefore, recommend this research work for anyone who is seeking for intimacy with God and the deepening of this intimacy through a personal encounter with the Holy Spirit.[3]

Rev. Dr. Benjamin Okon, MSP

---

[3] For concrete ways of deepening intimacy with God through the Holy Spirit, cfr. BENJAMIN OKON, *Seed of Glory: Journeying with the Holy Spirit,* Xlibris-Lightening Source, United Kingdom 2016, pp. 192-202.

Initial Understanding of
Charisms and General Introduction

M y ministry as a priest exposes me to experiences for which my spiritual, philosophical, and theological studies in the seminary did not prepare me. As I sought to resolve pastoral questions on *charisms* in the exercise of my ministry, it becomes clearer through reading some literature that the manifestations I see and experience were biblical and grounded historically in the Catholic tradition. It took me some years to have this understanding.

My initial understanding of *charisms* resonated with that of Cardinal Ruffini at the Second Vatican Council. He asserted that *charisms* were the extraordinary manifestations of the Holy Spirit in the early Church and were no longer necessary for the Church's existence.[4] Rufini's cessationist view, which was also held by Augustine, had profound consequences in Catholic theological schools. Many Catholic theologians and ecclesiastical leaders retain a dismissive attitude whenever the topic of *charisms* is mentioned. During my theological formation years, I was not exposed to any courses on *charisms* as manifested in the early Church. Most of my lecturers believed only saints possessed *charisms*. I personally assumed God compensated the saints with extraordinary gifts because of their ascetic and strange lifestyles. I thought the established sacramental structure of the Church was divinely instituted and fixed. I did not know the Church took years to evolve and is subject to the transformational molding of the Holy Spirit in each generation. When I read about the manifestations of *charisms* in the Old Testament, I thought they were mythical. My reaction to hearing about such happenings in Pentecostal churches was skepticism.

My understanding echoed with the traditional understanding of *charisms* as extraordinary signs of holiness.[5] I did not know ordinary people with common daily human experi-

---

[4] Edward P. Hahnenberg, *Ministries: A Relational Approach*. (New York: A Herder & Herder Book, The Crossroad Publishing Company 2003), 66.

[5] Francis A. Sullivan, *Charisms and Charismatic Renewal: A Biblical and Theological Study*. Eugene, Oregon: (Wipf & Stock Publishers 2004), 14..

ential struggles could have *charisms*. My worldview started changing when I encountered manifestations of *charisms* in my ministry and work with lay Catholics in the Church. This experience was reiterated by Cardinal Suenens's response to Cardinal Ruffini's refusal to appreciate that many lay faithful are gifted with *charisms* when he wrote, "Does not each and everyone of us here know of laymen and lay women in his diocese who are indeed called by the fields of catechesis, evangelization, apostolic action in all its ramifications, in social work and charitable activity ... Without these *charisms*, the ecclesiastical ministry would be impoverished and sterile."[6] I never envisioned that Pentecost could be reenacted and experienced in our age and time. The Holy Spirit is still in the business of releasing the tangible manifestation of God's merciful love on God's people. It is my quest to unravel how God can still use the most unlikely persons as God's instrumental healing love through God's outpouring of charismatic gifts for ministry in the Catholic Church.

The Spirit's story, which started with creation[7] gave birth to all things, made incarnation and the birth of the Church possible.[8] Consequently, the Church flourished through the willingness and openness of the early Christians to the Holy Spirit, who granted *charisms* to them for divine purposes.[9] The use of *charisms* was common and also part of the Liturgical life of the early Church.[10] However, manifestations and practice gradually disappeared. What happened? Were the *charisms* meant only for the early Church? I do not think so. Regrettably, Saint Augustine (354-430), John Chrysostom (AD 347-407), and some theological interpreters believe the doctrine of *cessationism*, which declares that the manifestations of the gifts of the Holy Spirit ended with the twelve apostles.[11] This perception has a

---

[6] Leon-Joseph Cardinal Suenens, Pp. 216-17. Quoted in Ibid., 11.

[7] Denis Edwards, *Breath of Life: A Theology of the Creator Spirit*. Maryknoll. (New York' Orbis Books, 2004), 64.

[8] Ibid., 30.

[9] Alan Schreck. *The Gift: Discovering the Holy Spirit in Catholic Tradition*. (Brewster, Massachusetts: Paraclete Press 2013), 12.

[10] Kilian McDonnell, K. & George T. Montague, *Christian Initiation and Baptism in the Holy Spirit: Evidence from the First Eight Centuries* (2nd ed.). (Collegeville, Minnesota: The Liturgical Press 1994), 115.

[11] See Philip Schaff, *The Complete Works of Saint Augustine* Edited. Translated by Marcus Dods. (Kindle Edition 2013) In City of God, Book 22 Chapter 8-10, Augustine alluded to the miracles that no longer persisted; "Why, they say, are those miracles, which you affirm were wrought formerly, wrought no longer? I might, indeed, reply that miracles were necessary before the world believed, in order that it might believe." See also the works of Saint John Chrysostom, translated edited by Philip Schaff and translated by Marcus Dods, Chrysostom in preaching on 1 Corinthians XII, 1&2, (Kindle Locations 68597-68600). Kindle Edition.

profound impact on the evolutionary understanding and practice of *charisms* in the Church today. Francis A. Sullivan, S.J., a theologian, noted with bewilderment that at the time of the Second Vatican Council, there were no articles published on *charisms* in the prestigious *Dictionnaire de Theologie Catholique!*[12] Nonetheless, the Lord, the giver of life, the Holy Spirit, cannot be concealed perpetually. The Holy Spirit will always find a way of self-revelation in people's lives. Accordingly, with the growing interest in a search for an experiential encounter with God, the person of the Holy Spirit has been rediscovered in recent times. Beyond the hustling and bustling for material acquisition that characteristically defines the modern person, there is a hunger for the exploration to experience the supernatural. Many Christians have delightfully experienced a fresh outpouring of the Holy Spirit on them in Pentecostal and Charismatic Churches. These manifestations are not new occurrences. Ecclesiastical historical scholars have shown that these happenings have always been a part of the Church's tradition. John Chrysostom asserted that during his time, *charisms* were received within the liturgy: "whoever was baptized at once spoke in tongues, and not only in tongues, but many prophesied; some performed many other wonderful works."[13]

In the fall of 1962, John XXIII convoked the Second Vatican Council. He invoked the Holy Spirit and prayed for a new Pentecost. While he entreated that the Holy Spirit renewed God's wonders on earth, he was asking for a total renewal of the Church. One of the renewals experienced by the Church was the introduction of ecumenical dialogue after the Council. The interactions with members of other Pentecostal Churches exposed some Catholics to Charismatic gifts. Some students and Catholic theology professors gathered at Duquesne University in Pittsburg for a retreat, and they were filled with the Holy Spirit as on the day of Pentecost. Their experience of the manifestation of the Holy Spirit and readiness to share their story gave birth to the Catholic Charismatic Renewal in 1967.[14] The Holy Spirit left an indelible print of the greatest of all the gifts on the beneficiaries, which was love (1 Cor. 13:13). In narrating the overwhelming impression of their Pentecostal experience, Patty Gallagher Mansfield said, "But the most important gift was the fruit of love which bound the whole community together. In the Lord's Spirit we found a unity we had long tried to achieve on our own."[15] The extraordinary nature of these experiences in Catholic circles raised questions about theological and doctrinal justifications. Nevertheless, it has

---

[12] Sullivan, Op. cit. 9.

[13] Quoted in Kilian McDonnell & George T. Montague, *Fanning The Flame: What Does Baptism in the Holy Spirit Have to Do with Christian Initiation?* (Collegeville, Minnesota: The Liturgical Press 1991), 18-19.

[14] Sullivan, op. cit., 14.

[15] Vinson Synan. *The Century of the Holy Spirit: 100 Years of Pentecostal and Charismatic Renewal.* (Nashville: Thomas Nelson 2001), 209-210. Patty Gallapher Mans eld was one of the Catholic students present at the Duquesne University on February 18, 1967.

been established that *charisms* are the Church's heritage as demonstrated by the works of Killian McDonnell, O.S.B. and George T. Montague, S.M.; Christian Initiation and Baptism in the Holy Spirit, evidence from the First Eight Centuries and Fanning the Flame. Though the Charismatic Catholic Renewal has brought many Catholics to have a tangible experience of the gifts of the Holy Spirit, the group is still viewed with suspicion among some members of the hierarchy and clergy. There has been a lingering mistrust regarding the use of *charisms* as manifested in the early Church. Consequently, this book demonstrates how *charisms* were part of the early Church's liturgical life with the evidence of manifestations and utilization in the first eight centuries of the Church.[16] It examines why the use of *charisms* disappeared and unravels how *charisms* can be recovered and restored for ministry in the Catholic Church today.

This book, through a scriptural-theological-exegetical method, traced what is now known as the Holy Spirit in the New Testament to be the Spirit of God in the OT. Though there were conceptual shifts in understanding, however, the basic perception of the Spirit as animator persists. This study explores, (a) the trails of the Spirit in the OT, which entails the evolutionary and conceptual understanding of the Spirit, (b) the footprints of Holy Spirit in the New Testament writings and particularly focuses on Luke's Gospel, Acts of the Apostles and also examines 1 Corinthians 12:8-11 and Romans 12:6-8 through a critical scriptural-theological-exegetical method. The theological-historical recovery approach was used to trace and retrieve a practice that evolved due to an experiential encounter with the Holy Spirit by the early Christians, by examining, (c) the manifestations and use of *charisms* in the first eight centuries of the Church, (d) the reasons for the disappearance of the use of charisms, (e) and established that charisms are not foreign but the Church's inheritance, and consequently, can be recovered and restored for ministry in the Catholic Church today.

Chapter one deals with an initial understanding of *charisms* and how my ministry as a priest exposed me to desire to understand more about the manifestations and use of *charisms*, especially as manifested and applied in the early Church. Through a theological reflection on the Trails of the Spirit in the OT, the chapter also explored how the understanding of *ruach* as the breath of life, the source of life in Hebrew Scriptures, trickled into New Testament theology as the Holy Spirit, the giver of life.

Chapter two studies the Spirit in the NT but focuses on how the theological understanding of the movements of the Spirit in the OT shaped Luke's pneumatology. Consequently, discovering how Luke's insightful universalization of the Holy Spirit created an opening for any Christian to have access to the *charisms* for ministry, this understanding, is contrary to the OT's understanding where the *charisms* were restricted to some special people alone.

---

[16] McDonnell and Montague, *Christian Initiation and Baptism in the Holy Spirit: Evidence from the First Eight Centuries*, 91-251.

What empowers anyone for the mission is the Holy Spirit who pours out God's gifts on all who are willing and ready to be used by God. The Corinthian and Roman communities showed us how God's gratuitous gifts can enable anyone to be God's instrument of blessings in the world. Just like the Corinthian and Roman communities, every community is given God's free gifts for ministry depending on the needs and openness of the community to access the gifts for the service and growth of a given society.

Chapter three deals with the manifestations and use of *charisms* in the first eight centuries of the Church, by exploring how baptism in the Holy Spirit unlocked *charisms* for ministry and was part of the Church's liturgical life. Furthermore, I expounded on the following reasons why the *charisms* disappeared, (a) the prohibition of *Montanism,* (b) the authority of the charismatics became a threat to Episcopal authority and the Church order, (c) the conversion of Constantine and the Edict of Milan in AD 313, which made legitimization of Christianity possible, thereby creating a way for the declaration of Christianity as universal religion of the Roman Empire by Theodosius in AD 380, and (d) the spread of infant baptism and the separation of confirmation from the rite of baptism.[17]

It is my opinion the Church needs to be ever open for rebirth that retrieves buried treasures that I consider *charisms*. Though the *charisms* seemingly vanished in the understanding and usage as expressed in chapter four, they were not meant to disappear but persist with each epoch's understanding and accessibility of the actions of the Holy Spirit. I believe that the *charisms* that seemed to have vanished in its understanding and usage can be reclaimed and reinstated for ministry in the Church today. The positive proof we have about the prospect of recovery and restoration of *charism* in the Catholic Church is in the testimonies of 100 years of Pentecostal and charismatic renewal in the world. Millions of Christians all over the world have an experiential encounter with the Holy Spirit and have been able to access their *charisms* for their churches and the good of humanity. Though the Church has functioned for centuries without the full activation of the charisms in her members, it cannot continue this way. Without these *charisms*, the ecclesiastical ministry would be impoverished and sterile."[18] The Holy Spirit is still in the business of releasing the tangible manifestation of God's merciful love for God's people. That is why there has been a

---

[17] John C. Haughey, "Connecting Vatican II's Call to Holiness with Public Life", *Proceedings of the* CTSA55 (2000): 8-9. See also Kilian McDonnell and George T. Montague, *Christian Initiation and Baptism in the Holy Spirit: Evidence from the First Eight Centuries* (Collegeville, Minn.: Liturgical Press, 1991), 83-342. Cited in Edward P. Hahnenberg, *Ministries: A Relational Approach.* (New York: A Herder & Herder Book, The Crossroad Publishing Company, 2003), 61.

[18] Leon-Joseph Cardinal Suenens, The Charismatic Dimension of the Church in Council Speeches of Vatican II, ed. Y. Congar, H. Küng, D.O'Hanlon, London/New York 1964, pp. 216-17. Quoted in Francis A. Sullivan. *Charisms and Charismatic Renewal: A Biblical and Theological Study.* (Eugene, Oregon: Wipf & Stock Publishers, 2004), 11.

resurgence of the *charisms* in the world among people of different Church denominations open up to God's gratuitous gifts.

In chapter four, I explored how the *charisms* can be recovered and restored, by proposing and elucidating on the following:

(a) The Body of Christ Includes Every Baptized Christian
(b) The Charismatic Renewal as a Revived Missing Part of the Church
(c) Baptism in the Holy Spirit as Part of Faith Formation and Parish Life.
(d) Intellectual and Experiential Balance of the Manifestations of the Holy Spirit
(e) Charismatic Spirituality as a Discipline of Study in Priestly Formation
(f) Expectant Spirituality

The entry of the Charismatic Renewal into the Catholic Church and the endorsement of all the popes since Pope John XXIII give us hope that one day, baptism in the Holy Spirit, which belongs intrinsically to Christian initiation, will be restored as part of the Church's sacramental life. It is baptism in the Holy Spirit that unlocks the *charisms* and without the manifestations and use of *charisms* by all members of the body of Christ, the body; the Church will not be holistic. I believe there is a perpetual need for an ongoing activation and bringing the hidden gifts of the Holy Spirit evident. For this purpose, Paul advised Timothy, "For this reason, I remind you to stir into flame the gift of God that you have through the imposition of my hands"[19] (2 Tim. 1:6).

---

[19] Senior Donald and Collins J. John, Eds., *The Catholic Study Bible*. Oxford: New York: Oxford UP, 2006), 1608.

Chapter One

The Trails of the Spirit in the Old Testament

⎯⎯⎯❧⎯⎯⎯

1.1 *Introduction*

> "Spirit, πνεῦμα (*pneuma*), spirit, wind; πνέω (*pneo*), to blow; πνοὴ (*pneo*), wind, breath; ἐκπνέω (*ekpneo*), breathe out; ἐμπνέω (*empneo*), to pant; πνευματικός (*pneumatikos*), spiritual; πνευματικως (*pneumatikos*), spiritually; θεόπνευστος (*theopneustos*), God-breathed, inspired by God."[20]

It is obvious from the above description that the word Spirit; *pneuma* in Greek and *ruach* in its Hebrew equivalent from the Septuagint (LXX), carry ambiguity of multiple meanings: "breath," "air," "wind," or "soul."[21] "As far as LXX translations of *rŭah* are concerned, *pneuma* predominates, for of the 377 instances of *rŭah* in Masoretic Text, 264 are translated by *pneuma*, the next most frequent rendering being *anemos*, wind, used 49 times."[22] *Rŭah* in the Old Testament carries the primary meaning of blowing air, which is the idea behind the implication of something immaterial but moves and impresses powerfully.[23] It denotes the

---

[20] Colin Brown, Ed. *The New International Dictionary of New Testament Theology, Vol. 3* (English language ed.). (Grand Rapids, Michigan: Zondervan and Exeter, Devon, U.K: The Paternoster Press Ltd 1986), 689.

[21] Veli-Matti Karkkainen, *Pneumatology: The Holy Spirit in Ecumenical International, and Contextual Perspective*. (Grand Rapids, Michigan: Baker Academic a division of Baker Publishing Group 2002), 25.

[22] Brown, op. cit., 690.

[23] Ibid.

force that gives life, acts and effects physical and spiritual activities.[24] The Priestly biblical tradition's pre-history account of Genesis revealed the breath of Yahweh as an enigmatic power of God in creation.[25] We see this power as the *Ruach Elohim* hovered over the formless void in Genesis 1:2, and from that, came forth creation.[26] *Ruach* is the dynamic, creative and active authority behind all things and the formation of the people of Israel. Furthermore, through the biblical metaphorical journeys of the Jewish people in the wilderness to their charismatic leaders, kings and prophets, *the Spirit of God* has always been the creative and abiding presence that orchestrates the history of the world.

As rendered above, the Hebrew word *ruach* mostly signifies both wind and spirit.[27] The implication of the variety of meanings some commentators believe can be resolved through a critical examination of each text of reference.[28] On the contrary, Pope John Paul II observed that, it is seldom feasible to resolve the exact meaning of the word *ruach* without confusion:

> *One might waver between wind and breath, between breath and spirit, or between created spirit and the divine Spirit. This multiplicity, however, has a certain wealth, for it establishes a fruitful communication between so many realities. In this regard it is better to give up in part the pretenses of neat reasoning in order to embrace broader perspectives. When we think of the Holy Spirit, it is useful to remember that his biblical name means "breath," and that it is related to the powerful blowing of the wind and to our own intimate breathing. Rather than clinging to an over-intellectual and arid concept, we will find it helpful to take in this wealth of images and facts. Unfortunately, translations are unable to convey them to us completely, for they are often obliged to choose other terms. To render the Hebrew word ruah, the Greek translation of the Septuagint uses twenty-four different terms,*

---

[24] Yves Congar, *I Believe in the Holy Spirit: The Complete Three-Volume Work in One Volume*. Translated by David Smith (New York: A Herder & Herder Book, 2006), 3.

[25] Lawrence Boadt, *Reading the Old Testament: An Introduction*. (New York, N.Y/Mahwah, N.J.: Paulist Press 1984), 20.

[26] Ibid.

[27] Raymond E. Brown, S.S., Joseph A. Fitzmyer, and Roland E. Murphy, O.CARM. Eds. *The New Jerome Biblical Commentary*. (Upper Saddle River, New Jersey: Prentice Hall 1990), 1290.

[28] John L. McKenzie, S.J., Ed. *Dictionary of the Bible*. (First Touchstone Edition). (New York. London. Toronto. Sydney: A Touchstone Book. Published by Simon & Schuster 1995), 840.

and so does not permit one to see all the connections between the texts of the Hebrew Bible.[29]

In the midst of varied uses of the term and interpretations of *ruach,* Pope John Paul II insists on the permeating principle of *ruach* as the source of life.[30]

Many commentators believe that the Old Testament authors used the word *ruach* as wind, breath, and spirit to express the different traits of their perceived understanding of the presence of God among them.[31] Interestingly, the use of *ruach* to designate the breath of God as the animating presence that gives and sustains life in all creatures has steadfastly and naturally influenced the evolutionary understanding of Spirit in New Testament theology as mentioned above.[32] The wind is the breath of God and also reflects the tangible manifestation of God's divine presence and dominance.[33] Because of the unpredictable nature of the wind, its mysterious might, and the way it enigmatically impacts nature, fittingly symbolized the divine in the Hebrew Bible.[34] In the Jewish understanding, the Spirit is a force that resides in the divine but displayed in astonishing external activities believed to have their origin in Yahweh. Consequently, the Spirit was not understood as a personal being in the Old Testament but a principle of action that belongs to Yahweh alone who communicates life to all living beings.[35] Life is considered to be a gift received from the divine and transferred through the breath of Yahweh. Thus, the Spirit becomes Yahweh's instrument of authority for creativity (Ps. 33:6), or a tool for the obliteration of the wicked[36] as seen in Isaiah 11:4, "He shall strike the ruthless with the rod of his mouth, and with the breath of his lips he shall slay the wicked."[37] Since all power is believed to come from Yahweh, the Spirit

---

[29] Pope John Paul II. *The Meaning of Spirit in the Old Testament.* Catechesis by Pope John Paul II on the Holy Spirit, General Audience, Wednesday 3 January 19. http://totus2us.com/teaching/jpii-catechesis-on- god-the-holy-spirit/the-meaning-of-spirit-in-the-old-testament/ (Accessed April 1, 2016).

[30] Ibid.

[31] http://danwebs.com/ruah/2NaturRuah&WritingsJPII.html Internet Resources (Accessed on April 1, 2016).

[32] Ibid.

[33] Brown, Fitzmyer, and Murphy, op. cit., 1290.

[34] Ibid.

[35] Ibid.

[36] McKenzie, op. cit., 840. The reference to the destruction of the wicked here points to the spirit of the messianic king (Isaiah 11:4).

[37] Collins and Senior, op. cit., 942.

becomes synonymous with anything that affects the people negatively, like anger.[38] Granted that it is anthropomorphic to attribute human vices to God, it was a way the Biblical authors expressed their understanding of the Divine at a time. The following text exposes this kind of thought: "At the blast of your nostrils the waters piled up, the flowing waters stood like a mound, the flood waters foamed in the midst of the sea" (Exod. 15:8).[39] Metaphorically, different kinds of spirits are perceived to emanate from Yahweh and they possess humans. Spirits are not visible but can be present at specific times and in certain places; they are beyond human control.[40] Both positive and negative spirits surpass human manipulative abilities. They are pictured at times in the Bible as if they have their personal beings, able to access human minds and hearts to influence them for good or evil. In 1 Kings 22:21-23, a lying spirit seduced Ahab, the book of Numbers 5:14 talks about the spirit of jealousy and in Zechariah 12:10, we read about the spirit of compassion and supplication.[41] Also 1 Samuel 16:14, speaks of the spirit of the Lord departing from Saul and an evil spirit from the Lord tormenting him. We see here the contingent nature of the spirits that possess the human person at different times.[42]

The Spirit is not inherently part of living beings but a gratuitous gift from the divine. It can come upon a person like it came upon Gideon (Judg. 6:34), and also fell upon Zechariah, son of Jehoiada the priest (2 Chron. 24:20). The Spirit can be poured out (Isa. 29:10; 44:3; Ezek. 39:29; Joel 2:28;), can leap upon (Judg. 14:6,19; 15:14; 1 Sam. 10:10; 11:6) and can be taken away at any time (Ps. 51:13) or depart from a person (1 Sam. 16:14).[43] It is noteworthy to acknowledge that the Spirit in the above texts is demonstrative of the enduring power from Yahweh that anointed the Judges, Kings and Prophets to exercise special missions at a particular point in time. With God's commanding absolute authority, the Biblical authors let us know that Yahweh can withdraw that spirit at will. In the case of Saul, it was because of his disobedience (1 Sam. 13-15). Saul's story validates the understanding that all living things receive life and sustenance from God, who has the power to determine when to take away their spirit (Ps. 104:29), which returns to Yahweh when they die (Eccles. 12:7).[44]

---

[38] McKenzie, op. cit., 840.

[39] Collins and Senior, op. cit., 87.

[40] Michael Downey, Ed. *The New Dictionary of Catholic Spirituality*. (Collegeville Minnesota: The Liturgical Press 1993), 911.

[41] Ibid.

[42] Collins and Senior, op. cit., 323.

[43] Brown, Fitzmyer, and Murphy, op. cit., 1290.

[44] Ibid.

In the texts above, the spirit of man and that of the beasts are not distinctive since they both receive life from Yahweh who can terminate that life at any time. Ecclesiastes 3:19 capture the common fate of man and beast alike:

> *For the lot of mortals and the lot of beasts is the same lot: The one dies as well as the other. Both have the same life breath. Human beings have no advantage over beasts, but all is vanity.*[45]

Man dies when the spirit is taken away and when Yahweh's spirit is removed from any other living beings, they die. Nonetheless, when Yahweh sends it forth His Spirit, they are created, and so renew the face of the earth.[46] Without prejudice to the Biblical authors' quest to moralize and teach about the consequential effects of disobedience being death, I believe the "*Creative Energy*"[47] of *Ruach* set in motion with the emergence of light is symbolized in the book of Genesis over fourteen billion years ago is still in progress.[48]

Genesis 1:2, records *Ruach Elohim*, the wind hovering over the chaotic waters. And in Genesis 1:3, the first creative activity of the divine is released through the expression, "Let there be light," and there was light."[49] The creative expression from Yahweh brought forth light from the chaos. From this light, all creation evolved. And in the metaphorical prediction of the destruction of the world through the flood the book of Genesis 6, verse 17 translates *Ruach* as the breath of life. The above text underscores that everything that enjoyed the breath of life from Yahweh would be destroyed. Our focus here is the life that comes from the breath of Yahwch.

Nevertheless, the term Spirit, *Ruach* has taken different expressions and interpretations all through biblical history. Conversely, it has retained the original impression the author of the book of Genesis implied of the spirit in the Old Testament, "a substantial source of force and activity," and the breath of God as the source of life.[50]

The story of the *Ruach Elohim, the spirit of God* (Gen. 1:2; Gen. 41:38; Exod. 31:3; 35:31; Num. 24:2; 1 Sam. 10:10; 11:6; 16: 15ff, 23; 18 19:20, 23; 2 Chron. 15:1; 2 Chr.

---

[45] Collins and Senior, op. cit., 829. See also Psalm 49:12.

[46] McKenzie, op. cit., 840.

[47] Thomas Berry, *The Dream of the Earth*. (San Francisco: Sierra Club Books 1988), 24.

[48] Ibid., 85.

[49] Collins and Senior, op. cit., 8.

[50] Donald L. Gelpi, S.J., *Pentecostalism: A Theological Viewpoint*. (New York/Paramus/Toronto: Paulist Press 1971), 43.

24:20), *Ruach Yahweh, the spirit of God* (Judg. 3:10; 6:34; 11:29; 13:25; 14:6, 19; 15:14; 1 Sam. 10:6; 16:13, 14; 19:20; 2 Sam. 23:2; 1 Kings 18:12; 22:24; 2 Kings 2:16; Isa. 11:2; 40:7, 13; 59:19; 61:1), *Ruach Adonai Adonai, the Spirit of the Lord God* (Isa. 61:1), *Ruach-El, the spirit of God* (Job 33:4), *Ruach Hakkodesh, the Holy Spirit* (Ps. 51:11),[51] unquestionably transcends the documented conceptual Jewish understanding in the Old Testament.[52] Though the author of the biblical book of Genesis did not set out to give a scientific account of the creation of the world, some schools of thought understand the account as a literal story. In Genesis, God created everything once and for all, which makes the universe, the earth, and the human persons finalized products. This worldview molded the pre-twentieth century science and theology.[53] However, with the introduction of contemporary biblical criticism, some scholars in the early 1900s started understanding the Genesis stories of creation as mythical, not to be understood literally.[54] This was a breath of fresh air in an age when old theologies could no longer stand the test contemporary scientific discoveries. Most ecclesiastical theologians are coming to grips with new discoveries about scriptural theological studies. Nonetheless, there are some apologetics that seek to establish and prove the historicity of everything in Jewish scriptures. From our knowledge of biblical scholarship and cosmology, the size and scale of the universe overshadow the worldview in the book of Genesis.[55] Against this background, I believe that the Old Testament's portrayal of the Spirit as the source of life has been insightful to science. Denis Edwards' quotation of Stephen Hawking succinctly brings out this point when he wrote: "What is it that *breathes fire* into the equations and makes a universe for them to describe?"[56] Denis Edwards asserts that God's spirit is the source of the fourteen billion years of the evolutionary process of the universe[57]. He calls this spirit, '*Creator Spirit.*'[58] Genesis 2:7, figuratively depicts the Spirit as the breath of God that makes the dust of the earth a living entity, breathes life into the dust

---

[51] Hebrew Names of God: *The Spirit of God as revealed in the Tanakh* http://www.hebrew4christians.com/Names_of_God/Spirit_of_God/Printer_Version/printer_version.html (Accessed April 1, 2016).

[52] Edwards, op. cit., 33.

[53] Brennan R. Hill, *Exploring Catholic Theology: God, Jesus, Church, and Sacraments.* (Mystic, Connecticut: Twenty–Third Publications 1995), 80.

[54] Ibid., 81.

[55] Ibid.

[56] Ibid.

[57] Ibid.

[58] Ibid.

of the earth and so becomes a living being.[59] It is explicable from this account that the action of the breath of God brought to life creatures on the face of the earth. In Jewish Scriptures, the Spirit is expressive of the presence and action of God as the one true God and maker of all things in the universe.[60] From our knowledge of cosmic science today, we know that the universe is still in the evolutionary process of attaining the fullness of God's full potential.

Consequently, there has also been an evolutionary process of understanding of the *Ruach* in Jewish Scriptures, which is not a static idea but has evolved to what we understand as the Holy Spirit today.[61] The God, who acts, works and gives life, did not reveal God-self in a single moment in history but through unceasing, progressive, and rough historical interactions between God and God's people.[62] The breath of God in the Old Testament is the basis of all life.[63] In the figurative account of human origin in the book of Genesis, the author creatively brings this understanding to light. The divine creator puts God's breath into the nostrils of the fashioned image of the human person to bring about life. The Jewish experience of a presence beyond the physical that protects and vivifies laid the foundation for the theological evolutionary understanding of Holy Spirit in the New Testament, which we shall treat in the next chapter. For now, let us continue to broaden our understanding of *Ruach*. Different biblical traditions and authors have used the term *ruach* but with nuances in their messages.

The spirit of Yahweh, *Ruach Yahweh* and the spirit of Elohim, *Ruach Elohim*, are understood and portrayed differently.[64] *Ruach Elohim* is a dispassionate force while *Ruach Yahweh* is an ardent force, which carries out the salvific works and judgment of Yahweh.[65] This spirit inspires prophecy (Num. 11:17ff; 24.2, 2 Sam. 23:2; 1 Chron. 12:18; Isa. 61:1; Mic. 3:8; Ezek. 2:2; 3:12, 14, 24; 8:3; 11:1, 5, 24; 37:1; 43:5; Neh. 9:30; Zech. 7:12)[66]. In the book of Joel 3:1-2, the messianic age will usher in a general outpouring of the spirit on all:

---

[59] Ibid., 35.

[60] Ibid.

[61] Pierbattistta Pizzaballa, OFM. *The Spirit in the Old Testament*. Franciscan Cyberspot, the "holy land" – quarterly published by the Franciscan Custody of the holy land. (Autumn 1998),–online version. http://www.christusrex.org/www1/ofm/mag/TSmgenB1.html (Accessed March 2, 2016).

[62] Ibid.

[63] Gelpi, op. cit., 43.

[64] McKenzie, op. cit., 841.

[65] Ibid.

[66] Ibid.

It shall come to pass, I will pour out my spirit upon all flesh. Your sons and daughters will prophesy, your old men will dream dreams; your young men will see visions. Even upon your male and female servants, in those days, I will pour out my spirit.[67]

It was *Ruach Yahweh* that inspired the prophetic Spirit that stirred up ecstatic worship in the sons of the prophets (1 Sam. 10:6, 10; 19:20, 23).[68] However, the Spirit of Yahweh that carried off Elijah cannot be said to be inspiring since it is an undisclosed agent (1 Kings 18:12; 2 Kings 2:16).[69] *Ruach Yahweh* is also depicted as a charismatic Spirit that imparts those chosen for ministerial offices in Israel the graces they need to carry out their assigned tasks:[70] "Judges (Judg. 3:10; 11:29; 6:34; 13:25; 14:6; 15:14), kings (1 Sam. 11:6; 16:13 f), in particular the messianic king (Isa. 11:2), the servant of the Lord (Isa. 42:1), Cyrus (Isa. 48:16), craftsmen (Exod. 31:3; 35:31)."[71] In the book of Judges, the Spirit was transient in allotting the gifts to those who were endowed with the Spirit for their assignments, but became permanent in David and the messianic king.[72]

1.2 *Metaphorical Expressions of the Spirit in the Old Testament*

Jewish scriptures present *Wind/Ruach* of the Lord as the fundamental instrument of God's activities on earth.[73] God's activities in the Old Testament were expressed in a Semitic language and in symbols and images because like all Semitic languages, Hebrew abhors abstract ideas.[74] There are different symbolic depictions of Spirit in the Old Testament. *Wind*, *Water* and *Fire* are the frequently used.[75] Water symbolizes purification and life-restoring

---

[67] Collins and Senior, op. cit., 1187.

[68] McKenzie, op. cit., 841.

[69] Ibid.

[70] Ibid.

[71] Ibid.

[72] Ibid.

[73] Lloyd Thomas, *Development in Understanding the Holy Spirit / Spirit of God*: As Reflected in the Old Testament Scriptures. http://www.lloydthomas.org/3-HolySpiritStudies/OTthink.html (Accessed February 2, 2016).

[74] Pizzaballa, op. cit., (Accessed March 2, 2016).

[75] Ibid.

grace of the Spirit of God: "I will sprinkle clean water over you to make you clean; from all your impurities and from all your idols I will cleanse you (Ezek. 36:25). "I will pour out water upon the thirsty ground, and the streams upon the dry land" (Isa. 44:3, 5-6). In John 3:1-21, the dialogue between Jesus and Nicodemus shows water as the symbol of God who purifies and gives life: " Amen, amen I say to you, no one can enter the kingdom of God without being born of water and spirit."[76] The blessing of water in the rite of Baptism in the Catholic Church beautifully sums up the grandeur of the Spirit of God in the waters:

> *Father, you give us grace through sacramental signs, which tells us of the wonders of your unseen power. In Baptism we use your gift of water, which you have made a rich symbol of the grace you give us in this sacrament. At the very dawn of creation your Spirit breathed on the waters, making them the wellspring of all holiness. The waters of the great flood you made a sign of the waters of Baptism, that make an end of sin and a new beginning of goodness. Through the waters of the Red Sea you led Israel out of slavery, to be an image of God's holy people, set free from sin by Baptism. In the waters of the Jordan your Son was baptized by John and anointed with the Spirit. Your Son willed that water and blood should flow from his side as he hung upon the cross. After his resurrection he told his disciples: "Go out and teach all nations, baptizing them in the name of the Father, and of the Son, and of the Holy Spirit." Father, look now with love upon your Church, and unseal for her the fountain of Baptism. By the power of the Spirit give to the water of this font the grace of your Son. You created man in your own likeness: cleanse him from sin in a new birth to innocence by water and the Spirit.[77]*

Fire is another significant symbolic illustration of the Spirit in the Old Testament. In Exodus 3:2, fire portrays the presence of God in the burning bush as God spoke to Moses. In Exodus 13:21-22, God's presence travelled with God's people as a pillar of fire at night and a pillar of cloud by day. In Isaiah 6:7, fire was used to purify the prophet of iniquity.[78] Consequently, the New Testament finds in the above symbolic expression the powerful manifestation of God on the day of Pentecost in Acts 2:3, "*Then there appeared to them*

---

[76] Ibid.

[77] St. Ladislav Catholic Parish! http://www.catholic.sk/main.php?page=183-en-Rite_of_Baptism (accessed March 2nd 2016).

[78] Pizzaballa, op. cit., (Accessed March 2, 2016).

tongues as of fire which parted and came to rest on each of them."[79] This understanding is also conveyed in the popular "Come Holy Ghost Creator Blest': "*O fount of life and fire of love, and sweet anointing from above.*"[80]

Nevertheless, the principal metaphor for *Ruach Yahweh,* Spirit of God in the Old Testament is wind; always connected with the manifestation of the activities of God.[81] Though *Ruach Yahweh* carries some vagueness as pointed out above,[82] we know that it denotes the life-vivifying force for humankind – the source of all living beings and finally, reflects the life of God-self, the power by which God acts and causes things to be at both the physical and spiritual level.[83] The appropriateness of this concept comes from the fact that, like the wind, Spirit cannot be seen physically, but remains God's active power in the universe and among God's people. In order to articulately present the reality of God's dynamic life giving-power,[84] the biblical authors used the Hebrew word, *ruah/ wind,* which always carries with it the concealed but visibly experienced presence of Yahweh.[85] While the Spirit is understood as God's breath of omnipotence, it is also a manifestation of the omniscience of God. This will later mirror in New Testament theology as it appropriates this dimension of the Spirit knowing all things. Saint Paul in his letter to the Corinthians expressed this thus: "For the Spirit scrutinizes everything, even the depths of God."[86]

The wind, on the other hand, represented the great *Breath/Nephesh* of God (2 Sam. 22:16), and the breath of the flesh is its *ruach*-wind (Gen. 6:17). The *Ruach* and *Nephesh* of Yahweh (Job 34:14) are used interchangeably but each with its own emphasis. God's breath is understood as God's life-giving power and will; it also conveys God's powerful presence among God's people.[87] This presence was the tangible manifestation of God's presence that was undeniably real as it is still apparent today. Like the wind, God cannot be seen; God's divine presence is strikingly visible in creation. In Romans 1:20, Paul says, "Ever since the

---

[79] Collins and Senior, op. cit., 1444.

[80] Pizzaballa, op. cit., (Accessed March 2, 2016).

[81] Ibid.

[82] Karkkainen, op. cit., 25.

[83] Congar, op. cit., 3.

[84] Edwards, op. cit., 35.

[85] Congar, op. cit., 3.

[86] Collins and Senior, op. cit., 1519.

[87] Thomas, op. cit., (Accessed on March 2nd 2016).

creation of the world, his invisible attributes of eternal power and divinity have been able to be understood and perceived in what he has made."[88]

In order to arrive at a real meaning of the word *ruach,* the particular context in which it refers to a given subject or intention has to be considered. "*ruah-pneuma,* for example, simply means the wind (as in John 3:8; Acts 2:1-4, 6). Elsewhere, it can mean the breath of God that communicates life (Exod. 15:8-10; Ps. 33:6) and consequently man's breath, the principle and sign of life (Gen. 7:22; Ps. 104: 29-30). It is also used very frequently in the book of Job.[89]

1.3 *The Evolutionary Understanding of the Spirit in the Old Testament*

The earliest understanding of Spirit as life-breath comes from the Old Testament Gen. 2:7.[90] This account metaphorically illustrates how the human person was fashioned out of the dust of the earth and breathed into. The author who is a Yahwist shows that life is a direct gift from God.[91] The author also perceived the Spirit as having a consuming influence that can make a person a seer, impact wisdom and inspire prophetic utterances. In the book of Numbers 24:2-4, a divine impulse came upon Balaam and made him prophesy in the name of the God of Israel.[92] The following Elohist accounts reflect how the spirit can come upon a person or persons. In Genesis 41:38, Pharaoh says of Joseph, "Can we find such a man as this who has the Spirit of God?"[93] Numbers 11:16ff records how God's Spirit came upon the seventy elders and also Eldad and Medad that were not in the camp, but they also prophesied. These men received the prophetic spirit in order to be effective pastoral leaders of the people of Israel.[94]

The word Spirit denotes God's creative, prophetic, or renewing presence to the people of Israel or to the world at large.[95] The spirit is known by what it produces. The Old Testament talks about the spirit of intelligence (Exod. 31:3), the spirit of wisdom (Deut. 31:3; 34:9), the spirit of jealousy (Num. 5:14) and 1 Samuel 16:14; 18:10 speaks of 'an evil spirit from the

---

[88] Collins and Senior, op. cit., 1496.

[89] George T. Montague, *The Holy Spirit: The Growth of a Biblical Tradition.* (Eugene, Oregon: Wipf & Stock Publishers 2006), 4.

[90] Ibid., 5-7.

[91] Ibid., 6-7.

[92] Ibid.

[93] Congar, op. cit., 5.

[94] Montague, *The Holy Spirit: The Growth of a Biblical Tradition*, 16.

[95] Edwards, op. cit., 35.

Lord.' It is only when its effect is prophecy, gifts of leadership and creation of religious men or women, can it be termed as Spirit or breath of God.[96] God is the life source and sustaining influence and strength of each person (Judg. 15:19; Num. 16:22). Everyone should consciously choose to worship God because the worship of idols amounts to nothing. They are lifeless; God's spirit is not in them (Jer. 10:14). All life resides in God (Ps. 33:6) because God is the giver and protector of life (Isa. 42:5; Ps. 31:5).[97] The worship of deities that are not the God of Israel is synonymous with being in bondage; and as such deities have no source of life. Psalm 106:28 declares in an outcry against the dumbness of the people's decision to worship Baal: "They joined in the rites of Baal of Peor, and ate food sacrificed to dead gods."[98]

1.4 *The Action of the Breath of Yahweh*[99]

The Deuteronomist tradition presents God's manifest powerful presence through God's breath upon individuals who experience a mighty charismatic surge of God's spirit taking over them (Judg. 14:6; 1 Sam. 16:13) and "clothe" (equip) them to perform powerful works (Judg. 3:34ff).[100] This same Spirit enables human beings to carry out extraordinary missions.[101] The book of Judges calls such charismatic leaders warriors. The following Judges are examples of charismatic gifts coming upon individuals.

Othniel: "The spirit (breath) of the Lord came upon him" (Judg. 3:10).
Gideon: "The spirit (breath) of the Lord took possession of Gideon" (6:34).
Jephthah: "The spirit (breath) of the Lord came upon Jephthah" (11:29).

Samson: "And the spirit (breath) of the Lord began to stir him … (13:25); 'And the spirit of the Lord came mightily upon him and he tore the lion asunder … and he had nothing in his hand' (14:6); 'And the spirit (breath) of the Lord came mightily upon him and he went down to Ashkelon and killed thirty men of the town.' (14:19).[102]

---

[96] Congar, op. cit., 4.

[97] Karkkainen, op. cit., 26.

[98] Collins and Senior Donald, op. cit., 760.

[99] Congar, op. cit., 5.

[100] Montague, *The Holy Spirit: The Growth of a Biblical Tradition*, 18.

[101] Ibid., 27.

[102] Congar, op. cit., 6.

The unusual and impulsive experiences of being overcome by the breath-spirit were common occurrences in the Old Testament times especially during and after the time of the Judges. Samuel, Saul, and David all experienced the sudden possession of the breath-spirit at different times. When David was anointed by Samuel, "the spirit of the Lord came mightily upon him from that day forward" (1 Sam. 16:13). David's destiny, without a doubt, took a resolutely good turn to fulfill God's divine plan and with God's spirit repeatedly protecting him from harm.[103] In 2 Samuel 7:12-16, Nathan prophesied about the family of David:

> *When your days have been completed and you rest with your ancestors, I will raise up your offspring after you, sprung from your loins, and I will establish his kingdom. He it is who shall build a house for my name, and I will establish his royal throne forever. I will be a father to him, and he shall be a son to me. If he does wrong, I will reprove him with a human rod and with human punishments; but I will not withdraw my favor from him as I withdrew it from Saul who was before you. Your house and your kingdom are firm forever before me; your throne shall be firmly established forever.*[104]

The prophecy of Isaiah 11:1-3, alluded to Nathan's prediction:

> *But a shoot shall sprout from the stump of Jesse, and from his roots, a bud shall blossom. The Spirit of Lord shall rest upon him: A spirit of wisdom and of understanding, A spirit of counsel and of strength, a spirit of knowledge and of fear of the Lord, and his delight shall be the fear of Lord.*[105]

The genealogies recorded in Matthew 1:1-16, and Luke 3:23-37, attest to the fulfillment of the above prophecy.[106] The Church fathers in formulating the Nicene Creed in AD 381, insightfully depicted the Holy Spirit has the one who has spoken through the prophets.[107] The early Christians believed the Spirit that brought the conception and birth of Jesus was the same Spirit that inspired the prophecies of old.[108] In his book, *I Believe in the Holy Spirit*, Yves Congar

---

[103] Ibid.

[104] Collins and Senior, op. cit., 347.

[105] Ibid., 942.

[106] Congar, op. cit., 6.

[107] Ibid.

[108] Ibid.

made reference to Targum on Isaiah 6 and H. Sahlin. He asserts that though prophecies were not always attributed to the breath of God during the ninth to the eighth centuries BC, the idea gained prominence during the Deuteronomic period and the exile, especially in Ezekiel (Ezek. 2:2; 11:5; see also Isa. 48:16; 61:1) and also in post-exilic Judaism (Zech. 7:12; 2 Chron. 15:1; 20:14; 24:20).[109]

1.5 *Spirit In the Prophetic Books*

Ruach Yahweh interestingly seems to have featured more in the prophecies of Isaiah, Ezekiel, and Joel.[110] In Isaiah, the word *rŭah* appears about fifty times,[111] and the prophet uses the word signifying creatures as having their source in the breath of God.[112] In the midst of catastrophic experiences of the people of Israel at a time, Isaiah prophesied hope and resurrection (7:10ff; 28:5-6; 31:3, 32:15-18; 37:21-35; 42:1; 60-61; 63:7-14).[113] In Ezekiel, the word *ruach* is used forty six times.[114] At the heart of the devastating pain of being in exile, Ezekiel gave hope to the people. He also envisaged their returning to normalcy and new life because Yahweh's Spirit could animate dry bones to come back to life.[115]

However, the pre-exilic prophets, Amos, Hosea, Jeremiah, and Micah, were disenchanted with the corrupt practices of professional prophets who were brought over to prophesy good fortunes for corrupt kings. They all distanced themselves from the phenomenal seizures of the spirit and focused on God's word in challenging the people to return to their God.[116] Isaiah was concerned with judgment and salvation (4:4; 28:5-6).[117] The prophet believed the coming messiah would establish God's eschatological kingdom of peace and justice (11:2) and the outpouring

---

[109] Ibid.

[110] Congar, op. cit., 7.

[111] Ibid. Taken from Congar's general introduction to Augustine's *Traites Antidonatises,* I, Bibl. August. Vol. 28 (Paris, 1963), pp. 104-109.

[112] Ibid.

[113] Ibid., 7-8.

[114] Ibid.

[115] Ibid., 8-9.

[116] Montague, *The Holy Spirit: The Growth of a Biblical Tradition*, 33-36.

[117] Ibid., 37-39

of the spirit would bring ethical rebirth in Israel (32:15-20).[118] For Ezekiel, God appears to the prophet in a storm wind (1:4).[119] The Spirit's power to restore God's people back to God-self (36:23-31) and the symbolism of restoring dried bones back to life was the restoration of Israel and the rebirth of a new nation after the exile (37:1-14).[120] Second Isaiah reaffirms that God's word for restoration will be fulfilled as the word of God is faithful and stands forever (40:6-8). The Spirit of the Lord is the agent of the restoration of Jerusalem and new creation.[121] Third Isaiah portrays the Spirit as anointing the servant of Yahweh for the salvation of all (61:1-3).[122]

In wisdom tradition, the spirit shares God's transcendence over the world and participates in the events of the world especially the events of sacred history as detailed in chapters 7-12 and in 15: 18-19:22. The wisdom tradition of the Old Testament exalted wisdom and the spirit to the point of personification and laid the foundation for the New Testament understanding of the Holy Spirit.[123]

1.6 *Conceptual Shifts*

God's Spirit was given to certain people and equipped them to perform specific tasks as cited above with reference to the spirit in the book of Judges. As God's people grew in their socio-religious-political self-awareness, two roles evolved and became considerably essential in the development of Israel's history: the office of prophet and the office of leader or king. However, Moses and Samuel combined these two positions.[124] A close look at the ministry of Moses shows that the prophetic office seems to have originated the from spirit-related phenomenon of prophesying rather than law-related teaching. In the book of Numbers 10:10, God confirmed the appointment of the seventy elders by putting the spirit of Moses on them and they prophesied together. Israel's early history reveals that those recognized by speech-enabling experiences of the Spirit of God were prophets to the nation (1 Sam. 19:20). Nonetheless, the prophetic ministry and the monarchy in early Israel seem to have been instinctive and casual. There were no structures, as such, until religion declined and the people became dissatisfied with Samuel's leadership. Thus, the people demanded a formally recognized king and a struc-

---

[118] Ibid., 40-42.

[119] Pizzaballa, op. cit., (Accessed March 2, 2016).

[120] Montague, *The Holy Spirit: The Growth of a Biblical Tradition*, 47-49.

[121] Ibid., 49-52.

[122] Ibid., 53 & 60.

[123] Ibid., 109-110

[124] Thomas, op. cit., (Accessed on March 2nd 2016).

ture of governance like other nations. The inauguration of a formal central leadership in Israel led to royal seers or prophets. As time went on, the kings of Israel started modeling after foreign kings and professional court-prophets that prophesied falsehood.[125]Consequently, Israel's monarchy's endorsement of the professionalization of the prophetic ministry and false prophecies plunged the kingdom into apostasy. The prophet Jeremiah cried out,

> *Do not listen to the words of the prophets who say to you, Do not serve the king of Babylon." They prophesy lies to you! I did not send them—oracle of the LORD—but they prophesy falsely in my name. As a result, I must banish you, and you will perish, you and the prophets who are prophesying to you.*[126]

The wantonness of the monarchy led to the Eighth-century's prophets' emphasis on morality. The prophets confronted Israel on the implications of their apostasy and abandonment of the covenant with God. Accordingly, the destruction of Israel by the Assyrians in 722 BC and the obliteration of Jerusalem and the Temple by the Babylonians between 590 and 587 BC generated the Messianic hope. The Spirit would renew Israel with a new covenant in their hearts.[127] The understanding of the spirit shifted from being the act of God to a wider theological concept because of the Babylonian exile, the destruction of the Temple, the end of the monarchy and loss of political independence.

1.7 *Conclusion*

It is clear that the studies of Jewish scriptures reveal that the Spirit of the Lord God, *Ruach Adonai Adonai* (Isaiah 61:1),[128] was present all through the history of Israel.[129] Consequently, this understanding of *ruach* as the breath of life, the source of life in Hebrew Scriptures, spilled into New Testament theology of the Holy Spirit as the giver of life. It is the Spirit of the Lord God that empowered the Messiah to fulfill his mission (Isaiah 11:2; 42:1; 61:1).[130] The Spirit of God has always been abiding, life-giving, creative, empowering and salvific.

---

[125] Ibid.

[126] Ibid. (See also (14:14; 29:9).

[127] Thomas, op. cit., (Accessed on March 2nd 2016).

[128] Hebrew Names of God: *The Spirit of God as revealed in the Tanakh* http://www.hebrew4christians.com/ Names_of_God/Spirit_of_God/Printer_Version/printer_version.html (Accessed April 1, 2016).

[129] Pizzaballa, op. cit., (Accessed March 2, 2016).

[130] Hebrew Names of God: *The Spirit of God as revealed in the Tanakh*, (Accessed April 1, 2016).

The understanding and application of the term *ruach* always changed with the socio-religious-political situations facing Israel at different times. This unchanging but transformational presence that has been interpreted all through biblical history as taking different forms and manifestations, remains God's self-revelation. It was through a theological-pastoral reflection that the early Church comprehended that the same presence that was revealed as a force is the same presence that manifested as the presence of God to be a person, the third person of the Blessed Trinity, God. The Old Testament had conceived this presence, not as a person but a substantial force that brought into being the creative ingenuity of God (Gen. 1:2; Jb 33:4), the saving power of Israel manifested by Yahweh's spirit (Zach. 4:6).[131] And God's abiding mysterious presence guides the affairs of Israel and permeates the world.[132] The early Christians later articulated this invisible, but life-changing presence as the Holy Spirit, the advocate, the comforter, and helper (John 14:16; 27), that rested on the disciples on Pentecost day in the metaphorical form of tongues of fire. This Spirit of God came to be understood as the giver of *charisms* for ministry.

---

[131] McKenzie, op. cit., 841.

[132] Ibid.

Chapter Two

The Holy Spirit in the New Testament

———————— ❧ ————————

2.1 *Introduction*

> *The revelation of the Holy Spirit as a person distinct from the Father and the Son, foreshadowed in the Old Testament, becomes clear and explicit in the New Testament.*[133]

The early Christians' success in spreading the good news was not necessarily centered on its teachings but in the impact, the transformational presence of God had through them on converts.[134] Jesus had promised that they would receive power when the Holy Spirit came down upon them (Acts 1:8). Consequently, Jesus' declaration was fulfilled when a people frightened and depressed by the memory of the cruel execution of their master on the cross, experienced a presence that emboldened them on the day of Pentecost (Acts 2:1-13). They were filled with joy and new fervor to carry out their mission of evangelization. Their experience could be likened to the lifeless dust that received God's breath in Genesis 2:7. Similarly, it could also be compared to Ezekiel's dry bones prophecy that made anything lifeless come back to life after receiving God's breath (37). Πνεῦμα *(pneuma)*, meaning spirit, the inherent power capable of bringing forth new birth[135] was at work on the day of Pentecost. However, the early Christians' experience of the outpouring of the Holy Spirit on

---

[133] *The Holy Spirit in the New Testament*. At the General Audience of Wednesday, May 20, 1988. http://www. vatican.va/jubilee_2000/magazine/documents/ju_mag_01061998_p-08_en.html (Accessed April 8, 2016).

[134] Luke T. Johnson, *The Writings of the New Testament: An Interpretation* (Revised Edition). (Minneapolis, MN: Fortress Press1999), 95

[135] Colin Brown, op. cit., 689.

the day of Pentecost was not exceptional to them alone. It was a historical continuity with the charismatic experience of judges, kings, and the prophets.[136] Comparably, Yves Congar asserts there is no doubt that the Spirit was active under the old disposition before Jesus.[137] I believe that the Spirit Congar referred is *Ruach Yahweh,* the breath of God that came to be understood as the Holy Spirit in the New Testament. Nevertheless, in the new dispensation, all those whom the Spirit of God animates are daughters and sons of God (Rom. 8:14-17), not necessarily as in judges, kings and prophets that were subject to the temporary action of the Spirit (Luke 1:15; 7:28), but an enduring act in the children of God in whom the Holy Spirit has found a dwelling (1 Cor. 6:11, 20; cf. 3:16ff).[138]

As a consequence, the synoptic tradition presents a developed theology of the Christian charismatic experience of the early Church.[139] In this theology, we recognize that the early Christian communities understood the Spirit that breathed life into creatures in Genesis was the same Spirit that overshadowed Mary at the conception of Jesus (Matt. 1:18; Luke 1:35), descended on Jesus in the form of a dove at His baptism (Mark 1:10), and who empowered the early Christians on the day of Pentecost (Acts 2:4).[140] Between the synoptic gospels, however, comparing the other two gospels, Luke reflects more advanced pneumatology.[141] In the synoptic gospels, John and other New Testament authors make their respective contributions to the understanding of the Holy Spirit in the New Testament. Though commentators may not agree on the New Testament author who has contributed more to pneumatology, I believe it is Luke's writings that gave credence to the Holy Spirit as fundamental to Christian Spirituality.[142] Luke records in Acts 2:1ff, the dramatic work of the Holy Spirit as the Church came to birth with the outstanding conversion of three thousand people.[143] No other evangelist showed a more captivating interest in the prominence of the Holy Spirit in the life and ministry of Jesus and the early Christian community as Luke did. This is reflected as Luke

---

[136] Gelpi, op. cit., 60.

[137] Congar, op. cit.,16.

[138] Xavier Leon-Dufour, (Ed). *Dictionary of Biblical Theology* (2nd ed.). (Frederick, Maryland: The Word Among US Press1988), 238.

[139] Gelpi, op. cit., 60.

[140] Edwards, op. cit., 37.

[141] *The Holy Spirit in the New Testament*. At the General Audience of Wednesday, May 20, 1988. http://www.vatican.va/jubilee_2000/magazine/documents/ju_mag_01061998_p-08_en.html (Accessed April 8, 2016).

[142] Downey, op. cit., 492.

[143] Karkkainen, op. cit., 31.

strategically positioned the Holy Spirit as the source of the life and mission of Jesus and the early Christians. Congar Yves in his book, *I believe in the Holy Spirit*, coherently affirmed this idea thus: "This Spirit, who, according to Luke, brought Jesus to life in Mary's womb, also brings the Church into the world. The same Spirit who sent Jesus on his mission after anointing him at his baptism also animates the apostolate from Jerusalem to the ends of the earth."[144] Though the Spirit of God was very active in the life and ministry of Jesus in the synoptic gospels, it was not understood as a distinct person. That understanding evolved later.[145] We see this in the evolutionary understanding of the Holy Spirit in the early Christian community. In the Gospel of John, Jesus speaks more clearly about the personhood of the Spirit (14:16, 26; 15:26; 16:7).[146]

The Spirit was always connected to the manifestation or action of God. It was the principal metaphor of God in the Old Testament[147] but came to be depicted as the unquestionable presence that gives life and meaning to Christianity. Correspondingly, the author of John's gospel portrayed the same Spirit as reflecting the presence of Jesus in the lives of Christians as their personal Advocate who abides with them forever (14:16).[148] In the words of Luke Timothy Johnson: "The Holy Spirit is an active power intervening in the progress of the mission, both impelling and guiding it" (Act 8:28, 39; 10:19; 11:15; 13:2; 15:28; 16:6; 20:22).[149] In this chapter, I shall examine the understanding of Holy Spirit in the New Testament writings but later focus more on the Theological development of the Holy Spirit in Luke's Gospel and Acts of the Apostles. In my effort to unravel how the manifest *charisms* in the early Church can be recovered and restored in the Catholic Church for ministry, I will also carry out an exegetical-theological study on *charisms* as in 1 Corinthians 12:8-11 and Romans 12:6-8.

2.2 *The Spirit in Mark's Gospel*

Mark's gospel's reference to πνεῦμα (*pneuma*) can be classified under three categories: (a), the Spirit of God or the Holy Spirit, which is mentioned six times (1:8,10,12; 3:29; 12:26; 13:11); (b), Evil and demonic spirits used concomitantly are identified ten times (1:23,26,27,32,34,39; 3:11,15,22,30; 5:2,8,13,18; 6:7,13; 7:25, 9:38; 16:9,17), and; (c), the

---

[144] Congar, op. cit., 44.

[145] Schreck, op. cit., 10.

[146] Ibid.

[147] Thomas, op.cit., (Accessed April 15, 2016).

[148] Edwards, op. cit., 37.

[149] Johnson, op. cit., 222.

human spirit is classified three times (2:8; 8:12; 14:38).[150] The Spirit of God communicates divine presence, impacts positively and evil/demonic spirits, on the other hand, come from the forces of darkness and they take possession, to inflict different kinds of maladies on the human person.[151] Though the mysterious afflictions of human beings are often attributed to evil spirits and demons, the New Testament authors never created the impression of evil being equal to God.[152] The evil spirits were always portrayed as inferior to God and subject to the Spirit of God working in God's agents as manifest in the ministry of Jesus (Mark 3:23-27).[153] However, the human spirit is that part of us that interacts with the spiritual realm, through which God most immediately encounters us (Rom. 8:16; Gal. 6:18; Phil. 4:23; 2 Tim. 4:22; Philm. 25; Heb. 4:12; Jas. 4:5)[154]. It is also that part that opens up a person for a divine experience (Matt. 5:3; Luke 1:47; Rom. 1:9; 1 Pet. 3:4).[155] Let's examine how the gospel of Mark uses the *Pneuma/Spirit* in the above classifications.

At the beginning of the gospel, the author starts with the prophecy of John the Baptist announcing the emergence of the Messiah whose Spirit-baptism is distinctive: He will not baptize with water but with fire and the Holy Spirit (Mk 1:4-8).[156] The metaphorical expression of fire and the Holy Spirit alludes to what would eventually take place on Pentecost whereby the disciples experienced what appeared like tongues of fire on each of them as they were filled with the Holy Spirit (Act 2:1-11).[157] In biblical symbolic usage, the fire was for purification and judgment.[158] It was understood that divine fire would burn out all imperfect nature of the human person and make a person holy in the sight of God.[159] Both

---

[150] Kenny Burchard, *Pneuma (Spirit) in Mark's Gospel*. http://thinktheology.org/2013/11/27/pneuma-spirit-marks-gospel/ (November 27, 2013). Accessed April 15, 2016.

[151] Ibid.

[152] Moises Silva, Ed. *New Dictionary of New Testament Theology And Exegesis* (2nd Ed.). (Grand Rapids, Michigan: Zondervan 2014), 808.

[153] Ibid.

[154] Brown, op. cit., 693.

[155] Ibid.

[156] Gelpi, op. cit., 50.

[157] McKenzie, op. cit., 842.

[158] Ibid.

[159] Ibid.

Matthew 3:11 and Luke 3:16 have the same expression found in Mark: "He will baptize you with the Holy Spirit *and with fire*."[160]

Furthermore, in his account, John the Baptist yields to the superiority of the baptism of Jesus and invokes his eschatological approach in his ministry as a precursor of the Messiah. John's end-time prophetic reproach was to condemn the misleading racial pride of the scribes and Pharisees.[161] Some commentators believe that the Marcan John the Baptist's eschatological pronouncement was for the total annihilation of the wicked. However, George Montague thinks Mark did not see the Spirit as that of judgment. He was more interested in directing his audience to the Messiah on whom the Holy Spirit reposed.[162] "His winnowing fork is in his hand, to clear his threshing-floor, and to gather the wheat into his granary; but the chaff he will burn with unquenchable fire" (Luke 3:17; cf. Matt. 3:12).[163] The above text finds resonance in both Matthew and Luke, employing the strict warning of the judgment of God in Isaiah 4:4, "where the prophet announces the coming judgment in terms of the Lord's *ruah* (breath, wind, "spirit") and fire."[164] The image of winnowing whereby the wind blows the chaff away to be burned is also in Isaiah 27:4,8 and 30:28.[165] In Matthew's portrayal of John the Baptist, the day of the Lord has no favorites; true Israel will not be based on racial descent but on the purifying presence of the Spirit of the Lord within individual's heart (Matt. 3:7-12; cf. Deut. 4:12; 5:4, 22, 24; Num. 16:35; 2 Kings 1:10-14; Isa. 66:15ff; Zech. 13:9).[166]

Mark's scenic account of the baptism of Jesus underpins the idea that creation was being reenacted anew as documented in the book of Genesis 1:2: God's Spirit hovers over the waters.[167] Mark uses "rend" or "split apart" in describing the opening of the heavens, which surfaces again toward the end of his Gospel; the splitting of the sanctuary after the death of Jesus (15:38).[168] The connection between the above-mentioned scenes suggests that the submission of Jesus to his ministry and death on the cross opens God's dwelling

---

[160] Ibid.

[161] Gelpi, op. cit., 50.

[162] Montague, *The Holy Spirit: The Growth of a Biblical Tradition*, 239.

[163] Ibid.

[164] Ibid.

[165] Ibid.

[166] Gelpi, op. cit., 50.

[167] Daniel Durken, O.S.B. Ed. *The New Collegeville Bible Commentary: New Testament*. (Collegeville, Minnesota: Liturgical Press 2009), 102.

[168] Ibid.

for humanity.[169] The Jews understood the expression, "the heavens are opened" to be indicative of God's readiness to pour out blessings on God's children.[170] When the heavens open up, God's presence is made manifest and endows whoever is disposed of the entire graces needed for ministry. Jesus opens up at His baptism and with heaven opening up and the Holy Spirit descending on him like a dove, He enacts the dawn of a new age.[171] Although the baptism of Jesus has been documented with different nuances due to the specific theological concerns of the evangelists, the four gospels record the account of the Holy Spirit descending like a dove on Jesus (Mark 1:10; Matt. 3:16; Luke 3:22 and John 1:32). Mark simply reports the baptism and describes the Holy Spirit descending upon Jesus as He comes out of the water. Luke situates Jesus at prayer and the Holy Spirit descending upon him after his baptism. Furthermore, Matthew creates a dialogue between John and Jesus who later submitted to John's baptism "to fulfill all righteousness" (Luke 3: 21-22; Matt. 3:13-17).[172] In John's account, however, it is John himself who testifies seeing the Holy Spirit descending like a dove on Jesus. All the evangelists use the metaphorical image of a dove as representing the Holy Spirit. The Old Testament writers or rabbinical authors never used the dove as a symbol of the Spirit.[173] It was in the Christian tradition that the dove came to be the symbol of the Holy Spirit[174]. Subsequently, after the Holy Spirit descended on Jesus in the symbolic form of a dove, a voice of authentication was heard from heaven: "You are my beloved Son, with you I am well pleased."[175]

Mark's narration of the confirmation and affirmation of Jesus from above and of his proclamation as the Son of God (1:9-12) ratify Jesus not only as a prophet but also as the Messiah and the Son of God who is endowed with power to heal and deliver the afflicted from evil spirits, and ultimately through his suffering and death redeem the world.[176] After his baptism, Jesus was anointed as a servant for the ransom of many (10:45). Through the

---

[169] Ibid.

[170] Ibid.

[171] Montague, *The Holy Spirit: The Growth of a Biblical Tradition*, 241.

[172] Ibid., 240.

[173] Gerhard Kittel, and Gerhard Friedrich, Eds. *Theological Dictionary of the New Testament* (Eng. tr.) Vol. VI, p.382, cited in Congar, *I Believe in the Holy Spirit*, 16.

[174] Congar, op. cit., 17.

[175] Senior, and Collins, op. cit., 1318.

[176] McDonnell, and Montague, *Christian Initiation and Baptism in the Holy Spirit: Evidence from the First Eight Centuries*, 14.

same authority, which he received from above, Jesus performed many signs and wonders and continued to do so after His death and resurrection. Mark recounts that Jesus did not start his salvific ministry until He had defeated the powers of darkness in the symbolic desert. Immediately after his anointing from above, the Spirit drove Jesus into the desert; and he remained in the desert for forty days, tempted by Satan (1:12-13). The Spirit drove Jesus into the desert; a place or state of struggle and Jesus was not exempt from temptation, just like the rest of humanity.[177] The mystical experience of Jesus at his baptism did not exempt him from temptation. His forty days in the desert parallel the trials of the Jews in the wilderness for forty years.[178] The Jews were a chosen people for a mission of being God's light to all the nations in the understanding of the Old Testament (Isaiah 42:6). God placed a salvific mission on Jesus at His baptism with the empowerment from above. Consequently, being chosen from above does not exempt anyone from the trials and tribulations of this life. Everyone must go through some hardship. The determinant factor to victory is the ability to remain in the Holy Spirit. Though Mark's account of the temptations of Jesus is not detailed like the other synoptic gospels (cf. Matthew 4:1-11 and Luke 3:2-16), he made it clear that the angels ministered to him in the midst of wild beasts (1:13).

Consequently, after the victorious outcome of His battle with Satan, Jesus started his ministry, filled with the Holy Spirit and authority. He took the battle to Satan's hold on ignorance by teaching, the possessed by casting out demons and the sick by healing them. He taught with authority, not like the scribes (1:22), unclean spirits obeyed him (1:27); and he cures Peter's mother-in-law (1:29-31).[179] Among the evangelists, Mark places more emphases in the ministerial authority of Jesus over Satan. For Mark, Jesus is the one anointed to challenge Satan.[180] He enthusiastically shares four specific cases:[181] *"the Cure of the Demoniac"* (1:22-28),[182] *"the Healing of the Gerasene"* (5:1-20),[183] *the healing of the Syrophoenician Woman' daughter*, (7:24-30),[184] and *"The Healing of a Boy with a Demon"* (9:14-29).[185] To

---

[177] Montague, *The Holy Spirit: The Growth of a Biblical Tradition,* 242-243.

[178] Ibid., 242.

[179] Ibid., 244.

[180] Ibid.

[181] Montague, *The Holy Spirit: The Growth of a Biblical Tradition,* 244.

[182] Senior, and Collins, 1319.

[183] Ibid., 1324-1325.

[184] Ibid., 1330.

[185] Ibid., 1334-1335

affirm the superiority of the authority of Jesus over unclean spirits, Mark notes at the beginning of his gospel message: "Unclean spirits would catch sight of him, fling themselves down at his feet, and shout, "You are the Son of God" (3:11).[186] Furthermore, in order to prove that his authority over unclean spirits came from above through the power of the Holy Spirit, Jesus was stern on those who likened his authority to that of Beelzebub: "Truly, I say to you, all sins will be forgiven the sons of men, and whatever blasphemies they utter. But whoever blasphemes against the Holy Spirit never has forgiveness, but is guilty of an eternal sin" (3:28-30).[187] In the above-mentioned exorcisms, there were healings in some of them.

In Mark, there are also healings not connected with demonic influences: "Peter's mother-in-law (1:29-31), a leper (1:40-45), the paralytic (2:1-11), the daughter of Jairus and the woman with the flow of blood (5:21-43), the deaf-mute (7:31-37), the blind man at Bethsaida (8:22-26), and the blind Bartimaeus" (10:46-52).[188] For Mark, healing and exorcisms are not only a confirmation of the teaching authority of Jesus. They also make up the very essence of the life and charismatic ministry of Jesus.[189] This ministry was not meant to disappear with the physical exit of Jesus from this world; it was meant to endure.

Subsequently, after His resurrection, Jesus empowered His disciples with charismatic authority to heal and set free all who are captives of demonic spirits. In concluding his gospel, Mark 16:17-18 asserted: "These signs will accompany those who believe: in my name they will drive out demons, they will speak new languages. They will pick up serpents (with their hand), and if they drink any deadly thing, it will not harm them. They will lay hands on the sick, and they will recover."[190] Believers are able to exercise the same charismatic ministry as Jesus did because openness to the baptism in the Holy Spirit empowers them. Besides, through the redemptive suffering and death of Jesus and by the power of his resurrection, those initiated into the faith by a participation in baptism in the Holy Spirit are empowered to continue in Jesus' charismatic ministry.[191]

---

[186] Montague, *The Holy Spirit: The Growth of a Biblical Tradition*, 245.

[187] Ibid., 246. (The quotation cited in Montague is from The Revised Standard Version).

[188] Ibid., 248.

[189] Ibid. Gelpi, *Pentecostalism: A Theological Viewpoint*, 58.

[190] Senior, and Collins, op. cit., 1348.

[191] McDonnell and Montague, *Christian Initiation and Baptism in the Holy Spirit*, 14.

2.3 *The Spirit in Matthew's Gospel*

Matthew's gospel in its present form is believed to have come after Mark, although it has enjoyed being placed first in the current order of the New Testament all through the centuries.[192] Many biblical scholars agree that Matthew's work is built on Mark's theology.[193] In Matthew's infancy narrative, he makes it clear that the powerful influence of the Holy Spirit on the life and ministry of Jesus can be traced back to his conception.[194] Both Matthew and Luke, in expanding Mark's basic theology of the Holy Spirit in their infancy narratives, confirm the virginal conception of Jesus.[195] Since God relates to humanity sacramentally, the virginal conception becomes an outward physical sign of an invisible inner reality, the birth of the Son of God.[196] God uses Joseph, the foster father of Jesus, as the one through whom the genealogy of Jesus is traced to Abraham (1:1-16). Matthew records that before cohabitation, which Judean law permits after betrothal,[197] Mary was found to be with child (1:18). In order to prevent Joseph from divorcing Mary quietly since that was his intention (1:20), the angel appeared to Joseph in a dream and said: "Do not be afraid to take Mary your wife in your home. For it is through the Holy Spirit that this child is conceived in her" (1:20).[198] The Spirit-filled Messiah of a divine origin, whose name is Emmanuel, meaning, 'God with us', cf. (1:23), with a divine origin, manifests God's salvific presence in human history and his interest to save us from our sins.[199]

Before the baptism of Jesus, John the Baptist announced Him as the one who will baptize "with the Holy Spirit and fire" (3:11).[200] Mark and Luke also recount Jesus as the one who baptizes with the Holy Spirit and fire (Mark 1:6; Luke 3:16). Without questioning which evangelist is more original,[201] it is good to recognize that these synoptic baptism-texts depict

---

[192] Montague, *The Holy Spirit: The Growth of a Biblical Tradition,* 302.

[193] Edwards, op. cit., 68.

[194] Ibid.

[195] Gelpi, op. cit., 58.

[196] Brown, Fitzmyer, and Murphy, op. cit., 635.

[197] Ibid.

[198] Senior, and Collins, 1253.

[199] Gelpi, op. cit.,58.

[200] Edwards, op. cit., 68-69.

[201] Ibid.

the Messianic longing of John the Baptist. He awaited the appearance of the Messiah in the Spirit of all His power.[202] He submits to the superiority of the ministry of Jesus. "I am baptizing you with water, for repentance, but the one who is coming after me is mightier than I. I am not worthy to carry his sandals. He will baptize you with the Holy Spirit and fire"(1:12).[203] Interestingly, John retains one of the traditional symbols, not readily accessible, i.e. *fire*.[204] Traditionally, fire has been understood in two ways: it is the same as the Spirit as experienced on the day of Pentecost (Acts 2:1-11) or the symbolism of eschatological judgment.[205] However, "Dunn thinks that this would have the element of both warning and promise—warning of judgment to the stiff-necked and promise and grace to the penitent."[206]

On the day of His baptism at the river Jordan, Jesus experienced the Holy Spirit descending on Him in the form of a dove (3:3-16). He also heard the voice of God's affirmation of him as God's beloved son (3:17). The divine voice from heaven anticipated the transfiguration experience of Jesus (17:5) and combined two scriptural texts—Psalm 2:7 and Isaiah 42:1—revealing to John the Baptist and the witnesses that Jesus is the Son of God.[207] Through this delightful experience, the Spirit led Jesus into the desert to be tempted by the devil (4:1). Enabled by the power from above in the Spirit, Jesus insistently chose to remain in God's divine plan, thereby creating the atmosphere for the angels to minister to him (4:11). Through the power of the Holy Spirit, Jesus is empowered to preach, teach, heal and do works of compassion (8:1-4, 5-13, 14-17; 9:1-13, 18-26, 27-31, 32-34; 12:22-32; 14:34-36, 15:21-28, 29-31; 17:14-21).[208] Through the power of the Holy Spirit, Jesus commissioned His disciples, gave them authority over unclean spirits (10:1), and also assured of the divine support in times of trials: "The Spirit of your Father will speak through you" (10:20).[209] Matthew concludes his gospel with a baptismal formula, which apparently reveals the baptismal form of his community, which later became quite fundamental in the development of

---

[202] Dufour-Leon, op. cit., 573.

[203] Senior, and Collins, op. cit., 1256.

[204] Dufour-Leon, op. cit., 573.

[205] John Barton, and John Muddiman, Eds. *The Oxford Bible Commentary.* (New York: Oxford University Press. 2000), 851.

[206] James D.G. Dunn, *The Christ and the Spirit,* volume 2, Pneumatology (Grand Rapids: Eardmans, 1998), 93-102. (Cited in Edwards, *Breath of Life: A Theology of the Creator Spirit*, 69).

[207] Barton, and Muddiman, op. cit., 851.

[208] McDonnell and Montague, *Christian Initiation and Baptism in the Holy Spirit,* 22.

[209] Edwards, op. cit., 69.

the doctrine of the Trinity. Christ commanded his disciples to baptize "in the name of the Father and of the Son and of the Holy Spirit" (28:19).[210] Many commentators believe that Matthew's Trinitarian formula is a reflection of an advanced liturgical tradition, which was different from the common form of baptism in the early Christian community (Acts 2:38; 8:12; 19:5).[211] This is also the only text that reveals a more developed form of belief and unambiguously depicts the most profound personal trait of Holy Spirit as a divine person in the entire New Testament.[212] Matthew also revealed the Trinitarian formula, which initiates converts into the ministry of Jesus and empowers them into continuing his mission of preaching and healing in the world.[213]

2.4 *The Spirit in the Gospel of John*

John the Baptist witnessed the Holy Spirit being conferred on Jesus at the moment of his baptism. He said, "I saw the Spirit come down like a dove from the sky and remain upon him … Now I have seen and testified that he is the Son of God" (1:32, 34).[214] Jesus became the anointed one on whom the Spirit of God rested from the beginning of his ministry, just as the synoptic gospels describe him.[215] The Holy Spirit experience of Jesus at his baptism then sets Him in motion for His divine mission to manifest God's healing presence in the world.[216]

The Johannine use and application of the Greek word, *pneuma,* encompasses its various meanings, 'air, wind, breath, and spirit.'[217] *Pneuma* refers to "wind" in John 3:8, "The wind blows where it wills, and you can hear the sound it makes, but you do not know where it comes from or where it goes."[218] *Pneuma* is the animating force of human life (3:6), the life force of Jesus (11:33; 13:21; 19:30), a sustaining gift that Jesus gives to the disciples (20:22),

---

[210] Ibid.

[211] Montague, *The Holy Spirit: The Growth of a Biblical Tradition,* 310.

[212] McKenzie, op. cit., 842.

[213] McDonnell and Montague, *Christian Initiation and Baptism in the Holy Spirit,* 22.

[214] Senior, and Collins, op. cit., 1405.

[215] Montague, *The Holy Spirit: The Growth of a Biblical Tradition,* 338.

[216] McDonnell and Montague, *Christian Initiation and Baptism in the Holy Spirit,* 72

[217] Felix Just, S.J., *The Spirit/Paraclete in the Johannine Literature.* http://catholic-resources.org/John/Themes-Spirit.htm (Accessed April 22, 2016).

[218] Senior, and Collins, op. cit., 1409.

the origin of which is God (1:32-33; 3:5-8; 15:26).[219] However, the expression "Holy Spirit" is not commonly used in John, as it appears only three times in contrast to its frequent use in Luke and Acts of the Apostles. But, "Spirit of Truth" appears only in John (14:17; 15:26; 16:13) and 1 John 4:6 but nowhere else in the New Testament.[220] Anointing is another metaphor, which John derives from the Old Testament (1 John 2:20, 27).[221] Though the word 'Spirit' is not mentioned in John's prologue in 1:1-18, it uses "Logos," which has the same role as the Spirit in the creation accounts of Genesis 1-2.[222] However, John also uses the Old Testament imagery of the Spirit related to the life-giving power of water and breath, which is apparent "in his metaphors of rebirth (3:3-8), springs of life (4:14; 6:63; 7:38-39), and reception of the Spirit as new life (20:22; cf. Gen. 2:7; Ezek. 37:9)."[223]

John's gospel also presents Jesus as the eternal One through whom the Word became flesh and dwelt amongst us (1:14), "the Son of God sent by God into the world (3:17), the Wisdom of God in our midst, who declares himself as: the bread of life (6:35),[224] "the light of the world" (8:12; 9:5), "the door of the sheep" (10:7), "the good Shepherd" (10:11), "the true Vine" (15:1), "the resurrection and the Life" (11:25), and "the Way, the Truth, and the Life" (14:6).[225]

The use of the word, *"Paraclete"* in John's gospel, is another distinguishing quality of Johannine pneumatology.[226] The origin of this word is not clear, but Colin Brown thinks that John may have created this word himself to express in a single word the various functions he attributed to the Spirit.[227] The Greek verb παρακαλέω (*parakaleo*) "to call to one's side" appears frequently in the New Testament, especially in Pauline letters.[228] Nonetheless, the derived noun παράκλητος (*parakletos*) is shown only in the Gospel and first epistle of John.[229] Outside of the New Testament, *parakaleo* and *parakletos* are used mostly in jurid-

---

[219] Just, op. cit., (Accessed April 22). 2016

[220] Ibid.

[221] Ibid.

[222] Ibid.

[223] Karkkainen, op. cit., 34.

[224] Ibid.

[225] Johnson, op. cit., 542-543.

[226] Karkkainen, op. cit., 35.

[227] Brown, 704.

[228] Just, op. cit., (Accessed April 22, 2016).

[229] Ibid.

ical/courtroom contexts. The Holy Spirit is "another Advocate" (14:16), denoting that Jesus himself was the first "Advocate " (cf. 1 John 2:1). Consequently, the Paraclete accomplishes several of the same things that Jesus said and did.[230] The Spirit/Paraclete performs different functions in John's Gospel: Acts as a *companion*; being with the disciples for all eternity even after Jesus leaves them physically (14:16-18; cf. 1John 3:24; 4:13); a *teacher*, who reminds the disciples of the teachings of Jesus (14:26); an *advocate*, a *legal witness* who gives testimony to the disciples and the world about Jesus (15:26); a judge who convicts the world of sin and righteousness and judgment (16:8-11); and a revealer, who leads the disciples to the complete truth about Jesus (16:13-15; cf. 1 John 5:6-8).[231] For John, the *Paraclete* as revealer denotes that new revelation and original teaching are to be held in constant tension, so that the Spirit's role is never simply that of repeating the original teaching as it was given and received initially, but, that of illuminating new truth utterly unconnected to the old, but that of re-deciphering the old to give it modern meaning and that of revealing the new in a way coherent with the old.[232]

Consequently, the multifaceted advocate who comes from the Father will testify to Jesus (15:26) and glorify Him (16:14).[233] For John, the Spirit is only given through His glorification (7:39), which will take place through His death and resurrection (3:4).[234] As Jesus approached his ultimate departure from this world and became convinced of Judas betrayal, which eventually led to his death and resurrection, he said: "Now is the Son of Man glorified, and God is gloried in him. If God is glorified in him, God will also glorify him at once" (13:31-32).[235] After his crucifixion, Jesus bowed his head and gave up His spirit (19:30). One of the soldiers pierced his side with a spear, and at once blood and water came out (19:34). Some commentators believe that this was a way of fulfilling what is in John 7:39, that those who believe in Jesus will receive a Spirit which is symbolized by the "rivers of living water that flowed from within him at the piercing of the soldier (7:38).[236] Consequently, after his resurrection, Jesus appeared to his disciples and gave them his Spirit as he breathed on them:

---

[230] Ibid.

[231] Ibid.

[232] Brown, op. cit., 704.

[233] Edwards, op. cit., 74.

[234] Ibid.

[235] Senior, and Collins, op. cit., 1429.

[236] Edwards, op. cit., 74

Peace be with you. As the Father has sent me, so I send you. "When he had said this, he breathed on them and said to them, "Receive the Holy Spirit. If you forgive the sins of any, they are forgiven them; if you retain the sins of any, they are retained (20:21-23).[237]

Through his creative use of these two Old Testament metaphors, breath and water, John makes a contribution of the two key sacramental symbols required for the kingdom of God. Jesus says, "No one can enter the kingdom of God without being born of water and Spirit" (3:5).[238] To be born of water and the Holy Spirit is an empowerment to be God's embodied presence in the world and always ready to forgive others their sins and bring all into the kingdom of God.

2.5 *The Spirit in Pauline Writings*

In Paul's pneumatology, the Spirit captures a primary place of importance.[239] Amazingly, Paul did not know Christ according to the flesh, had no experience of Pentecost, but based his experience of the Spirit entirely and candidly on the event of Easter, the resurrection and glorification of Jesus as Christ and Lord.[240] From his encounter with the risen Christ, Paul presented the most comprehensive and integrated teaching on the Spirit.[241] This experience radically transformed him from a persecutor of Christians (Acts 8:3)[242] to the greatest evangelist the world has ever known. Many scholars believe that Paul's entire message was a result of the unfolding implication of the religious conversion experience he had (Acts 9:1-19).[243] Absolutely, I wish to isolate what made all the difference. It is Paul's encounter with the Holy Spirit through the laying on of hands by Ananias (Acts 9:17) that empowered him with the Holy Spirit:

---

[237] Ibid.

[238] Senior, and Collins, op. cit., 1409.

[239] C.D. Stampley Enterprises, INC. *The New World Dictionary-Concordance to the New American Bible* (World Bible Publishers 1970), 655.

[240] Congar, *I Believe in the Holy Spirit,* 30.

[241] Silva, op. cit., 815.

[242] Wayne A. Meeks, and John T. Fitzgerald, Eds. *The Writings of St. Paul; A Norton Critical Edition* (2nd ed). (New York. London: W.W. Norton & Company, Inc.2007), xxii.

[243] Ibid.

> *Ananias said, "Saul, my brother, the Lord has sent me, Jesus who appeared*
> *to you on the way by which you came, that you may regain your sight and be*
> *filled with the Holy Spirit. Immediately things like scales fell from his eyes*
> *and he regained his sight. He got up and was baptized, and when he had*
> *eaten, he recovered his strength (Acts 9:17-19).*[244]

Paul was baptized in the Holy Spirit through the laying on of hands, which was character-istic of the method the early Christians used for baptizing new converts with baptism in the Holy Spirit (Acts 6:6; 13:3; 28:8; 1 Tim. 4:14; 2 Tim. 1:6). Paul's transformational experience of the Holy certainly impacted his writings. The number of times *pneuma* is used in Paul's writings reveals to us the fundamental role the Spirit plays in Paul's pneumatology. Πνεῦμα *(pneuma)* appears 146 times in Pauline writings out of the 399 times the word appears in the New Testament.[245] Paul used the term more than any New Testament writer. Consequently, some commentators believe that Paul deserves the title, "theologian of the Spirit."[246] Others may have a contrary view since there is no remarkable development of the Holy Spirit in Paul's thought. However, I think Paul, through his charismatic experience of the Holy Spirit and application of his creative ingenuity in expressing his thoughts, enriched New Testament pneu-matology and the contemporary Christians understanding of the workings of the Holy Spirit.

The Spirit is the distinguishing mark of belonging to Christ. The experience of the early Christians, especially Paul, proves that the gift of the Spirit is what makes an individual a member of Christ (Rom. 8:9; cf. 1 Cor. 2:12; 2 Cor. 11:4; 1 Thess. 4:8).[247] The Spirit makes us children of God through adoption (Rom. 8:14-16). Our union with Christ through the Spirit (1 Cor. 6:17) makes us sharers in his Lordship (Rom. 8:14-16; Gal. 4:6).[248] The Christian life begins with the reception of the Spirit through faith (Gal. 3:2-3), which fulfills the promise of Abraham (3:14), and God's Spirit washes, sanctifies and justifies us (1 Cor. 6:11); and because we drink of the one Spirit, believers become members of the body of Christ (1 Cor. 12:13). Christians, who receive Christ through their baptism in the Holy Spirit, walk according to the Spirit (Gal. 5:25). The Holy Spirit leads them (Rom. 8:4) and they produce the fruits of the Holy Spirit (Gal. 5:22).[249] For Paul, what distinguishes a Christian

---

[244] Senior, and Collins, op. cit., 1459.

[245] Just, op. cit., (Accessed on April 22, 2016).

[246] Silva, op. cit., 815.

[247] Ibid.

[248] Ibid.

[249] C.D. Stampley Enterprises, op. cit., 655.

from an unbeliever is surely the gifts of the Holy Spirit (Rom. 2:29; 7:6; 2 Cor. 3:6-8; Gal. 4:29; Phil. 3:3).[250] Believers' experience of the Holy Spirit brings about an inward transformation that makes the Spirit the glory of Christ that dwells in us (Rom. 8:10).[251] Thus, Paul asserts: "I live, no longer I, but Christ lives in me; insofar as I now live in the flesh, I live by faith in the son of God who has loved me and given himself up for me"(Gal. 2:20).[252] Life in the Spirit is not abstract; it is a real presence that can be experienced with manifest external manifestations of divine gifts (*charisms*).[253] These *charisms* enable believers to perform miracles and also serve in different ministries in the Church and in the whole world (Rom. 12:6-8; 1 Cor. 12-14; Eph. 4:7-16). One of the gifts of Holy Spirit is discernment (1 Cor. 12:10; Phil. 1:9-10). From Paul's writings, his perceptive use of the gift discernment makes clear what the Spirit does. The Spirit enlivens our life of charity (Rom. 5:5; 15:30; Gal. 5:13; Col. 1:8) and our faith (2 Cor. 4:13). The Spirit creates in us an awareness of the mysteries of God (1 Cor. 2:10-16).

Although, Paul, as mentioned above, didn't know Christ physically and was not among the disciples who experienced the Holy Spirit on Pentecost Day, his writings, however, reflect a profound impact the Holy Spirit had on him and his communities. Many of his communities manifested and used the gifts of the Holy Spirit but not without problems that prompted Paul's writings aimed at resolving some of the problems concerning the use of spiritual gifts. The abuses notwithstanding, Paul's communities were lively and functional. Paul made it clear that the gifts of the Holy Spirit are from the same Spirit and the same God, working in all and for all (1 Cor. 12:4-11). All the gifts are given to serve all and they form an integral part of Christian initlation,[254] and that is why for Paul they were part of what makes a believer belong to the body of Christ. The excitement of being filled with the Holy Spirit and the eagerness to share the gifts with the world has sustained the Church for many centuries. Believers taught, preached and testified to the power of the presence of the risen Christ in their lives because of the indwelling Spirit they experience (Rom. 8:11), and they knew they were temples of the Holy Spirit (1 Cor. 3:16; 6:19). They fulfilled the mandate of Christ in Matthew 28:19-20: "Go, therefore and make disciples of all nations, baptizing them in the name of the Father, and of the Son, and of the Holy Spirit, teaching them to observe all that I have commanded you. And behold, I am with you always, until the

---

[250] Silva, op. cit., 815.

[251] Leon-Dufour, op. cit., 575.

[252] Senior, and Collins, op. cit., 1564.

[253] Leon-Dufour, op. cit., 575.

[254] McDonnell and Montague, *Christian Initiation and Baptism in the Holy Spirit: Evidence from the First Eight Centuries*, 55.

end of the age."[255] Matthew's Trinitarian formula persists in Paul's communities as shown in his several Trinitarian formulae (2 Cor. 13:14; Gal. 4:6; Rom. 8:9,11; 1 Cor. 12:4-6).[256]

In conclusion, Paul's pneumatology asserts the superiority of the Spirit over the law and the flesh. He practically reflects ways that the Spirit dwells in us, making us temples of the Holy Spirit (1 Cor. 3:16; 6:19; 2 Cor. 6:16; Rom. 8:9), leading us to the imitation of Christ (1 Thess. 1:6; 1 Cor. 11:1; 4:16; 1 Thess. 2:14), and how the gifts of the Holy Spirit make each part of the body function with *charisms* for the good of the whole body. For Paul, the Spirit continues to be with believers as a helper when they cannot pray (Rom. 8:26-27), and when they go through temptations (2 Thess. 3:33), and even at the difficult moments of their death (Rom. 8:11).

2.6 *The Spirit in other New Testament writings*

The writings of Luke, John, and Paul on the Holy Spirit seem to have over-dwarfed whatever the other New Testament epistles have to say about the Holy Spirit.[257] However, a close look at the other epistles shows that they also have made some contribution to the early Christians pneumatology.[258]

(a) *The Letter to the Hebrews*

The word *Pneuma*/Spirit in Hebrews is mentioned only seven times (2:4; 3:7; 6:4; 9:8, 14; 10:15, 29). Nonetheless, the Holy Spirit is vital to the authors' vision of reality.[259] Hebrews reflects on the charismatic vitality of the early Christians (2:4),[260] and how "God confirmed the gospel with signs and wonders and the gifts of the Holy Spirit (2:4)."[261]

---

[255] Senior, and Collins, op. cit., 1315.

[256] C.D. Stampley Enterprises, op. cit., 656.

[257] Larry L. Lichtenwalter, *The Holy Spirit in the General Epistles and the Book of Hebrews: The First-Century Church's Understanding of the Holy Spirit was Central to its Theology and Practice*. http://www.perspectivedigest.org/article/130/archives/19-2/the-holy-spirit-in-the-general-epistles-and-the-book-of-hebrews Accessed April 22, 2016.

[258] Ibid.

[259] Ibid.

[260] Silva, op. cit., 706.

[261] Karkkainen, op. cit., 34.

Hebrews associates the Spirit with the inspiration of the Scripture (3:7; 9:8; 10:15) and with Christ offering of self through an eternal Spirit (9:14).[262]

(b) *James*

Pneuma/Spirit scarcely features in the letter of James. It appeared only twice, (2:26 and 4:5).[263] The two references are vague,[264] and many scholars still contend with their meaning, the human spirit or the Spirit of God. Some commentators believe that James' first reference is in 2:26 alludes to the human spirit, thereby concluding that the second reference means the same. However, others believe that only the second reference could refer to the Holy Spirit: "Or do you suppose that the Scripture speaks without meaning when it says, the Spirit that he has made to dwell in us tends towards jealousy" (4:5).[265] Nevertheless, numerous commentators suggest that this passage refers to the Holy Spirit's reaction to the believer's envious worldliness.[266]

(c) *1Peter*

The Holy Spirit may not have featured prominently in 1 Peter. Nevertheless, he begins with a Trinitarian structure (1:1) and ends with the Father and Jesus (5:10).[267] Peter's understanding of the Holy Spirit is characteristic of the New Testament pneumatology.[268] The Holy Spirit inspires mission and it is the power of the gospel (1:12) that consecrates people for God (1:2) and transforms them into the image of God's glory through the despair and oppression (4:4), and though Christ was put to death in the body, he is brought back to life in the Spirit (3:18).[269] Peter's reference to the Spirit of the Old Testament as the Spirit of Christ is unique to him but more creatively is his portrayal of Christian witness as dominated by the Spirit

---

[262] Ibid.

[263] Lichtenwalter, op. cit., (Accessed April 22, 2016).

[264] Karkkainen, 34.

[265] Senior, and Collins, op. cit., 1642.

[266] Lichtenwalter, op. cit., (Accessed April 22, 2016).

[267] Ibid.

[268] Silva, op. cit., 822.

[269] Ibid.

of the glory of Christ.[270] The author gives the impression through his writing that baptismal grace is saving and charismatic.[271] The author attributes Old Testament prophecy to the Spirit of Christ (1:11), speaks of an experiential dimension of the new Christian life (2:2-3) and of varied gifts received by each Christian for the service of the community (4:10-11).[272]

(d) *2 Peter*

2Peter 1:20-21 depicts the most powerful statement of Scriptural inspiration:[273] "There is no prophecy of scripture that is a matter of personal interpretation, for no prophecy ever came through human will, but rather human beings moved by the Holy Spirit spoke under the influence of God."[274] We see here the functional link that Peter brings between the Old and New Testaments. The same Spirit that inspired the prophets still speaks through God's word.

(e) *Jude*

The book of Jude is a one-chapter book that only makes one reference to the Spirit in 19-20.[275] The author's admonition to his community resonates with how Paul challenges some of his communities (cf. 1 Cor. 2:12-3:4).[276] He reprimands members that are unspiritual as the source of division in the community but enjoins the faithful to build on faith and to pray in the Holy Spirit. This is the only text outside Pauline epistles to exhort his audience to pray in the Holy Spirit (cf. Eph. 6:18).[277]

(f) *Revelation*

In the book of Revelation, the author portrays the source of his vision as the Spirit (1:10; 4:2; 14:13; 17:3; 21:10; 22:17). He believes the same Spirit that inspired his visions

---

[270] Montague, *The Holy Spirit: The Growth of a Biblical Tradition*, 314.

[271] McDonnell, and Montague, *Christian Initiation and Baptism in the Holy Spirit*, 56.

[272] Ibid., 88.

[273] Silva, op. cit., 822.

[274] Senior, and Collins, op. cit., 653.

[275] Silva, op. cit., 822.

[276] Ibid.

[277] Ibid

commanded him to write to the seven Churches (2:7; 11, 17, 29; 3:6, 13, 22).[278] However, the expression Holy Spirit is not in the book of Revelation as the author often uses "spirits" in the plural, and even when he speaks of "the Spirit" in the singular, commentators are not sure if his understanding resonates with other New Testament authors.[279] Prophecy is central to the book of Revelation, and the author considers himself a prophet (22:9), and his book prophecy (1:3; 10:11; 22:7, 10, 18).[280] The Spirit is called the Spirit of life in 11:11, and makes reference to the breath of life from God and the Spirit communicates messages of God and Jesus through the gift of prophecy (1:10; 4:2; 17:3; 19:10; 21:10), and when Jesus and the Spirit speak to the church.[281] Each of the messages to the churches contains the phrase "He who has an ear, let him hear what the Spirit says to the churches" (2:7, 11, 17, 29; 3:6, 13, 22). One fascinating thing about Revelation is its remote but evident Trinitarian trajectories (1:4-5; 22:16-17); the book begins and ends with references to the Spirit.

2.7.1 *Theological Development of the Holy Spirit in Luke's Gospel and Acts of the Apostles*

Many New Testament scholars agree that the Gospel of Luke is anonymous.[282] However, earliest Church tradition identifies Luke as the author of the only gospel with a sequel: the Acts of the Apostles. Irenaeus was the first writer to attribute Acts to Luke.[283] Many commentators agree that Mark is the primary source of Luke's work, though some assert that Luke's work is a combination of Mark, Matthew and Q sources with special creative insights to make his message meaningful to his Gentile community.[284] The author was adept in Greek, uses sources innovatively to employ various literary devices to connect traditions and sources together.[285] He engages in literary promise and fulfillment, and he delights in the use of inclusion and

---

[278] Montague, *The Holy Spirit: The Growth of a Biblical Tradition*, 321-323.

[279] Ibid.

[280] Ibid.

[281] Angel M. Rodriguez, *The Holy Spirit in Revelation*, https://www.adventistbiblicalresearch.org/materials/holy-spirit/holy-spirit-revelation Accessed April 22, 2016.

[282] William R. Farmer, Ed. *The International Bible Commentary: A Catholic and Ecumenical Commentary for the Twenty-First Century.* (Collegeville, Minnesota: The Liturgical Press 1998), 1368.

[283] Ibid.

[284] Barton, and Muddiman, op. cit., 924.

[285] Brown, Fitzmyer, and Murphy, op. cit., 676.

parallelism.[286] Luke writes to resolve his community's difficulty in understanding God's faithfulness, which came as the result of the destruction of the Temple. Robert J. Karris, captures this in a question: "If God has not been faithful to the promises made to God's elect people and has allowed their holy city and Temple to be destroyed, what reason do Gentile Christians, who believe in this God, have to think that God will be faithful to promises made to them."[287] In an ingenious fashion, the author reveals in Luke-Acts that God was faithful through Jesus to the promises made to Israel, which includes the Gentiles, the unclean, the poor, women, the Samaritans, tax collectors and the social outcasts of the society.[288] However, some commentators think that Jesus' inclusiveness of the Gentiles, sinners and the outcasts was unexpected. I believe that Luke was clear in his theological thought process as he wrote his Luke/Acts. Accordingly, his genealogy account makes Jesus a descendant of Adam (3:23-38), while Matthew's account (1:1-17), traces Jesus' ancestry to Abraham. Consequently, Adam is inclusive of all humankind while Abraham was exclusively for Jews alone. Nevertheless, while not discarding Judaism, Luke cleverly writes about a reconstituted Israel, how Jesus selected twelve apostles (6:12-16), modeled after the twelve tribes and how the twelve apostles were restored to that initial twelve even after the death of Judas (Acts 1:15-26).[289] Interestingly and metaphorically, the gospel originates from the Temple in Jerusalem, and from Jerusalem the good news goes out to all the nations (Acts 1:8).[290] Luke skillfully acknowledges at the presentation of Jesus in the Temple in Jerusalem that Jesus is a light for revelation to the Gentiles, and glory for God's people Israel (2:32).

The Jesus portrayed in Luke is a universal Jesus, who is loving, compassionate, merciful and kind to all. In Luke's Jesus, the world sees a loving God who has been veiled for ages through erroneous teachings and religious bigotry. Luke's Jesus reveals God's salvific plans for everyone to be saved and come to the knowledge of the truth (1 Tim. 2:4). Jesus is the image of the unseen God (Col. 1:15), who desires not the death of a sinner but that sinners will come to be reconciled and have new life. When the Scribes and the Pharisees did not understand why he should eat with sinners and tax collectors, Jesus told a parable of God's merciful love (Luke 15:1-32). Luke's Jesus embraces Gentiles, sinners, tax collectors, women, and children, thereby creating a vision of holistic Christianity and a better world. We are better off with the world without racism and religious narrow-mindedness. After God ministered to Peter in a dream in an attempt to purify his prejudice, he said: "In

---

[286] Ibid.

[287] Ibid.

[288] Ibid.

[289] Ibid.

[290] Ibid.

truth, I see that God shows no partiality. Rather, in every nation whoever fears him and acts uprightly is acceptable to him" (Acts 10:34).[291] Peter was still speaking when the Holy Spirit came upon all members of the household of Cornelius (Acts 10: 44-49), showing us that God's Spirit cannot be confined to a particular people alone. Luke does an awesome job through this account in making the Holy Spirit accessible to the household of Cornelius thus, making the Holy Spirit available to everyone. Luke's pneumatology in this regard is insightful for the future of Christianity. Let us explore furthermore, the theological development of the Holy Spirit in Luke/Acts.

In his book, *The Charismatic Theology of St. Luke: Trajectories from the Old Testament to Luke-Acts*, I agree with Roger Stronstad that in order to articulately understand the Holy Spirit in Luke-Acts we need to contemplate how the Hebrew and Greek Bibles affected Luke's theology of the Holy Spirit in two fundamental ways; (a) charismatic motives such as the transfer, (b) sign and vocational motif and (c) how the Septuagint (LXX), the translation of the Hebrew Bible used by Luke and the early Church provided Luke with most of the terms used to depict the activity of the Holy Spirit in the New Testament.[292] However, I disagree with Stronstad that Luke has an Old Testament pneumatology.[293]

Congar also asserts that to say that Luke has an Old Testament understanding of the spirit may be dangerous as Luke goes beyond the understanding of the Spirit as a breath of Yahweh to developing the idea of the personification of the Holy Spirit and universalizing access to the Holy Spirit.[294] Though Luke's idea of the Holy Spirit came mainly from the Old Testament, his understanding metamorphosed as the Holy Spirit came to be seen as a person. Luke's pneumatology may not express the totality of the New Testament theology of the Holy Spirit; yet, his contribution has a great influence on our understanding of charismatic spirituality today, especially the need for *charisms* for ministry.

2.7.2 *Luke's Source of Pneumatology*

Luke's pneumatology is rooted in the theological understanding of the movements of the Spirit in the Old Testament.[295] Those called to leadership positions at different times

---

[291] Senior, and Collins, op. cit., 1461.

[292] Roger Stronstad, *The Charismatic Theology of St. Luke: Trajectories from the Old Testament to Luke-Acts*. (Grand Rapids, Michigan: Baker Academic, a division of Baker Publishing Group 2012), 15.

[293] Roger Stronstad, *The Holy Spirit in Luke-Acts: A Synthesis of Luke's Pneumatology*. http://enrichment-journal.ag.org/top/Holy_Spirit/200611.cfm Accessed April 27, 2016.

[294] Congar, op. cit., 46-47.

[295] Stronstad, op. cit., 89.

in Israel were endowed with charismatic gifts to enable them to carry out explicitly their assigned tasks. I concur with Stronstad's explanation of the term, *charismatic* as God's gift to his servants, either individually or collectively, to anoint, and empower for divine service.[296] The success of God's servants, from Moses, the founder of the nation of Israel, to the judges, the kings, the pre-exilic and post-exilic prophets and priests were anchored on the unction they received from God through the outpouring of God's Spirit upon them. Moses had the Spirit of God upon him as a prophetic-founder-leader of Israel (Num. 11:17) and the Lord "took of the Spirit upon him and placed upon the seventy elders" (Num. 11:25). Among the seventy elders was Joshua who was also filled with the spirit of wisdom for leadership (Num. 27:18; Deut.34: 9).[297] During the turbulent and tragic period of the early history of Israel, the judges were exclusively given charismatic graces to deliver Israel from their oppressors. Othniel, Gideon, Jephthah and Samson received charismatic gifts to be the Judges of Israel (Judg. 3:10; 6:34; 11:29; 13:25; 14:6,19; 15:14).[298] These charismatic activities continued with the anointing of the first two kings of Israel, Saul, and David. As Samuel anointed Saul, the Spirit of Lord came upon him and his tongue was unlocked and he prophesied (1 Sam. 10:1-10).[299] There were two other occasions that the Spirit of the Lord came upon Saul before he lost his crown to David (1 Sam. 11:6; 19:23).[300] The Spirit of the Lord also came upon David as Samuel anointed him (1 Sam. 16:13; 2 Sam. 23:2).[301] As the kingship in Israel became hereditary with David's descendants after his death, the charismatic character that was apparent in Saul and David disappeared. Though there were no specific references of how the Spirit of the Lord came upon Elijah, the manifest power of the Spirit of the Lord in his ministry clearly showed that he was charismatically endowed as he performed many miracles (1 Kings 16-18). Elisha was also granted his request for a double portion of Elijah's spirit before he was taken up to heaven (2 Kings 2:9,15).[302] Elisha lived to be a man of signs and wonders. The prophet Isaiah envisioned that the coming messiah on whom the Spirit of the Lord would rest would be the one to establish God's eschatological kingdom of peace and justice (11:2) and the outpouring of the spirit of renewal

---

[296] Ibid., 16.

[297] Ibid., 18.

[298] Ibid.

[299] Ibid.

[300] Ibid.

[301] Ibid.

[302] Ibid.

that would bring about ethical rebirth in Israel will also be upon him (32:15-20).[303] The kings and the people of Israel sinned repeatedly against God and they lost their land to the Babylonians who sent them into exile.

During the exile, Ezekiel, whose spiritual eyes were opened to see the reason why Israel was punished with the exilic experience (7-11), wrote about the Spirit's power to restore God's people back to God-self (36:23-31), and the symbolism of restoring dried bones back to life was the restoration of Israel and the rebirth of a new nation after the exile (37:1-14).[304] Second Isaiah reaffirms that God's word for restoration will be fulfilled as the word of God is faithful and stands forever (40:6-8), and the Spirit of the Lord will restore Jerusalem and make anew.[305] Third Isaiah portrays the Spirit as anointing the servant of Yahweh for the salvation of all (61:1-3).[306]

The Chronicler of the postexilic period associated the gift of the Spirit with inspired speech, with particular emphasis on prophets and priests to instruct and witness to the people (1 Chron. 12:18; 2 Chron. 20:14-15; 24:20; Neh. 9:30).[307] The above summarily lays the foundation to Luke's pneumatology, charismatic motifs, sign motifs, vocational motifs, and the Spirit of the messianic age.

2.7.3 *The Holy Spirit in Luke-Acts*

Luke-Acts provide more references to the Holy Spirit than any other New Testament books. "Holy Spirit" is referred to 13 times in the Gospel of Luke and 41 times in Acts of the Apostles, which many commentators believe was composed by the same author as mentioned above.[308] The gospel of Luke shows the importance of the Holy Spirit as the Angel Gabriel announced to Zechariah that the child to be conceived by Elizabeth would be filled with Holy Spirit even in his mother's womb (1:15). The same angel told Mary that her conception will be by the Holy Spirit who will overshadow her from on high (1:35). Interestingly here, the Angel Gabriel appears to Mary, showing how Luke takes the same story of Matthew 1:18-25, where the Angel appears to Joseph, and contextualizes it, making women relevant in his community. A study of Luke shows that among the evangelists, Luke

---

[303] Montague, *The Holy Spirit: The Growth of a Biblical Tradition*, 40-42.

[304] Ibid., 47-49.

[305] Ibid., 49-52.

[306] Ibid., 53 & 60.

[307] Stronstad, op. cit., 19.

[308] Felix Just, (Accessed April 27, 2016).

honors women more, and provides them with unique roles to play in the life and ministry of Jesus.[309] To mention a few, he talks about the role of Anna the prophetess (2:36-38), the public woman, Mary of Magdala (7:36-50), the ministering women in Galilee (8:1-3), Mary and Martha (10:38-42), the women in various parables, weeping women in Jerusalem after he was condemned to death (23:49), and women who took spices to the tomb (23:55-56).[310] Luke shows in his community that a woman can equally have access to the Holy Spirit and be a minister of Jesus.

Mary was the first woman to access the Holy Spirit as a bearer of Jesus for ministry. The Holy Spirit overshadows Mary from on high and anoints her for a mission/task of birthing Jesus and giving him to the world. Jesus is a blessing to be shared with the world. Comparably, chosen people in the Old Testament were filled with *Ruach Yahweh* for a particular mission/task. They were empowered by the Spirit of God to minister in their fields of endeavors. More importantly, Mary carried out her mission as the first messenger of good tidings, bearing Jesus, the Good News. As Mary visited her kinswoman Elizabeth, she was filled with the Holy Spirit (1:41). Luke carefully presented Jesus as the medium to the Holy Spirit even in the womb of Mary and as John the Baptist came in contact in the spirit with Jesus, he rejoiced and leaped for joy (1:44). John the Baptist will later declare in 3:16, "I am baptizing you with water, but one mightier than I is coming. I am not worthy to loosen the thongs of his sandals. He will baptize with the Holy Spirit and fire."[311] Absolutely filled with the Holy Spirit, Mary rejoiced as she proclaimed, "My soul proclaims the greatness of the Lord; my spirit rejoices in God my savior" (1:46-47).[312] Filled also with the Holy Spirit, Zechariah's tongue was released to proclaim, "Blessed be the Lord God of Israel" (1:67).[313] At his presentation in the Temple, Simeon came into the Temple in the Spirit, blessing God and prophesying upon the life of Jesus (2:25-27). We read that at his baptism, the Holy Spirit descended upon Jesus in the bodily form of a dove (3:22). Consequently, before he started his public ministry and after his temptations in the desert, Jesus returns to Galilee "in the power of the Spirit" (4:14).[314] In the synagogue at Nazareth, his hometown, Jesus reads from the scroll of the prophet Isaiah: "The Spirit of the Lord is upon me, because

---

[309] Farmer, op. cit., 1371.

[310] Ibid.

[311] Senior, and Collins, *The Catholic Study Bible,* 1358.

[312] Ibid., 1353.

[313] Ibid.

[314] Ibid., 1359.

he has anointed me to bring good news to the poor" (4:18);[315] after finishing the reading, Jesus declared, "Today this scripture has been fulfilled in your hearing" (4:21),[316] implying that he is indeed the anointed one, the Messiah. In order for any minister or messenger of God to function, he or she has to be empowered from above. In fulfillment of the prophecy of Isaiah 61, Jesus is anointed to carry out his mandate from his Father. Therefore, in his public ministry, Jesus casts out from many people several *"unclean spirits" and "evil spirits"* (4:33, 36; 6:18; 7:21; 8:2; 8:29; 9:39, 42; 10:20; 11:24, 26; 13:11).[317] Soon after the seventy disciples return from their mission, Jesus "rejoiced in the Holy Spirit" and thanks God for hiding things from the wise but revealing them to infants (10:21).[318] Jesus taught his disciples that God the Father gives the Holy Spirit to those who ask him (11:13). In 12:10, Luke personifies the Holy Spirit as one who can be blasphemed and in 12:12, and shows the Holy Spirit as a teacher. At his death on the cross, Jesus gave up his spirit to the Father as he cried out; "Father into your hands I commend my spirit; and when he had said this he breathed his last" (23:46).[319]

Many commentators believe that the Acts of the Apostles could also be named Acts of the Holy Spirit because it is the Holy Spirit who prompts, empowers and carries out different missions through the various human agents. Jesus instructs the disciples "through the Holy Spirit" (Acts 1:2). The Holy Spirit takes over after the resurrection of Christ and even speaks through his mouth to the disciples of Jesus. The disciples cannot do anything unless they are empowered from above as Jesus instructed them to wait. At the appointed time, when Pentecost Day arrives, the first disciples were baptized with the Holy Spirit (1:5, 8; 2:1-4; 11:15-16). Filled with the Holy Spirit, the apostles exercised their ministry of preaching (1:8; 2:4; 4:8, 31; 11:24; 13:9, 52). Comparably, the Holy Spirit spoke through King David and the prophets in ancient Israel (1:16; 4:25; 28:25), God "will pour out" his Spirit on all people and all nations in the last days (2:17-18, 33; 10:45). Believers, including Gentiles, receive the Holy Spirit when they repent and are baptized (2:38; 15:8; 19:5-6). In fulfillment of the prophecies of Old, reception of the Holy Spirit even precedes baptism (10:44-48). Some people "test" or "lie to" or "oppose" the Holy Spirit, with dire consequences (5:1-11; 7:51). Deacons and other ministers must also be open to being filled with the Spirit" (6:1-6), especially when they prophesy (6:10; 7:55-59; 11:28; 21:4). The Spirit is conferred through the "laying on of hands" (8:17-19; 9:17; 19:6). The Spirit "speaks to"

---

[315] Ibid., 1360.

[316] Ibid.

[317] Felix Just, *The Holy Spirit in Luke/Acts*, Accessed April 27, 2016.

[318] Ibid.

[319] Senior, and Collins, op. cit., 1399.

the apostles and prophets (8:29; 10:19; 11:12; 13:1-4; 21:11). The Spirit leads and guides the decisions and actions of the Christian leaders (15:28; 16:6-7; 19:21; 20:22-23)."[320] We see from the beginning that the Holy Spirit is the principal agent that enlivens, empowers, teaches, inspires, commissions and sustains.

2.7.4 *Transfer Motifs*[321]

In Old Testament biblical history, it was strategically feasible to transfer duty from a leader or leaders to others and there is also a corresponding transfer of the Spirit.[322] For example, Moses shared his leadership responsibilities with the 70 elders; the Lord "taking some of the Spirit that was on Moses, he bestowed it on the seventy elders; and as the spirit came to rest on them, they prophesied" (Num. 11:25).[323] There are similar transfers of the Spirit from Moses to Joshua (Num. 27:18–20; Deut. 34:9), from Saul to David (1 Sam. 16:13-14), and from Elijah to Elisha (2 Kings 2:9–15). The transfer of the Spirit from Moses to the elders can be compared to the transfer of the Holy Spirit from Jesus to his disciples on the Day of Pentecost; each of these transfers anticipates the Day of Pentecost.[324] Peter likened the outpouring of the Holy Spirit on the apostles on the day of Pentecost to the fulfillment of the prophecy of Joel, "I will pour out a portion of my spirit upon all flesh. "Your sons and your daughters shall prophesy, young men shall see visions, your old men shall dream dreams" (Acts 2:17-18).[325] The apostles carried on this transfer motif and they made other disciples by laying their hands on them to receive the Holy Spirit for the mission (Acts 6:6; 8:17).

Though the transfer of the Spirit through the laying of hands is only officially practiced at liturgical ceremonies in the Catholic Church, at confirmations and ordinations, however, transfer of the Spirit is also exercised in Charismatic ministries and Churches all over the world. Before one can manifest the gifts of the Holy Spirit as experienced in Charismatic ministries in the Catholic Church, one has to go through Life in the Spirit Seminar, which prepares aspirants for this special encounter with the Holy Spirit. During the process, hands

---

[320] Ibid.

[321] Stronstad, op. cit., 23.

[322] Ibid.

[323] Senior, and Collins, op. cit., 167.

[324] Stronstad, op. cit., 24.

[325] Senior, and Collins, op. cit., 1446.

are laid on candidates and through this impartation; they manifest the gifts of the Holy Spirit for ministry.

2.7.5 *The Sign Motifs*[326]

The sign and transfer motifs are elements of the charismatic motifs and are complementary to one another. Stronstad explains the purpose of sign to be twofold: (1) to validate to the recipient of the Spirit that his or her call to leadership is of divine origin, and (2), to witness to others that he or she is chosen by God. The sign is frequently, though not always, a surge of prophecy. Thus, for example, when the Spirit rested upon the elders, they prophesied (Num. 11:25).[327] Another instance is when Samuel anointed David king over Israel, "from that day on, the spirit of the LORD rushed upon David" (1 Sam. 16:13).[328] David later declared, "The spirit of the LORD spoke through me; his word was on my tongue" (2 Sam. 23:2).[329] Peter declared later, "My brothers, the scripture had to be fulfilled which the Holy Spirit spoke beforehand through the mouth of David, concerning Judas, who was the guide for those who arrested Jesus" (Acts 1:16).[330] The sign of succession for both Joshua and Elisha seem to have been the ability to part the Jordan River (Josh. 3:7; 4:14; 2 Kings 2:14,15).[331] The manifest sign for the early Christians was speaking in tongues and prophecy; however, that still holds today in charismatic ministries and churches. This understanding has remained problematic as individuals can have other charismatic gifts without first manifesting the gift of tongues. Some charismatic commentators even believe that one cannot claim to have the Holy Spirit without speaking in tongues. I believe that is a false assertion since one can have the Holy Spirit without speaking in tongues.

2.7.6 *The Vocation Motifs*[332]

Each time the Spirit of the Lord filled anyone in the Old Testament, it was for a purpose or a mission. God endows each person called for a specific assignment with all the graces

---

[326] Stronstad, op.cit., 24

[327] Ibid.

[328] Senior, and Collins, op. cit., 323.

[329] Ibid., 366.

[330] Stronstad, *The Holy Spirit in Luke-Acts*, (Accessed April 27, 2016).

[331] Ibid.

[332] Stronstad, op. cit., 26.

they need to function as commissioned.[333] Subsequently, Luke's pneumatology has a dominant vocational dimension attached to it. Jesus was filled with the Holy Spirit for a mission as he declared in his inaugural manifesto quoting Isaiah 61:1-2:

> *The Spirit of the Lord is upon me because he has anointed me to bring glad tidings to the poor. He has sent me to proclaim liberty to captives and recovery of sight to the blind, to let the oppressed go free, and to proclaim a year acceptable to the Lord (Luke 4:18-19).*[334]

From the above introductory declaration of the mission of Jesus, it is clear that he is anointed to bring about restoration especially to the poor and the marginalized. After his resurrection, he transfers this mission to his disciples but guarantees them of the bequeathing power of the Holy Spirit, "But you will receive power when the Holy Spirit comes upon you, and you will be my witnesses in Jerusalem, throughout Judea and Samaria, and to the ends of the earth" (Acts 1:8).[335] The promise of the Holy Spirit establishes that their empowerment from above was for a mission of being witnesses of Jesus through their preaching, testimonies, and practice of their faith from Jerusalem to the ends of the earth. Just like Jesus was empowered by the Holy Spirit for his mission, his followers also experience the surge of the Holy Spirit for their ministry. In the mission of the apostles, the Holy Spirit instructs them on their mission as Philip was instructed to join the chariot of the Ethiopian (Acts 8:29) and also commands Peter visit the household of Cornelius (Acts 10:19). At a gathering of prayer in Antioch, the Spirit sends Barnabas and Saul out upon their missionary journeys, beginning at Cyprus (Acts 13:1–4). The Holy Spirit lead the disciples in their mission as new missionary endeavors were initiated at different times for the salvation of the world.[336] Nobody receives the Holy Spirit and stays inactive. When Mary received the Holy Spirit, she was moved to visit her kinswoman Elizabeth (Luke 1:39-45); that is a model and the beginning of her ministry. Consequently, all who have the Holy Spirit have the tools for ministry and also bear the urgency of taking the Good News of Christ to the ends of the earth.

The power to perform signs and wonders did not end with Jesus; it was transferred to the disciples also as part of their mission. Consequently, after the disciples received the power of the Holy Spirit on the Day of Pentecost, Acts 2:43 records that many wonders and signs were done through the apostles. Peter and John healed a cripple at the entrance of

---

[333] Ibid.

[334] Senior, and Collins, op. cit., 1360.

[335] Ibid., 1443.

[336] Stronstad, *The Holy Spirit in Luke-Acts,* (Accessed April 27, 2016).

the Temple in Jerusalem (Acts 3:1-10); and in Acts 9:32, Peter heals Aeneas at Lydda (Act 9:33) and restores Tabitha to life (Acts 9:36).[337] When people wondered about the source of their power, Peter was glad to let them know that they are witnesses of Jesus who was anointed with the Holy Spirit and power and he went about doing good and healing all who were oppressed by the devil (Acts 10:38). The mission of the disciples was not only limited to preaching and healing but encompasses a variety of functions (1 Cor. 12-14, Rom. 12, and Eph. 4). In Luke-Acts Stronstad expounds on how a variety of gifts were manifest among the disciples who were filled with a wide range of offices and functions: apostles (Acts 1:2), deacons (6:1ff), elders (14:23), bishops (20:28), and evangelists (21:8). Twice Luke mentions groups of prophets (11:27; 13:1). He names as prophets, Agabus (11:27, 28), Barnabas, Simeon, Lucius, Manaean, and Saul (13:1), Judas and Silas (15:32), and daughters of Philip (21:9).[338] There were some other occurrences of prophesying, especially with regard to Paul's final journey to Jerusalem (20:23; 21:4). Besides, groups like the disciples on the Day of Pentecost (2:4,17ff), the household of Cornelius at the visit of Peter (10:46), and the disciples of Ephesus (19:6) spoke in tongues and prophesied when the Holy Spirit came upon them.[339]

2.7.7 *The Septuagint Terminology in Luke-Acts*[340]

A close study of Luke-Acts reveals that the terms Luke uses to describe the activities of the Spirit are almost totally derived from the Septuagint. Stronstad asserts that of the nine verbs Luke employed to describe the activity of the Spirit, eight are derived from the Septuagint. These are: "to fill" (Luke 1:15, and others), "to come upon" (Luke 1:35, and others), "to lead" (Luke 4:1), "to give" (Luke 13:13, and others), "to clothe" (power = Holy Spirit, Luke 24:49), "to speak" (Acts 1:16, and others), "to fall upon" (Acts 10:44, and others), and "to witness" (Acts 15:8). Only the verb "baptized" in the Holy Spirit is not Septuagintal.[341]

Conclusively, most scholars agree that the Spirit is not personalized in the Old Testament. Consequently, deriving his pneumatology from the Old Testament, it seems that the Holy Spirit in Luke-Acts is not a person but a power or a substance, since Luke often uses impersonal language to describe the activity of the Holy Spirit. Nevertheless, Luke balances his impersonal language by repeatedly describing the activity of the Holy Spirit in intimate

---

[337] Ibid.

[338] Ibid.

[339] Ibid.

[340] Stronstad, op. cit., 90.

[341] Stronstad, *The Holy Spirit in Luke-Acts,* (Accessed April 27, 2016).

terms. For example, the Holy Spirit witnesses through the signs and wonders that filled Jerusalem after the outpouring of the Holy Spirit on the Day of Pentecost (Acts 5:32). In addition to speaking to or addressing the Holy Spirit, one can lie to the Holy Spirit (Acts 5:3). The Holy Spirit forbids (Acts 16:6) and prohibits (Acts 16:7). The Holy Spirit can also be tested (Acts 5:9) or resisted (Acts 7:51); and the Holy Spirit makes elders the overseers of the Church (Acts 20:28).[342]

The universalization of the Holy Spirit is the major contribution of Lukan pneumatology. While the Old Testament restricted *charisms* to some special people, Luke insightfully lets his community know that one does not need to be a Jew or specially chosen to have access to the Holy Spirit. Luke's unique reports of the Good Samaritan (Luke 10:25-37) and the experience of Cornelius (Acts 10:36-48) demonstrate that everyone is called to be God's embodied presence for the healing and salvation of the world. What empowers one for mission is the Holy Spirit who pours out God's gifts on all who are willing and ready to be used by God.

2.7.8 *Exegesis of 1 Corinthians 12:8-11*

Due to the invigorating presence of the Holy Spirit in the Corinthian community, members experienced an unprecedented manifestation of the gifts of the Holy Spirit (*charismata*, χαρισματα—gracious gift).[343] Unfortunately, from their over-enthusiasm for the powers of the Spirit, a form of spiritual superiority infected the community.[344] This was not the only problem facing the Corinthian community. Many commentators believe that in answer to the problems facing the Corinthian community, Paul wrote his first letter to them. Nonetheless, this section is not going into an exegetical exploration on the whole Corinthian problem, but we shall confine ourselves to the part where Paul uses the purpose of *charisms* to resolve some of the issues facing the community. Consequently, this section is limited to the study of *charisms* in 1 Corinthians 12:8-11, which is a part of the complete text of Paul's response. The chosen text for exposition helps to uncover Paul's understanding of *charisms*. This is helpful for our objective since this thesis is centered on how the *charisms* that were manifest in the early Church can be recovered and restored. In as much as I am taking an exegetical approach to unravel Paul's elucidation of the term, *charism*, it will be limited to Paul's application of the word to resolve the disunity in the Corinthian community. I will explore

---

[342] Stronstad, op. cit., 94.

[343] Paul K. Njiru, *Charisms and the Holy Spirit's Activity in the Body of Christ: An Exegetical-Theological Study of 1 Corinthians 12,4-11 and Romans 12,6-8.* (Tesi Gregoriana Serie Teologia 86). (Rome: Editrice Ponti cia Universita Gregoriana 2002), 7.

[344] Johnson, op. cit., 297.

the origin and Paul's use of the term and accentuate how *charisms* are still relevant in the Catholic Church today.

2.7.9 Background and Overview of 1 Corinthians

Among the books of the New Testament are two letters addressed to the Church of God in Corinth by the apostle Paul. Its history can be divided into two phases. The first is "that of the Greek city-state, which flourished in the fifth century BC and was destroyed by the Roman Consul Lucius Mummius in 146 BC."[345] The second historic phase is "that of the Roman city, the thriving political and mercantile community founded in 44 BC by Julius Caesar.[346] The importance of the strategic location of the ancient city is such that the Roman poet, Horace, described it as *bimaris Corinthus*,[347] that is, a city (Corinth) on two seas. In fact, according to Joseph Fitzyman,

> *The ancient city of Corinth lay just a short distance south of the narrow isthmus that joins the Peloponnesus to the central part of Greece. Its location thus enabled it to achieve an importance in ancient Greece that few other cities could have rivaled. Anyone traveling from Macedonia, Attica, or Athens to Arcadia, Argos, Achaia, or Sparta, would have had to travel across the isthmus of 5,950 meters and pass Corinth en route. Its strategic location also enabled it to dominate two important harbors, one on each side of the isthmus. Eight and a half kilometers to the east was Cenchreae (Kenchreai) on the Saronic Gulf, which gave access to ships traveling from Asia and the Aegean Sea (Apuleius, Metamorphoses 10.35); and two kilometers to the north was Lechaeum (Lechaion) on the Gulf of Corinth, which gave access to the Adriatic Sea and Italy … Consequently, after classical Athens, Corinth was the second most important city in ancient Greece, but in the first century a.d. it would have been more important than Athens. Along with Rome, Alexandria, and Antioch on the Orontes (Syria), it would have been one of the four most important cities of the Mediterranean world.[348]*

---

[345] Collins F. Raymond, Ed. *First Corinthians*. (Minnesota: The Liturgical Press 1995), 22.

[346] Ibid.

[347] Horace Carm 1.7.2. Cited in Fitzyman Joseph. *First Corinthians: A New Translation with Introduction and Commentary*. (New Haven University Press, 2008), 21.

[348] Ibid.

However, the resistance of the Corinthians and their refusal to dissolve the Achaean League precipitated a great war with Rome in 146 BC. In the Achaean war that ensued, "the city was sacked, burned, and razed to the ground; all the male citizens were killed, and the women and children sold into slavery ... City-states such as Corinth, Euboea, Phokis, came under Roman domination, rule, and taxation. So ended the early era of Corinth."[349]

The second era of Corinth witnessed the rebuilding of the city as a Roman colony at the order of Julius Caesar in 44 BC, imbuing the new city with Roman law, custom, and architectures.[350] Thus, "in time, Roman Corinth became the capital of the province of Achaia and the seat of the Roman governor, the center for assizes and the collection of taxes ... and its character of a crossroad between East and West made it necessary for the Roman occupiers to rebuild the city ... Romanitas and a prolonged pax Romana reigned until Byzantine times"[351] Not only was Corinth the metropolitan seat of the proconsul governing the Roman province of Achaia by the time Paul visited and evangelized the city, it has also recovered the administration of the Isthmian Games whose importance is second only to the Olympics.[352] However, "like many modern cities, the city was intellectually arrogant, materially affluent. Also, the city was given to the worship of idols such as, Isis, Serapis, and many other gods and goddesses. In the city, religion and vices were intertwined. Pagan temples stood everywhere dedicated to Aphrodite, the goddess of love and lust. The city of Corinth was known in and around the Mediterranean world for its corrupt practices, and it was at this city that Paul established his church which later became a force to be reckoned with in the whole province."[353]

Paul's first letter to the Corinthians is comprehensive and lengthy, written from Ephesus, in response to ethical, doctrinal and socio-cultural issues most probably in the fall of AD 54.[354] Many Scriptural historians contend about this date as different dates are speculated. 1 Corinthians 12:8-11, our chosen text, is part of a complete text on the whole question of the use of *charisms* that was written as a proposed solution to some of the issues the Corinthian Christian community faced. In the different analogies, Paul insists on the unity of the body of Christ as he explained that all the gifts come from the same Spirit and should function for the good of the body of Christ, the Church.[355]

---

[349] Ibid., 24

[350] Ibid., 25.

[351] Ibid.

[352] Ibid.

[353] Ibid.

[354] Farmer, op. cit., 1601.

[355] Njiru, op. cit., 19.

2.7.10 *The City of Corinth at the Time of Paul*

Corinth at the time of Paul's visit in AD 51, about the year the Church was founded (Acts 18:1-11), was modern, beautiful, industrious, and prosperous; and it attracted sailors from different parts of the known world.[356] There was a flourishing Jewish community and also other religious groups with temples dedicated to the gods of Egypt, Rome, and Greece.[357] Though the Temple of Aphrodite, the goddess of love had fallen into ruins during Paul's time, its 1,000 cult-prostitutes successors continued and earned Corinth the reputation in immorality.[358] Many commentators believe that Paul was attracted to Corinth in order to make right her lewd lifestyle.

2.7.11 *Authorship, Place, Date and Addressees*

The introductory paragraph of 1 Corinthians suggests that Paul and Sosthenes wrote the letter (1:1).[359] However, many scholars accept Paul as the author of 1 Corinthians.[360] Scholars dispute the date of the publication of the letter. It is nevertheless estimated that the letter may have been written in Ephesus between AD 52-55 in the spring before Pentecost (1 Cor. 16:8), on a high possibility that he founded the Corinthian Church in AD 50-51 (Acts 18:1-7), and that he was in Ephesus for two or three years.[361]

2.7.12 *The Problems of the Corinthian Community*

The problems of the Corinthian community as expressed in 1 Corinthians were many and varied. There were different factions in the Church (1:2). Some believed in the disciple that baptized them (1:13-17) and despised the others; others considered "wisdom and eloquence" the ultimate and wondered about Paul's wisdom.[362] The community was besieged with the issues of incest, members frequenting brothels (6:9-20), some rejecting sex entirely (7), sacrificing to idols (8-10), and some were contentious of the role of women (11:2-16; 14:34-36). There was confusion about the celebration of the Lord's Supper (11:17-34) and

---

[356] Meeks, and Fitzgerald, op. cit., 21.

[357] Brown, Fitzmyer, and Murphy, op. cit., 252.

[358] McKenzie, op. cit., 148.

[359] Barton, and Muddiman, op. cit., 1108.

[360] Njiru, op. cit., 26.

[361] Barton, and Muddiman, op. cit., 1109.

[362] Meeks, and Fitzgerald, op. cit., 21.

the use of *charisms*, especially the gift of tongues (*glossolalia*) that endangered the unity of the community (12-14).[363] The Corinthian problems can be summed up as follows: immorality, abuse of sexuality, Idolatry, sexism, wrong liturgy and abuse of *charisms*.

2.7.13 *Paul's Response: Different Kinds of Charismata 1 Corinthians 12:8-10*

Paul, tackling the ethical and doctrinal questions of paramount importance, which the Corinthian community raised,[364] reiterates his central message of the gospel: Christ crucified (1:18-25), the true way of love (13:1-13) and the hope of the resurrection of the believer (15:12-34).[365] Without delving into the details of Paul's solution to the numerous Corinthian problems, it is noteworthy that Paul had the opportunity to expose the beauty of the abundant manifestations of charismatic gifts that abound in the early Christian group. However, self-importance and pride that gave birth to elitism are part of the problems facing the Corinthian community. They judged the gracious gifts of the Holy Spirit received for ministry with the standard of the world. They prized their giftedness more in wisdom and eloquence that expressed the moral philosophies of the times. In response, Paul makes it clear that all wisdom and knowledge comes from God who gives gratuitous gifts to people for the good of the community and not for self-aggrandizement. Paul offers a list of *charisms* to show how the Spirit manifests in the Christian community. He lists nine gracious gifts, *charisms*.[366]

The RSV Text of 1 Corinthians 12:8-11

> *To one is given through the Spirit the utterance of wisdom, and to another the utterance of knowledge according to the same Spirit,[9] to another faith by the same Spirit, to another gifts of healing by the one Sprit,[10] to another the working of miracles, to another prophecy, to another the ability to distinguish between spirits, to another various kinds of tongues, to another the interpretation of tongues.[11] All these are inspired by one and the same Spirit, who apportions to each one individually as he wills.*[367]

---

[363] Ibid., 22.

[364] Farmer, op. cit., 1601.

[365] Ibid., 1602.

[366] Njiru, op. cit., I30.

[367] The Holy Bible. *Revised Standard Version* (Kindle Edition, Second Catholic Edition). Retrieved from Amazon. (San Francisco: Ignatius Press 2002), Loc. 55496.

Many commentators believe that the Revised Standard Version Bible is the corrected English of the original text in Greek. Consequently, it is preferred to others in this section for citation. A close exegetical study is, however, done with Greek text for a philosophical and syntactical purpose.

(a) 1 Corinthians 12:8

ᾧ μὲν γὰρ διὰ τοῦ πνεύματος δίδοται λόγος σοφίας, ἄλλῳ δὲ λόγος γνώσεως κατὰ τὸ αὐτὸ πνεῦμα.[368]

To one is given through the Spirit the utterance of wisdom, and to another the utterance of knowledge according to the same Spirit.[369]

In verse 8 as seen above, Paul begins with a conjunction particle, μὲν ... δὲ, which has the grammatical effect of putting two things being compared side by side, and could be left without being translated or sometimes translated as "while." So, while one is given λόγος σοφίας, (word of wisdom), the other is given λόγος γνώσεως (word of knowledge).[370] The term λόγος has various meanings: a statement or utterance (Matt. 12:32, 37; 1 Cor. 14:19; a spoken word (Mark 7:13; Luke 24:19; 2 Cor. 11:6); computation or reckoning (Luke 16:2; Rom. 14:12; 1 Pet. 3:15); subject, matter or thing under discussion (Matt. 5:32; Acts 8:21; 19:38); a prophetic announcement, (John 12:38); an account, statement, (1 Pet. 3:15), a story, report (Matt. 28:15; John 4:39; 21:23; 2 Thess. 2:2), a written narrative, a treatise (Acts 1:1), a set of discourse (Acts 20:7), doctrine, (John 8:31, 37; 2 Tim. 2:17); a motive (Acts 10:29), reason, (Acts 18:14), ὁ λόγος, the word of God, especially in the gospel, (Matt. 13:21,22; Mark 16:20; Luke 1:2; Acts 6:4), ὁ λόγος, the divine Word has its highest theological usage in Johannine gospel, the divine λόγος that existed at the beginning, which dwelt among humans (John 1:1, 14).[371] The spoken word in verse 8 retains the meaning of the normal sense of the spoken word. However, it is the Holy Spirit that gives humans the ability to speak words of wisdom and knowledge.

[368] Aland B., Aland K., Karavidopoulos J., Martini M. C., and Metzger B. Eds. *The Greek New Testament*. (Fifth Revised Edition). (Deutsche Bibel Gesellschaft, American Bible Society, United Bible Society 2014), 576.

[369] The Holy Bible, op. cit., Loc. 55489.

[370] Njiru, op. cit., I30.

[371] William D. Mounce, *The Analytical Lexicon to the Greek New Testament: Zondervan Greek Reference Series*. (Grand Rapids, Michigan: Zondervan 1993), 303. See also, Silva, *New Dictionary of New Testament Theology And Exegesis* (2nd ed). (Grand Rapids, Michigan: Zondervan 2014), 157.

Σοφία (Wisdom), means wisdom in general, knowledge (Matt. 12:42; Luke 2:40, 50; 11:31; Acts 7:10), practical wisdom, prudence (Col. 4:5), professed wisdom, human philosophy, 1 Cor. 1:19, 20,22; 2:4, 5, 6), superior knowledge and enlightenment (Col. 2:23), divine wisdom (Rom. 11:33; Eph. 3:10; Col. 2:3), revealed wisdom (Matt. 11:19; Luke 11:49; 1 Cor. 1:24, 30; 2:7), Christian enlightenment (1 Cor. 12:8; Eph. 1:8, 17; Col. 1:9, 28, 3:16; James 1:5).[372] Every rational being by nature should have natural wisdom. However, λόγος σοφίας, a word of wisdom from the Holy Spirit is an extraordinary gift because it comes the divine. The difference between wisdom and knowledge is tenuous. While intellectual knowledge is more of acquiring information and data through experience and study, wisdom, on the other hand, has more to do with right thinking, judgment, and decision-making.

Many commentators believe that λόγος σοφίας (word of wisdom) is a gift that enables a person to gain insight into the depth of the things of God. George Montague asserts that it is a special insight given in a transitory way by the Holy Spirit to an individual of a community by way of directive or a counsel on how best to live the Christian life.[373] The gifts of wisdom and knowledge that Paul begins with have to do with the supernatural enlightenment of the mind.[374] In 1 Corinthians 2:5, 13, Paul writes about the "wisdom of men"; and in 2:7, he writes about "the wisdom of God," thereby differentiating between the wisdom of men and that of God. The wisdom of God is hidden from the rulers of this world (2:7-10).[375] For Paul, wisdom as the gift of the Spirit transcends limited human understanding to having divine insights into the mystery of redemption through Christ.[376]

Curiously, a close look at the text shows that Paul does not just speak of wisdom and knowledge as *charisms* separately, but in both cases, it is the *logos*, the word or utterance that he mentions as a *charism*.[377] Since Paul uses λόγος σοφίας (word of wisdom) and λόγος γνώσεως (word of knowledge) simultaneously, is there a difference as such? Paul's use of the terms is not always evidently apparent as some commentators think there is no clear difference in Pauline usage.[378] However, contemporary use and application of the terms differ. While knowledge deals with the intellectual acquisition of perceptible facts, wisdom, on the other hand, is the ability to discern how best to use the knowledge or insights received.

[372] Ibid., 419.

[373] Montague, *The Holy Spirit: The Growth of a Biblical Tradition*, 149

[374] Ibid.

[375] Sullivan, op. cit., 31

[376] Ibid., 32.

[377] Ibid., 31.

[378] Ibid.

Nevertheless, word of knowledge in Pauline corpus is not limited to what is known intellectually but opens up the human intellect to the supernatural realm into gaining insight of divine reality.[379] Paul believes that since certain spiritual realities are inscrutable: "O the depth of the riches and wisdom and knowledge of God! How unsearchable are his judgments and how inscrutable his ways!" (Rom. 11:33),[380] and consequently, the unassisted mind cannot totally comprehend the mind and the knowledge of God (cf. Rom. 11:34).[381] More importantly, since no human person can grasp the thoughts of God unless aided by the Spirit of God, Christians who have received the Holy Spirit are made capable through the Holy Spirit to understand the things of God.[382] However, the gift of knowledge is for service to the community and not something to boast. Paul reminds his Corinthian audience that even knowledge will eventually come to an end because of its limitations and inability to communicate the whole picture sufficiently in words.[383]

Considering also how Christians have interpreted λόγος γνώσεως (word of knowledge) in history, two meanings have been attached: (a), inspired knowledge of fact and (b), insight into the Christian mystery given for the purpose of teaching. For example, Nathan learned of David's sin with Bathsheba and used an insightful parable to get David to admit his guilt (2 Sam 12:1-12).[384] Likewise, in Daniel 13:44-49, we read about the story of Daniel, another figure in the Old Testament with a charismatic gift of knowledge who knew about the innocence of Susanna and called for the examination of her accusers.[385] However, from Paul's subsequent epistles, we can deduce that knowledge is the object of the Christian faith that helps a believer to appreciate better all that God has supplied in Christ (Phil. 1:9; Col. 1:9, 10, 2:2; 3:10). It helps to bring about unity through a common understanding of the faith (Eph. 4:13) and thereby nurtures love also in the community (Eph. 4:16).[386] Consequently, knowledge in Paul is not the same as intellectually acquired knowledge as noted above. When the gift of knowledge is applied in Paul's understanding, and used for

---

[379] Ibid.

[380] The Holy Bible, Loc. 64920.

[381] Njiru, op. cit., 136.

[382] Ibid.

[383] Ibid., 139.

[384] Montague, *The Holy Spirit: The Growth of a Biblical Tradition*, 151.

[385] Ibid.

[386] Ibid., 151-152.

teaching through the anointing of the Holy Spirit, in the words of Montague, "it leads the listener to prayer, worship, and glorification of the Father."[387]

(b) The Gifts of Faith and Healing (v. 9)

ἑτέρω πίστις ἐν τω αὐτω πνεύματι, ἄλλω δὲ χαρίσματα ἰαμάτων ἐν τω ἑνὶ πνεύματι[388]

... to another faith by the same Spirit, to another gift of healing by the one Sprit[389]

The gift of πίστις (faith) is mentioned in verse 9. Πίστις (faith) entails trust, commitment, faithfulness, loyalty, and reliability, especially with regard to God (Matt. 9:2; Luke 18:8, 42; 23:23; Gal. 5:22)[390]. It also includes confidence or solemn promise (1 Tim. 5:12).[391] Faith has to do with the reality, which is not yet clearly seen; and as such faith goes with ἐλπὶς (hope). The letter to the Hebrews defines this beautifully: "Now faith is the assurance of things hoped for, the conviction of things not seen" (11:1).[392] In his letter to the Romans, Paul opines, "Now hope that is seen is not hope. For who hopes for what he sees?" (8:24).[393] Faith also means conviction (Rom. 14:22-23). It is the Holy Spirit that gives this supernatural gift of faith, which enables a believer to rely entirely on God even if things seem to be falling apart. The gift of faith is so fundamental that without it, one cannot function as a Christian. The letter to the Hebrews even says, that without faith it is impossible to please God (11:6).[394] Consequently, this is why the apostles asked the master, "increase our faith"

---

[387] Ibid. 152.

[388] Aland, B., et al., 576.

[389] The Holy Bible, Loc. 55489.

[390] Gingrich Greek Lexicon, (2006) 159, in BibleWorks 7, available from CD-rom, Norfolk, VA: BibleWorks, LLC. See also Mounce, *The Analytical Lexicon to the Greek New Testament: Zondervan Greek Reference Serie*, 375.

[391] Ibid.

[392] The Holy Bible, Loc. 57645.

[393] Ibid., Loc. 54749.

[394] Ibid., Loc. 57662.

(Luke 17:5);[395] and Jesus replied, "If you had faith as a grain of mustard seed, you could say to this sycamore tree, "Be rooted up, and be planted in the sea,' and it would obey you" (Luke 17:6).[396] (This is the faith that moves mountain (Matt. 17:20).

The gift of faith, healing, and working of miracles for Paul are closely related.[397] Beneficiaries of most miracles accessed their healing and miracles in the gospels by faith (Mark 5:34; 10:54; Luke 17:19). Faith as the gift of the Spirit is better expressed in Hebrews 11:1, as mentioned above, "the realization of what is hoped for and evidence of things not seen." It is the kind of faith that Romans 1:17 says, "The one who is righteous by faith will live." It is the faith without which it is impossible to please God (Heb. 11: 6). It is the faith that moves mountains and performs miracles (1 Cor. 13:2)[398]. 'Mountain' here is not physical but an obstacle to a blessing. For Paul, it is the Spirit that enables the recipient of *charisms* to be God's instrument of healing the sick and afflicted. For healing to take place at times, the obstacles of doubt, fears, confusion have to be moved. Jesus refers to this in Mark 11:22 as the faith that could move a mountain. The Spirit empowers ministers to move out of the way every obstacle between God's children and God's healing love. It was the kind of faith Elijah used to defeat 450 prophets of Baal (1Kgs 18:33-44); and in the Acts of the Apostles (3:1-10), it is the faith that Peter and John exercised in healing the cripple at the Temple gate. [399]

Still, in verse 9, the Spirit is the giver of χαρίσματα ἰαμάτων (*charisms* of healing). Χαρίσματα ἰαμάτων (*charisms* of healing) and ἐνεργήματα δυνάμεων (working of miracles) are classified under the gift of faith.[400] It takes faith to be God's instrument of healing and miracles. In order to perform healing and miracles, one has to operate under the gift of the Holy Spirit. In 1 Corinthians 13:2, Paul speaks also of the faith that can move a mountain.[401] It is through the Holy Spirit that God gives to the believer the spiritual gifts of effecting physical and spiritual healing or finding a remedy to problematic situations. It means therefore that the Pauline χαρίσματα ἰαμάτων (*charisms* of healing) is not limited to the miracles of physical healing alone. It could be spiritual healing or even finding a solution to a problem. Whoever has the grace of healing and miracles is God's instrument to demonstrate

---

[395] Ibid., Loc. 51530.

[396] Ibid., Loc. 51530-51538.

[397] Montague, *The Holy Spirit: The Growth of a Biblical Tradition,* 152.

[398] Sullivan, op. cit., 32.

[399] Montague, *The Holy Spirit: The Growth of a Biblical Tradition,* 152.

[400] Njiru, 145.

[401] Ibid.

God's divine power to deliver and save those in severe bodily or spiritual conditions. It is not based on human abilities or wisdom but on God's gratuitous grace that enables whoever God chooses to be God's instrument of healing presence in the world.

1 Cor. 12: 10

"ἄλλῳ δὲ ἐνεργήματα δυνάμεων, ἄλλῳ (δὲ) προφητεία, ἄλλῳ (δε) διακρίσεις πνευμάτων, ἑτέρῳ γένη γλωσσῶν, ἄλλῳ δὲ ἑρμηνεία γλωσσῶν."[402]

To another workings of miracles, to another prophecy, to another ability to distinguish between spirits, to another various kinds of tongues, and to another interpretation of tongues.[403]

The first gift mentioned in v. 10 is ἐνεργήματα δυνάμεων (working of power). The word ἐνεργήματα has the meaning of an effect, a thing effected, activity, operation, working[404] and it is specifically a Pauline vocabulary found only in 1 Corinthians 12:6 and 10 in the whole Bible.[405] On the other hand, δύναμις is a rampant word, both in the OT and the NT, with various shades of meaning: army, host, force (Gen. 26:26; Exod. 6:26; Mark 13:25; Luke 21:26), power, might, strength (Num. 1:20-42; Acts 1:8; Heb. 7:16) and Power as a divine being or angel (1 Cor. 15:24; Rom. 8:38). Δύναμις also means 'deed of power' or 'miracle' (Matt. 11:20-21; Mark 6:5; 2 Cor. 12:12; Heb. 2:4).[406] It is in this sense that Paul uses it here in verse 10. The Holy Spirit gives to some people the gift of working of miracles. The gift of miracles lays bare God's miraculous intervention in the plight of humanity. Miracles are God's mediation in the affairs of humans, bringing to normalcy whatever may be deformed. This certainly refers to an exceptional show of what the power of God can do through those endowed with the gift of a miracle as seen in Acts 9:40, where Peter raised Dorcas from the dead back to life and the raising also of Eutychus to life by Paul (Acts 20:10).[407]

---

[402] Aland, B., et al., 576.

[403] The Holy Bible, Loc. 55495.

[404] Mounce, op. cit., 188.

[405] *Gingrich Greek Lexicon*, 52, in BibleWorks 7.

[406] Ibid.

[407] Montague, op. cit., 153.

Another gift is that of προφητεία (prophecy). The biblical idea of προΦητεία, which Paul expresses as an action of the Spirit, derives from the etymology of the word itself. The word is a combination of the preposition, προ (pro) – 'in front of' or 'in place of' – and Φημι (phēmi) – 'speak'.[408] Thus, prophecy is an utterance made for God, and the prophet is a spokesperson for God. Consequently, the identification of prophecy as a gift of the Holy Spirit by Paul is a redirection to the real biblical concept of the word. It is also an affirmation that it is the Spirit that gives Christians the grace to speak the mind of God to the world, just as Moses did to the Egyptians. Hence, the Pauline and Christian sense of the word "prophecy" must "be understood as a Spirit-inspired dynamic and effective preaching of the Scriptures and the gospel, as Paul makes clear below, in 14:1, 3–6, 24, 29, 31."[409] Accordingly, Paul's understanding flows from prophecy in the OT that was focused on the proclamation of the word of God, to exhort, comfort, teach and counsel the people in order to bind the people to God alone.[410] The popular concept of a prophet is the one who foretells the future. However, prophecy in Israel must not be confused with soothsaying. The prophets of Israel deal with religious matters, correcting a person's behavior in the light of expected events.[411] The noun προφητεία is found only 19 times in the NT, of which 9 times are in Paul; including 5 times in 1 Corinthians and twice in 1 Timothy, and 7 times in Revelation, once in Matthew and twice in 2 Peter and only Paul uses the term for the gift of prophecy (*charisma*; Grace (Rom. 12:6).[412] The NT associates the prophet with the teacher and presents prophets as people who speak to God's people under the inspiration of the Holy Spirit.[413] Consequently, the type of prophecy, which Paul has in mind here, is most probably the gift of discerning the mind of God and speaking to the people about it in such a way that they are edified. It is the exposition of inspirational words from God uttered for the benefit of the community.[414] In other words, it is the inspiration to speak God's word in such a way that it impacts people's lives positively. The early Christians who had the gift of prophecy were considered manifest signs of the presence of the Spirit in the Church, which presumably was the early stage this charismatic, impulsive prophecy was institutionalized and prophets

[408] Fitzyman, op. cit., 467.

[409] Ibid.

[410] Brown, op. cit., 79.

[411] Ibid., 76.

[412] Ibid., 81.

[413] Njiru, op. cit., 156.

[414] Montague, op. cit., 154.

became prominent in holding spiritual offices.[415] The Corinthian community used the gift of prophecy in their service (1 Cor. 14:23f.), to exhort (1 Cor. 14:3, 24f., 31), to comfort (1 Cor. 14:3), and to edify the Church (1 Cor. 14:3), and to communicate knowledge and mysteries (1 Cor. 13:2).[416] Though prophecy in Paul consists of spontaneous, intelligible messages, orally delivered in a gathering for the purpose of building the community, it could at times lead unbelievers to repentance.[417] However, the community has to discern all prophecies with the *charism* for discernment and interpretation and judging prophetic expressions.[418]

Also in verse 10a comes the διακρίσεις πνευμάτων (discernment of spirits). Apart from Job 37:16, διακρίσεις does not appear in any other place in LXX. It is basically Pauline and appears only three times (1 Cor. 12:10; Heb. 5:14) with the meaning, "distinguishing, and differentiation" and Rom. 14:1, where it means 'quarrel or dispute'.[419] The πνευμάτων (spirits), which are to be discerned here are states of mind and dispositions and inner forces, that impel one to act in one way or the other. It is quite pertinent to discern these forces or states of mind so as to act morally in the right way. Discernment is the grace to judge what is of God and what is not of God. And the variety of tongues can be for prayer, praise or prophecy.

Speaking in Tongues and the Interpretation (v. 10b)

Another gift in verse 10 is γένη γλωσσῶν (various kinds of tongues). According to Gingrich Lexicon, the expressions γλῶσσαι, γένη γλωσσῶν, ενη γλωσσηλ λαλεῖν etc. "refer to the ecstatic speech of those overcome by strong emotion in a cultic context. The latter expression is usually rendered 'speak in tongues', Act 19:6; 1 Cor. 12:10; 13:1,8; 14."[420] The gift of speaking in tongues was very prominent among the challenges of the Corinthian Church. Paul did not make a categorical assertion on it in this text. Rather, he drew attention to its place in the community. This approach gives us an allusion into what Paul really meant by the gift of tongues. First and foremost, his reference to the tongue in γενη γλωσσων is not to the bodily organ of taste, but it is a figurative allusion to a speech or a language. Furthermore, on the specific speech or language that 'speaking in tongue' entails in this text, Fitzyman explains that

---

[415] Ibid., 84.

[416] Ibid.

[417] Njiru, op. cit., 156.

[418] Ibid., 157.

[419] Walter Bauer, *A Greek-English Lexicon of the New Testament and Other Early Christian Literature*, 2nd ed., trans. Arndt W. F., and F. W. Gingrich (Chicago/London: The University of Chicago Press, 1979), 185.

[420] *Gingrich Greek Lexicon*, 40, in BibleWorks 7.

"gene glōssōn could denote different foreign languages spoken by human beings (xenologia), but, in referring it to pneumatikon, someone who speaks in such "tongues," Paul means vocal utterances of unusual nature not understood by others, as it becomes clear in chapter 14."[421] Therefore a good description of the concept shall be either as utterances made outside the normal patterns of intelligible speech, that is, utterances of persons in religious ecstasy or as foreign and unintelligible human utterances.[422] It is the type the utterances the apostles received on the day of Pentecost (Acts 2). However, the spirit also gives the gift of ἑρμηνεία γλωσσῶν (interpretation of tongues). Ερμηνεία is a Pauline term, occurring only in 1 Corinthians 12:10 and 14:26 in the NT,[423] apart from its appearance in Sirach 47:17 and Daniel 5:1. It means 'interpretation or translation'. For Paul, the gift of tongues that is devoid of interpretation does not edify the faithful (1 Cor. 14). This is why he says; "In Church, I would rather speak five words with my mind, in order to instruct others, than ten thousand words in a tongue" (1 Cor. 14:19). The variety of tongues can be praise, prayer or prophecy. Every manifestation of the gift of tongues must have an interpreter.

2.7.14 *Conclusion*

In verse 11, Paul caps up his discussion on the itemized charismata, "All these are inspired by one and the same Spirit, who apportions to each one individually as he wills." With the phrase παντα δε ταυτα (all these), which is not just a rhetorical emphasis, but also Paul's way of summing up all the gifts mentioned in verses 4-10. The introduction of δε, a postpositive conjunction serves to "mark the contrast of transition from the manifold gifts and powers to the one Source of them all"[424] Paul strategically, he is emphasizing that all the gifts are products of the benevolence of the Spirit, as such, "Paul's stress is on 'all these' gifts in order to show that such characteristics that individual Christians possess are not personal achievements, but endowments derived solely from a divine source (Spirit, Lord, or Father) and destined for the good (12:7) of the whole community."[425]

The Spirit apportions to each person according to his or her ability. Personalities differ and consequently, one is given gifts as the Holy Spirit deems fit. The Spirit, who searches

---

[421] Fitzyman, op. cit., 468.

[422] Ibid., 470.

[423] Bauer, *A Greek-English Lexicon of the New Testament and Other Early Christian Literature*, 310.

[424] Olugbenga Olagunju, *Exegesis of 1 Cor. 12:1-11*, http://www.biblicaltheology.com/Research/ OlagunjuO02. pdf Accessed on August 8, 2016.

[425] Fitzyman, op. cit., 471.

and knows each person knows and offers each what is needed to be dutifully God's embodied presence to bless the world through whatever charismatic gift one has.

Self-importance, pride, and elitism are some of the problems that Corinthian community faced. They judged the gracious gifts of the Holy Spirit received for ministry with the standard of the world. They prize their giftedness more in wisdom and eloquence expressed in the moral philosophies of the times. In response, Paul makes it clear that all wisdom and knowledge comes from God who gives gratuitous gifts to people for the good of the community, but not for self-aggrandizement.

Paul's discourse on *charisms* emphasizes the Spirit as the source of the gifts for ministry and underscores the need for harmony in the community that is in chaos. However, it is admirable to know about the openness of the Corinthian community to allow God's gratuitous gifts that enable anyone to be God's instrument of blessings in the world. I believe that each Christian community also has access to God's gratuitous gifts.

Paul accentuated the need for mutual respect among members because each gift is important and indispensable. Given that the same Spirit gratuitously gives each person gifts for serving the body of Christ and humanity, bearers of these gratuitous gifts are to use them humbly for God's glory and the good of humanity. There are enough spiritual gifts in each Catholic Christian Community to invigorate the body of Christ. By our baptism, each person receives gifts of the Holy Spirit for ministry in the Church and the world. The question is: can we still manifest today the gifts of the Holy Spirit, as they were apparent among the Corinthians and the early Church? The Holy Spirit and the gifts are indispensable if we have to fulfill our calling to be fruitful in God's kingdom.

2.7.15 *Reflection on Romans* 12:6-8

Paul's letter to the Romans has long held a prominent position amongst all his other letters.[426] It is the longest and most theological exposition of Paul's thought on the gospel of God's righteousness that redeems all who believe (1:16-17). It has a universal outlook, with a particular implication for Israel's relation with the Church (Chapters 9-11).[427] The letter to the Romans is certainly not a systematic summary of Paul's theology,[428] but rather an essay presentation of his evolutionary understanding of the salvation history, rooted in God's righteousness and love, given to humans through Jesus Christ.[429]

---

[426] Senior, and Collins, op. cit., 1493.

[427] Ibid.

[428] Johnson, op. cit., 344.

[429] Brown, Fitzmyer, op. cit., 830.

2.7.16 *The Roman Church*

Someone other than Paul founded the Roman Church; but he did not mention the founder (15:20; cf. 1:8, 13).[430] Converts from Palestine or Syria may have formed the community at an early date.[431] Many commentators believe that the Roman Church was a mixture of Jewish and Gentile converts, but predominantly Gentile,[432] possibly after Emperor Claudius expelled the Jews from Rome (ca. AD 49) due to an argument in the Jewish community over Jesus as the Messiah (*Christus*)[433].

2.7.17 *Authorship, Place and Addressees*

Paul's authorship of the letter to the Romans is not in dispute as most scholars are in agreement. However, some scholars doubt the relationship between chapter 16 and the rest of the letter. [434] The accurate date of the letter cannot be verified; however, many commentators are in consensus that Romans may have been written probably in Corinth, during Paul's final visit in mid AD 50, making it one of Paul's final letters.[435] The letter addresses all God's beloved in Rome.[436]

2.7.18 *Occasion and Purpose*

Apparently, mindful of the end of his apostolate in the eastern Mediterranean area, Paul looked forward to visiting Spain but desired to stop in Rome to fulfill his age-long desire (1:13; 15:22, 24, 28).[437] Paul wrote to introduce himself before arriving Rome since he was known by name alone. He also wanted the Roman Church to know his theological thoughts on certain salvific and ecclesiastical issues, which he had discussed in some of his

---

[430] Ibid., 831.

[431] Ibid.

[432] Ibid.

[433] Senior, and Collins, op. cit., 1493.

[434] Barton, and Muddiman, 1084.

[435] Ibid.

[436] Ibid.

[437] Ibid., 830.

Churches.[438] Some commentators speculate that he desired to win the support of the Roman Church for his missionary exploits in Rome; and since he sees himself as a 'minister of the Gentiles' (Gal. 2:7), he felt some responsibility for the Gentile Christian.[439] From the many assumptions about Paul's purpose of writing to the Romans, it can be summed up as, theological, pastoral and missionary.[440]

2.7.19 *The Exegesis of Romans 12:6-8*

The exegesis done on this text is only to complete the one on 1 Corinthians 12:8-11. The two texts bear on the charismata of the Holy Spirit. Only issues that are new and absent in the already analyzed text are considered. In Romans, Paul gives an impelling elucidation of the doctrine of the supremacy of Christ and of faith in Christ as the source of salvation.[441] He calls on the Roman Christians to be unwavering in their faith, and resist any doctrine of salvation that insists on the works of the law.[442] Furthermore, he reminds them of the significances of the gospel that they have embraced, especially the aspect of presenting themselves exclusively to God by a life of selfless sacrifice.[443] Apart from using the analogy of human body to emphasize the importance of unity in diversity in the community, he highlights his concerns about the Roman Church and enjoins them to live in harmony. His listing of all seven gifts, namely, prophecy, ministry, teaching, exhortation, almsgiving, leadership, and works of mercy, in Romans 12:6-8 are all for the purpose of exhorting the members of the community.[444]

The RSV Text of Romans 12:6-8

[6] ἔχοντες δὲ χαρίσματα κατὰ τὴν χάριν τὴν δοθεῖσαν ἡμῖν διάφορα, εἴτε προφητείαν κατὰ τὴν ἀναλογίαν τῆς πίστεως, [7] εἴτε διακονίαν ἐν τῇ διακονία,

---

[438] Johnson, op. cit., 344.

[439] Barton, and Muddiman, 1085.

[440] G. Bornkamm, "The Letter to the Romans, 2-14, referenced in Njiru, *Charisms and the Holy Spirit's Activity in the Body of Christ,* 224.

[441] Senior, and Collins, op. cit., 1494.

[442] Ibid.

[443] Njiru, 284.

[444] Ibid., 285-293.

εἴτε ὁ διδάσκων ἐν τῇ διδασκαλίᾳ, [8] εἴτε ὁ παρακαλῶν ἐν τῇ παρακλήσει ὁ μεταδιδοὺς ἐν ἁπλότητι, ὁ προϊστάμενος ἐν σπουδῇ, ὁ ἐλεῶν ἐν ἱλαρότητι[445]

[6] *Having gifts that differ according to the grace given to us, let us use them: if prophecy, in proportion to our faith; [7] if service, in our serving; he who teaches, in his teaching; [8] he who exhorts, in his exhortation; he who contributes, in liberality; he who gives aid, with zeal; he who does acts of mercy, with cheerfulness.*[446]

Gifts According to Χάρις (Grace) (v. 6)

The gifts of the Holy Spirit are given κατὰ τὴν χάριν (according to grace). Χάρις means 'graciousness' (Luke 4:22), 'favor, grace, and goodwill' (Luke 1:30; Acts 2:47; Eph. 2:5).[447] Grace brings divine favor (1 Pet 2:19-20). It is the effect of God's favor (Rom. 12:6; 2 Cor. 8:1). Χάρις also expresses 'thanks or gratitude' (1 Tim. 1:12; 2 Tim. 1:3; Heb. 12:28). In verse 6, it used in the sense of grace or favor. What is given by grace is a gratuitous gift but not given by merit. The individual gifts, which God has given to us, are therefore not by our merit but by God's graciousness. Paul exhorts his audience to be humble in discharging whatever *charisms* one has received gratuitously according to one's measure of faith and grace, without thinking of oneself better than the other (12:3). The recipient of gifts should acknowledge that God's gifts are gratuitously given, and everyone has his/her according to the grace given to one.

The Gifts of Service (διακονία) and Teaching (διδασκαλία), v. 7

Διακονία is a famous theological word, the basic meaning of which is 'service'. It encompasses domestic service like serving at the table. Service or ministry here is not in a generally categorized term for all the gifts as in 1 Corinthians 12:5 but a particular gift, which may be waiting at table or serving the community (Acts 6:1 and Luke 10:40).[448] The seven deacons were elected to serve at table, while the apostles were to concentrate on the preaching of the word (Acts 6:3-4). Both are forms of service. It entails office work or

---

[445] Aland, B., et al., 576.

[446] The Holy Bible, Loc. 54966.

[447] Bauer., op. cit., 877.

[448] Montague, 214

ministry (Acts 1:17; 20:24; 1 Cor. 12:5).[449] All kinds of aid, support and contribution come under the term, διακονία (service). Paul enjoins all who are endowed with any kind of service to do it with dedication.

The gift of διδασκαλία (teaching) entails the imparting of knowledge. The teaching could be in any sphere of life, but the highest teaching is the one on divine realities. The word διδασκαλία appears often in 1 and 2 Timothy, letters purportedly written by Paul to his disciple Timothy, instructing him on how to lead the Church entrusted to his care, and on how leaders of the Church should behave. A teacher gives instructions on the right things to be done (Rom. 15:4; 1 Tim. 1:10; 2 Tim. 3:10, 16). Those who have the *charism* of teaching should exercise the gift according to the measure of the grace given to them in service to the community. Likewise, one should prophesy only to the extent that one receives the guarantee that the word received is from God.[450] Though Romans does not mention discernment as in 1 Corinthians 12:10, prophecy entails proper discernment to ascertain its authenticity.

The Gifts of Exhortation and Sharing/Generosity (v. 8a) The gift of παράκλησις (exhortation) has several meanings. This noun comes from the verb, παράλαλεω, which has a lot of connotations: called to one's side (Act 8:31; 16:9), appeal, exhort, encourage (Rom. 12:1,8; 2 Cor. 10:1; Heb. 3:13), entreat, implore, appeal to (Matt. 8:5; Luke 8:31-32; Philem. 9), comfort, encourage, cheer up (Luke 16:25; Eph. 6:22; 1 Thess. 4:18), console, conciliate (1 Cor. 4:13; 1 Thess. 2:12).[451] Just as the verb, the noun παράκλτος, comes from it has varied meanings: the one who exhorts, one who journey with another, an advocate, comforter, intercessor, implorer, etc. This is the term that the Johannine gospel uses exclusively to designate the Holy Spirit (John 14:16, 26; 15:26; 16:7; cf. 1 John 2:1). So, the Holy Spirit is actually the first comforter or the one who exhorts. Those who are gifted in this direction are to imitate the Holy Spirit. The one who exhorts is like a prophet who encourages the community with words from God in order to inspire and strengthen them (1 Cor. 14:3).[452]

The participial phrase, ὁ μεταδιδοὺς (the one giving) stands for those who have a special gift of generosity. Paul advises that this gift should be exercised with ἁπλότητι, (*simplicity, sincerity, frankness*). This means that gifts should be given with sincerity (Col. 3:22; 2 Cor. 1:12). One should neither give in order to blot one's ego nor give grudgingly, out of compulsion. There should be no strings attached to gifts of this sort (Rom. 12:8; 2 Cor. 9:11), for God loves a cheerful giver. Contributing with liberality has to do with sharing

---

[449] Bauer, op. cit., 184. See also, Mounce, *The Analytical Lexicon to the Greek New Testament: Zondervan Greek Reference Series, 323*.

[450] Sullivan, 43.

[451] *Gingrich*, 7.

[452] Montague, 214.

one's goods with others. Paul particularly encourages the Roman Church to help in making contributions to the Church in Jerusalem, and he expects everyone to generously take part. Those who give alms and perform works of mercy should do such with zeal and cheerfulness.

The Gifts of Leading/Giving Aid and Mercy (8b)

In verse 8b, the participial phrase, ὁ προϊστάμενος, has two possible meanings: It could mean a) "the one leading, directing and ruling (1 Tim. 3:4-5; 5:17) and/or b) the one who is caring and giving aid (Rom. 12:8; 1 Thess. 5:12). Consequently, different Bible versions have varied translation of this part of verse 8. Both actions are gifts of the Holy Spirit. Anyone who is gifted in these ways should act with σπουδῇ, (eagerness, diligence, enthusiasm, 2 Cor. 7:11; Heb. 6:11; 2 Pet. 1:5) and with devotion (2 Cor. 7:12).[453] Likewise, the one having mercy (ὁ ἐλεῶν) should do that in ἱλαρότητι (cheerfulness, graciousness, without reluctance). This word, ἱλαρότητι, is an hapax in the entire NT, occurring only here in Romans 12:8. In the OT, it appears only in the Wisdom books of Proverbs (18:22) and Psalms (4:5; 16:12), where they have the same meaning.

2.7.20 Conclusion

Paul's treatment of gifts of the Spirit in Romans seems to be a development his discussion on the same theme in 1 Corinthians 12-14. Though they are complementary, they differ in three ways: (a) In Romans, διακονία is a specific gift, but not an umbrella term comprising all varieties of gifts as in 1 Corinthians 12:5; (b) Paul urges his audience in Romans to use gifts in proportion to the measure of their faith; and (c) He gives directives on how the gift of prophecy should be carried out.[454] Paul encourages his audience to exercise good judgment and discernment in carrying out the *charisms* and to do all for the glory of God and for the spiritual development of the community.

In concluding this section, I affirm the complementarity between Paul's treatment of *charisms* in 1 Corinthians 12-14 and Romans 12. However, I think that Paul's expansion and unique categorization of the gifts of the Holy Spirit in Romans goes a long way to show that each community is unique. For each Christian community to function and make a Godly impact on the world, there has to be an openness to God's gratuitous gifts for service in the Church and the world. Every community is given God's gratuitous gifts for ministry, depending on the needs and readiness of the community to access the gifts for its nourishment and growth. Nonetheless, there has to be mutual respect in the body of Christ

---

[453] Bauer, 763.

[454] Ibid.

through the appreciation and treasuring of the gifts that each person has for the promotion of God's kingdom.

Chapter Three

The Manifestations and the Use of Charisms in the First Eight Centuries of the Church[455]

❦

3.1 *Introduction*

All through biblical history, authors have insightfully documented that no chosen person goes on a divine assignment on his or her own. It is God who calls each person by name. Everyone selected for a mission by God is equipped with special graces to carry out given tasks. Graces are the unmerited favors from the God who gratuitously made a choice of a person or people unqualified as they were and used them for God's divine purposes. In a special way, God endowed people with the favor that enabled them to accomplish inexplicable deeds, at times beyond human comprehension. Consequently, the apparent activities of God seen in a person or persons in the Old Testament clarify what was operational, which I believe is grace, χαρις (*charis*) in Greek.

χαρις (*charis*), grace, gracefulness, graciousness, favor, goodwill; χαριζομαι (*charizoma*i), show favor or kindness, gives a favor, to be gracious to someone, to pardon; χαριτόω (*charitoŏ*), endure with grace.[456]

The term χαρις (*charis*) occurs sparingly in the New Testament writings but features more in Paul's epistles, and Luke/Acts.[457] Paul's use of *χάρις* signifies the core of God's decisive saving act in Jesus Christ on the cross, and also of all the consequences in the present

---

[455] McDonnell and Montague, *Christian Initiation and Baptism in the Holy Spirit,* i.

[456] Brown, op. cit., 115.

[457] Silva, op. cit., 656-657.

and future (Rom. 3:24-26).[458] God's gratuitousness is manifest on the cross through the Christ event that confirms the availability of grace to the sinner (Rom. 3:23-31; 5: 7-10, cf. Gal. 2:17-21; Rom. 11:32), which is the totality of salvation (2 Cor. 6:1). Every Christian possesses it as a precious gift.[459] We are saved by grace.[460] Salvation entirely dependent on grace was such a fascinating and delightful experience for Paul that the word χάρις/grace occupies a prime place in his greetings.[461] Χάρις ὑμῖν καὶ εἰρήνη means grace and peace to you (Rom. 1:7), and in a similar fashion in the final greetings: χάρις τοῦ Κυρίου ἡμῶν Ἰησοῦ Χριστοῦ μεθ' ὑμῶν, which means the grace of our Lord Jesus Christ be with all of you (1 Thess. 5:28).[462] Paul's use of χάρις/*grace* for his salutations at the beginning and end of his letters demonstrate how grounded his understanding of God's gratuitousness was in his life and for all humanity.[463] He tried very much to impress the idea of grace on his audience especially the Jews. At the climax of communicating his theology of grace in Galatians 2:21 and in divergence to those who see the Mosaic Law as the core of life, he repudiates the idea to "set aside the grace of God, for if righteousness could be gained through the law, Christ died for nothing" (Gal. 3:18, 21)[464]. By the way of dissimilarity, Paul believes that the Galatians, even though they were called by divine grace (1:6; cf. v. 15), fell away from grace inasmuch as they succumbed to the regulations of circumcision in order to be justified by the law.[465] Furthermore, Paul contrasts God's grace with "worldly wisdom" (2 Cor. 1:12). Grace is not only opposed to Jewish self-confidence based on the law, but also distinctive

---

[458] Ibid., 658.

[459] Gerhard Kittel, and Gerhard Friedrich, Eds. *Theological Dictionary of the New Testament.* 10 vols. (Grand Rapids, MI: Wm. B. Eerdmans Publishing 2006), 394. Cf. Silva, New *Dictionary of New Testament Theology and Exegesis*, 658.

[460] Ibid.

[461] On the Gk, epistolary formula cf. O. Roller, "Das Formula d. paul. Briefe," BWANT, 58 (1933). 46-91; Wendland Hell. Kult., 411-417. On Paul's formula cf. E. Lohmeyer, "Probleme paulinischer Theologie. 1: *Briefliche Grussuberschriften*," ZNW, 26 (1927), 158-173; G. Friedrich, "Lohmeyers These über d. paul. Brief-Präskript kritisch beleuchtet," ThLZ, 81 (1956), 343-6. Cited in Kittel, and Friedrich, (Eds). *Theological Dictionary of the New Testament*, 393.

[462] Ibid.

[463] Silva, op. cit., 658.

[464] Ibid., 659.

[465] Ibid.

from the Greeks proud self-sufficiency.[466] Ultimately, everything about the Christian life is governed by grace (Rom. 5:2; 2 Cor. 6:1-9).[467] It is God's grace that grants success in ministry. Paul attributes his vocation and mission to being of a special grace (Rom. 1:5; 12:3; 15:15 cf. 1 Cor. 3:10).[468] It is God who gives those called to ministry the special graces they need for specified tasks and these graces are called charisma.

The noun Χάρισμα (charisma) is cited almost solely in the Pauline corpus.[469] Besides, it is used in reference to a divine grace in a general sense (Rom. 5:15-16; 6:23; 11:29).[470] However, the usage here is different because of its particular and manifold outworking of the one grace in individual Christians through one and the same Spirit.[471] The word *charisma* comes from the verb χαρίζομαι (charidzomai), "to bestow a gift or favor," which means free gift, a spiritual capacity stemming from God's grace (*charis*).[472] Paul applies *charisma* to the gifts of the Holy Spirit but first of all relates it to the total gift of salvation received by believers as mentioned above (Rom. 5:15-16; 6:23: "the *charisma* of God is eternal life in Christ Jesus our Lord").[473] Paul stresses that each person has a specific gift/*charism* from God (1 Cor. 7:7, 17; 12:7) that is meant for the benefit of others "so that in all things God may be glorified through Jesus Christ" (1 Pet. 4:10-11), and offers lists of *charisms* (1 Cor. 12-14), and also how the gifts are used (Rom. 12:6-8; Eph. 4:4-11).[474] These gifts/*charisms* have been God's effective, ministerial, saving tools throughout human salvific history. Whenever God wanted to carry out a mission in the OT among a people, God used people and gave them special graces to accomplish it. In chapter two we explored the trails of the Spirit in the OT. We saw how God endowed chosen persons with charismatic graces for specific responsibilities. Emphasis was placed on leaders who were special recipients of these gifts/*charisms*.[475] However, there is a shift in understanding and application in the NT.

---

[466] Ibid.

[467] Ibid.

[468] Kittel, and Friedrich, op. cit., 396.

[469] Silva, op. cit., 660.

[470] Ibid.

[471] Brown, op. cit., 121.

[472] Downey, op. cit., 140. Cf. Kittel, and Friedrich, op. cit., 396-398.

[473] Ibid.

[474] Ibid.

[475] Ibid., 141.

This shift comes from the fulfillment of a number of prophecies in the OT. On the day of Pentecost, the promise made by the prophets that one day the gifts would be given to everyone was fulfilled (Isa. 42:1; 44:1-3; Joel 2:28-29; Ezek. 36:26-27; Jer. 31:31-33).[476] The prophetic fulfillment process started at God's appointed time (Gal. 4:4), with the birth of Jesus (Matt. 1:18-25; Luke 2:1-20), who was filled with the Holy Spirit at his baptism (Mark 1:9-11; Matt. 3:13-17; Luke 3:21-22). Peter captures the intensity and power of the mission of Jesus: "God anointed Jesus of Nazareth with the Holy Spirit and power. He went about doing good and healing all those oppressed by the devil, for God was with him" (Acts 10:38).[477] Subsequently, the early Christians continued the salvific charismatic ministry of Jesus through their openness to the Holy Spirit who gave them *charisms* for ministry in the world. They used their gifts to evangelize the known world with remarkable success. Unfortunately, all that excitement and enthusiasm as recorded in the early Church dwindled and eventually died out in fewer than 10 centuries.

Notwithstanding, the abiding presence of God manifested in the workings of the Holy Spirit's gifts/*charisms* in the early Church, was not meant to fade with each age, but was to remain constant with developmental twists in each epoch's understanding and accessibility of the actions of the Holy Spirit. With God's creation not absolutely fixed and determined and God's Spirit still moving and willing to work with the creative human freedom in the Church to make the Church eternally new, the Church needs to be ever open for renewal.[478] The only presence capable of bringing about the revitalization needed in the Church is the Holy Spirit who is still professed as the giver of life. Unfortunately, most members of the Catholic Church have not experienced the manifestations of the Holy Spirit, whose activities seem to be doctored, confused and suppressed. How can we remain confused about the actions of the Holy Spirit? Pope Francis reminds us that ever since Pentecost the "protagonist of the Church" has been the Holy Spirit, it is he who "moves all things" and he repeatedly calls on Catholic Christians to open up to the Holy Spirit who makes all things new.[479] We always need the invigorating presence of the Holy Spirit, but the Holy Spirit cannot impose herself on us. Pope Francis said recently in his homily at Santa Marta chapel on April 28, 2016, "Be open to the surprises of the Holy Spirit."[480] Yes indeed, the God of surprises who brings about transformation and renewal to whatever the Holy Spirit touches awakens

---

[476] Ibid.

[477] Ibid.

[478] Prusak, op. cit., 5 & 332.

[479] Mass at Santa Marta, http://www.news.va/en/news/mass-at-santa-marta-innovation-and-resistance Accessed on May 3, 2016.

[480] Ibid.

newness, enthusiasm, and purposefulness in each generation. I believe the Church needs an ongoing Pentecostal experience, what Kilian McDonnel calls *A Perpetual Pentecost*,[481] to remain ever new and relevant in the world of each era. The Church does not need a new movement or a special spirituality.[482] However, the Church needs an introspective openness to retrieve buried treasures that I consider *charisms*/gifts of the Holy Spirit and allow God's children to blossom to full manifestations for effective ministry in the world today. These *charisms* I believe are forgotten riches of the Church, which are suppressed, and not necessarily lost but appear extraneous to many in the ecclesiastical leadership circles. It is encouraging to know that Kilian McDonnel, George Montague, and some other theologians through ecclesiastical, historical, and scientific biblical research have shown evidence of the manifestations and use of the *charisms* in the first eight centuries of the Church. Nonetheless, there seems to be a discontinuity. This chapter seeks to unravel the truth of the rich Catholic ecclesiastical history that was inspired by the early Christians' experience of the Holy Spirit and establish that *charisms* were part of the early Church's liturgical life. The chapter will also propose how *charisms* are still relevant in the Church today for active ministry in the world.

3.2 *The Holy Spirit, a Fact of Human Experience Before Being a Doctrine*

> *Long before the Spirit was a theme of doctrine, He was a fact in the experience of the community.*[483]

All Christian doctrines develop from a person or a people's authentic spiritual experience of God, Jesus Christ or the Holy Spirit. From Luke's historical, theological narratives, we can construe that the apostles and disciples of Jesus had the tangible experience of the transforming touch of the workings of the Holy Spirit in their lives. However, they never left a well-defined teaching or doctrine of the nature of the Holy Spirit. Nevertheless, through the theological insightful documentations of authors of the gospels, Acts of the Apostles and the Epistles, we understand the functioning manifest mechanisms of the Holy Spirit

---

[481] Kilian McDonnel, Ed. *Open the Windows: The Popes and Charismatic Renewal.* (South Bend, Indiana: Greenlawn Press 1989), X.

[482] Heribert Mühlen, *A Charismatic Theology: Initiation in the Spirit.* (London: Burns & Oates and New York, Ramsey, NJ, Toronto: Paulist 1978), 15.

[483] Eduard Schweizer, "πνεῦμα," TDNT, 6:396. Quoted in Veli-Matti, Karkkainen, *Pneumatology: The Holy Spirit in Ecumenical International, and Contextual Perspective.* (Grand Rapids, Michigan: Baker Academic a division of Baker Publishing Group 2002), 38. Also quoted in McDonnell and Montague, *Christian Initiation and Baptism in the Holy Spirit*, 87.

in their different established Christian communities. No Christian doctrine was packaged from above. It took years of prayerful theological reflections, Synodal Councils' deliberative conferences and discernment for the early Christians to finally articulate that the enduring presence of God manifested in diverse forms, and understood through different symbols and images in different biblical OT generations and NT writings, is the Holy Spirit.[484]

One of the doctrinal developments of the fourth century was the resolution that the Holy Spirit is Lord and giver of life. This doctrine was expressed and formulated from two Councils: Nicaea (AD 325) and Constantinople (AD 381), called the Nicene-Constantinopolitan Creed.[485] Catholics still uphold and profess their faith in the above resolution at each Sunday's liturgy, "I believe in the Holy Spirit, the Lord, the giver of Life."[486] Though the Church now understands the Spirit that was revealed in the OT as the principle of life, our profession in the Holy Spirit as the "giver of life" affirms the early Christians tangible experience which is expressed differently from what the ancestors of our Jewish roots believed of Spirit, breath as a sign of life (Gen. 1:2).[487] The Holy Spirit as a lived experience among the early Christians was authenticated by their love for one another.

After the crucifixion and death of Jesus, the disciples were disheartened and terrified, not knowing what their future would be. However, after the resurrection of Jesus, and their revitalizing experience on Pentecost Day (Acts 2:1-13), their joy was restored, and everything became new again. In John 6:63, Jesus affirms that it is the Spirit that gives life, and in 2 Cor. 3:6, Paul declares, "the Spirit brings life,"[488] and this life, which is God's love has been poured into our hearts (Rom. 5:5). The early Christians understanding captured the fundamental essence of the Holy Spirit as the animator of all things.[489] They did not keep their experience to themselves but took the good news of salvation to the ends of the earth sharing the love and joy of the risen Lord. The onus of sharing the good news is on Christians who are the principal agents in the world in assuring that all God's creatures are

---

[484] Patout T. Burns, and Gerald M. Fagin, *The Holy Spirit*. (Eugene, Oregon: Wipf & Stock Publishers 2002), 228-234.

[485] Ibid., 155.

[486] United States Catholic Bishop Conference confirmed by the Apostolic See. *The Roman Missal*, English Translation According to the Third Edition. (Libretria Editrice) Vaticana, Vatican City State 2011), 527.

[487] Kenneth Baker, *The Holy Spirit: Lord and Giver of Life*. http://www.catholiceducation.org/en/culture/ catholic-contributions/the-holy-spirit-lord-and-giver-of-life.html Accessed May 5, 2016.

[488] Ibid.

[489] United States Catholic Bishops Conference. *Catechism of the Catholic Church*. (New York: Catholic Book Publication Co 1994), 703.

in harmony with God's will. Christians receive God's life in order to be God's embodied presence to make the world a Godly place for all God's creatures. Christians have all it takes through the power of the Holy Spirit that has been given to us to be God's life in the world. All we need is a renewed openness to a fresh outpouring of the Holy Spirit as experienced by the early Christians. They were able to surmount trials and tribulations through their missionary expedition in the known hostile world. The world is still hostile to Christians. Nevertheless, as we live out the love of God poured into our hearts, living in the Spirit, we can even in the midst of antagonism still bear the fruits of the Holy Spirit: love, joy, peace, patience, kindness, generosity, faithfulness, gentleness, and self-control (Gal. 5:22). This was the lived experience of the early Christians who in Antioch were first called Christians (Acts 11:19-26).

3.3 *The Experience of the Holy Spirit in the Early Church.*[490]

The author of Luke as mentioned above is also considered by many scholars also as the author of Acts of the Apostles records and impresses on his audience how the Holy Spirit is an enabler and founder of the early Christian Church. Filled with the gifts of the Holy Spirit, the early Church saw herself as subject to the activity of the Spirit[491]. The Holy Spirit filled and confirmed the disciples in their faith. They were inflamed with the passion for publicly witnessing through preaching and urging others to repent and be baptized.[492] They took directives and acted on the Holy Spirit's mission. In his speech at the Areopagus, Paul said of God, "For in Him we live and move and have our being" (Acts 17:28).[493] This could be said of the early Christians experience of the Holy Spirit as it was the Holy Spirit that empowered the disciples, founded the Church, initiated and sustained their mission of evangelization in the world. In order to meaningfully proclaim Christ as the Messiah to the ends of the hostile world, the disciples opened up to the Holy Spirit, who caused an astonishing change in their lives. They were transformed from naive and fearful men and women into willing instruments that were motivated to preach the good news of salvation to the ends of the earth.[494] Their experience of the freshness of purpose and mission sustained them in the midst of all odds. The spread of Christian communities around the known world attests to the

---

[490] Congar, op. cit. 65.

[491] Ibid.

[492] Thomas Bokenkotter, *A Concise History of the Catholic Church*. (New York, London, Toronto, Sydney, Auckland: Image Books Doubleday 2005), 17.

[493] Senior and Collins, op. cit., 1474.

[494] Sullivan, op. cit., 59.

success of their ministry. They succeeded because they had the Holy Spirit, the "Promise of the Father, their helper" who not only empowered them with the tools they needed for their missions but also was steadfast with them all through their afflictions. This was to fulfill what Jesus said in Matthew 28:20: "I am with you always, until the end of the age."[495] The abiding presence of Jesus was made real through the manifest gifts of the Holy Spirit that worked through the members of different early Christian communities.

The different early Christian communities experienced the charismatic gifts of the Holy Spirit, which they used to serve their communities. As enumerated in Chapter two, there were manifestations of multiple charismatic gifts in Paul's communities, which he recognized for service in love (1 Cor. 12:4-11, 27-31 and Rom. 12:6-8). All the gifts were operative, as members used their gifts for the glory of God, however, not without misunderstanding as was pointed out in the previous chapter. Some early Christian writings give us a clear and invaluable picture of how the gifts were noticeable and used in the early Church. One of them is the *Didache*.[496]

The *Didache*, also known as the teaching of the twelve in ancient times[497] dates back to the end of the first century. It was composed by a Jewish-Christian author of western Syria or eastern Asia Minor and the work centers on discernment, baptism, fasting, prayer, prophets and the Eucharist.[498] In the *Didache*, an important place was given for the ministry of prophets and provides criteria to determine those who could carry out this ministry.[499] The rules of discernment that was created by the *Didache* also show how to treat a prophet, and how to differentiate between a true prophet and a false one.[500] It was alleged that Justin Martyr maintained that prophecy and charismatic gifts still existed in the Church during his time.[501] The gift of prophecy was so prominent and beneficial to the Church that it was

---

[495] Senior, and Collins, op. cit., 1315.

[496] Gerald O'Collins, S.J. Edward G. Farrugia, S.J. Eds. *A Concise Dictionary of Theology*. (New York/ Mahwah, N.J.: Paulist Press 2000), 17.

[497] Burgess, op. cit.,5- 6.

[498] Burns, and Fagin, op. cit., 64.

[499] *Didache*, XI, 8-12; XII. Quoted in Congar, *I Believe in the Holy Spirit*, 65. See also, Stanley M. Burgess, *Christian Peoples of the Spirit: A Documentary History of Pentecostal Spirituality from the Early Church to the Present*. New York and London: New York University Press 2011), 5-7.

[500] J.B. Lightfoot and J.R. Harmer, Eds. *The Apostolic Fathers*, 2nd Ed., Grand Rapids, MI: Baker, 1989, Quoted in Burgess, *Christian Peoples of the Spirit*, 6.

[501] Justin, *Dial*. 82; G. Bardy, p. 132. Quoted in Ibid.

believed the prophets would accompany the Church until the end of time.[502] In his epistle of AD 95, Clement of Rome refreshed the Corinthians' minds of the abundant outpouring of the Holy Spirit on them (II, 2; see also XLVI, 6) and gave them this rule: "Let each one of us respect in his neighbor the *charisms* that he has received' (XXXVIII, 1).[503] Nevertheless, the ecstatic form that prophecy took in the early Church declined to some extent because of the increasing emphasis on the authority of the bishops.[504] That notwithstanding, some bishops manifested and used the *charisms* because there was no sharp contrast between charismatics and the hierarchical ministers, Ignatius of Antioch declared that he preached under the influence of the Spirit.[505] Polycarp of Smyrna was referred to as "teacher who was both an apostle and a prophet"[506] and Melito of Sardis was believed to have lived entirely on the Holy Spirit.[507] Many of the clergies manifested the gifts of the Holy Spirit, as did most members of the hierarchy, who exercised the *charisms* at this time. The bishop's active participation in the manifestation and use of the *charisms* also helped to promote the activities of the Holy Spirit in the early Church.[508] Their spiritual demeanor made them fit into Paul's categorization of spiritual men (1 Cor. 2:10-15).[509] As a follow up to this understanding, Irenaeus went further to say: "Those who have received the pledge of the Holy Spirit and who behave correctly in everything are rightly called by the Apostle spiritual men."[510] The characteristic traits of the manifest presence of the *charisms* of knowledge and teaching in the bishops also contributed to why they were considered spiritual men.[511]

More importantly, *charisms* flourished like flowers because the bishops as shepherds guided their flock and judiciously used their charismatic gifts for the glory of God in the

---

[502] Miltiades, an opponent of Montanism, quoted by Eusebius, Hist. Eccl. V, XVII, 4. Referenced in Congar, *I Believe in the Holy Spirit*, 65.

[503] Ibid.

[504] A.J. Ash, *The Decline of Ecstatic Prophecy in the Early Church*, 227-252. Cited in Congar, *I Believe in the Holy Spirit*, (vol. 1), 65.

[505] Ignatius, *Philad*, 7. Cited in Ibid.

[506] Mart, *Polycarpi*, XVI, 2. Quoted in Congar, *I Believe in the Holy Spirit*, 65.

[507] Eusebius, *Hist. Eccl.* V, 24, 2, 5, quoting Polycrates. Cited in Ibid.

[508] Congar, op. cit., 65.

[509] Ibid.

[510] *Irenaeus, Adv. haer.* V, 8, 2 (PG 7, 1142; ed. W.W. Harvey, II, p339); IV, 33 (PG 7, 1072ff.; Harvey, II, p. 256). Quoted in Congar, *I Believe in the Holy Spirit*, 65-66.

[511] Congar, op. cit., 66.

Church. This helped to promote the Church's mission of evangelization, as many miracles experienced, were believed to have been performed by prophets.[512] However, the widespread use of *charisms*, especially that of prophecy, was not without its problems. The rise of Montanus, who had a considerable faction when he started prophesying in about AD 172, brought about some tensions in the early Church.[513]

Montanus was a native of Asia Minor who claimed that the Paraclete demanded a life of rigorous asceticism in preparation for the impending coming of the Lord.[514] His prophecies appealed to many people who were enthralled with his non-traditional method of prophesying—losing consciousness, speaking in tongues and falling into frenzy and trance when he prophesied.[515] Some of his disciples, like Alcibiades and Theodotus, also acquired prophetic status as the miracles that were done through them swayed many to believe that the wonder-workers were also prophets.[516] His followers came to be known as the Montanist sect, who claimed exclusive possession of the Spirit and of full revelation about Jesus.[517] Their teachings and practices and openness to women's prophetic ministry impressively drew Tertullian to the group.[518] In Tertullian's own writing he describes Montanist church service as follows:

> We have among us now a sister who has been granted gifts of revelations, which she experiences in church during the Sunday services through an ecstatic vision in the Spirit ... And after the people have been dismissed at the end of the services it is her custom to relate to us what she has seen ... "Among other things," says she, "there was shown to me a soul in bodily form, and it appeared like a spirit; but it was no mere something, void of

---

[512] Ibid.

[513] Ibid.

[514] Burns, and Fagin, op. cit., 19.

[515] Burgess, op. cit., 25.

[516] Eusebius, *His. Eccl.* V, III, 4; Fr. Tr. P. de Labriolle, *Les sources de l'histoire du Montanisme. Testes grecs, latins, syriaques* (Fribourg and Paris, 1913), p. 68; *idem, La crise montaniste, op. cit.* (note 4); R.A. Knox, *Enthusiasm* (Oxford, 1950), pp. 25-49; H. Kraft, 'Die altkirchiche Prophet und die Entstehung des Montanismus', TZ, 11 (1955), 249-271. For the latest stage in research into the subject, see F. Blanchetiere, 'Le montanisme originel', *RSR*, 52 (1978), 118-134, and 53 (1979), 1-22. Quoted in Congar, *I Believe in the Holy Spirit*, 66.

[517] Burns, and Fagin, op. cit., 19-20.

[518] Congar, op. cit., 66.

.qualities, but rather a thing which could be grasped, soft and translucent and of ethereal color, in a form at all points human."[519]

Many commentators believe Tertullian might have been describing a twentieth-century charismatic Church.[520] Contrary to Tertullian's experience and view, Hippolytus wrote forcefully against the Montanists:

> *They have been deceived by two females, Priscilla and Maximilla by name, whom they hold to be prophetesses, asserting that into them the Paraclete spirit entered … They magnify these females above the Apostles and every gift of Grace so that some of them go so far as to say that in them there is something more than Christ … They introduce novelties in the form of fasts and feasts, abstinences and diets of radishes, giving these females as their authority.[521]*

The Catholic Church rejected most of their teachings and oracular mannerisms, like convulsions, cries, and suspension of judgment.[522] Unfortunately, the decision of the Church to put away the charismatic Montanist group played a role in the distrustful attitude of the Church toward the manifestation and use of *charisms* in the Church today. Many commentators believe that the Church seemed to have also scorned some valuable *charisms* that came with the charismatic Montanist sect. I agree with Congar that "a rejection of this kind was dangerous if it meant building up the life of the Church without *charisms* and without the Holy Spirit."[523]

Anyhow, the Pentecost Day event unquestionably helped to give the early Church a solid foundation in knowing and appreciating her mission on the face of the earth. The sustaining grace of the early Church was also the unwavering openness of the early Christians to the manifestations of the gifts of the Holy Spirit that molded them continually in all they needed to direct their ecclesiastical and mission endeavors. Irenaeus testified and wrote about the miraculous charisms that existed in the Church, which were prophetic pronouncements,

---

[519] Henry Bettenson, Ed. *Documents of the Christian Church* (London: Oxford, 1963), 78. Cited in John, F. MacArthur, *Chrismatic Chaos: Signs & Wonders, Speaking in Tongues, Health, Wealth & Prosperity, Charismatic Televangelism, Does God Still Speak Today?* (Michigan: Grand Rapids, Zondervan Publishing House, 1992), 74.

[520] MacArthur, op. cit., 74.

[521] Bettenson, op. cit., 77. Cited in MacArthur, op. cit., 73.

[522] Congar, op. cit., 66.

[523] Ibid.

speaking in tongues and the gift of knowledge to reveal and expose the mysteries of God.[524] In AD 248, Origen asserted that there were people who had the marks of the Holy Spirit that appeared on them in form of a dove and they healed the sick, drove out demons and predicted certain events according to the will of Christ.[525] By the same token, Saint Augustine (354-430), who was alluded to in Chapter one as a cessationist later changed his position after experiencing some manifestations of charismatic gifts and miraculous healings in his cathedral in Hippo for which he acknowledged the universal Church's need for *charisms* in his Church.[526] Subsequently, Saint Augustine later testified in his *Retraction,*

> *It is indeed true that the sick are not always healed ... But what I said should not be taken to mean that no miracles are believed to happen today in the name of Christ. For at the very time I wrote ... a blind man in the city (of Milan) was given back his sight; and so many other things of this kind have happened, even in this present time, that it is not possible to know all of them or to count up all those we do have knowledge of.*[527]

Saint Augustine also recounted the numerous remarkable healings that he witnessed in his book, *The City of God.*[528] He described how a brother and sister were miraculously healed of a dreadful sickness, and expressed the pleasant surprise of his congregation:

> *Such wonders rose up from men and women together that the exclamations and tears seem as if they would never come to end ... They shouted God's praises without words, but with such a noise that our ears could scarcely stand it.*[529]

Also prominent among the *charisms* of the early Church were visions, warnings, and

---

[524] Ibid., 66-67.

[525] Origen, *Contra Cels.* I, 46. Quoted in Ibid. 67 but paraphrased here.

[526] *Baptism in the Holy Spirit*: International Catholic Charismatic Renewal Services Doctrinal Commission (Vatican City: Palazzo San Calisto 2012), 56.

[527] *Reactions*, 1.13,7. Quoted in Ibid.

[528] *The City of God*, XXII.8. Cited in *Baptism in the Holy Spirit*: International Catholic Charismatic Renewal Services Doctrinal Commission, 56.

[529] *The City of God*, XXII.8.Quoted in *Baptism in the Holy Spirit*: International Catholic Charismatic Renewal Services Doctrinal Commission, 56.

suggestions attributed to the Spirit.[530] Cyprian whose life was adorned with supernatural visions and warnings,[531] said in reference to the council held at Cartage in the spring of 252: "It has pleased us, under the inspiration of the Holy Spirit and according to the warnings given by the Lord in numerous clear visions."[532] This clearly shows the early Church's strong belief in the guidance and inspiration of the Holy Spirit in all her undertakings.[533]

Consequently, the Church that was formed by the gathering of 12 apostles[534] and sustained in the charismatic gifts of the Holy Spirit still needs the *charisms* if she has to survive the future. We have seen that *charisms* motivated the missions of the early Church. There was a persistent liturgical practice in the Church through which *charisms* were applied for many centuries. Though these *charisms* may not be in full manifestations and practice in the Catholic Church today, they are readily experienced in Pentecostal and charismatic Churches. While these manifestations and exercise of *charisms* may be unfamiliar to many Catholics; they are part of the Catholic Church's heritage. More importantly, many Ecclesiastical historians have done much work to unravel this fundamental truth.

Considering the above post-biblical early Christian experience, we have seen how *charisms* were part of the Church's life and ministry of which many commentators are in agreement. Consequently, Kilian McDonnell and George T. Montague a few among many who have demonstrated in their theological works that *charisms* maintained a place in preaching and in baptismal liturgies as a normal and expected dimension of the Christian life.[535] Nonetheless, the use of the gifts of the Holy Spirit visibly disappeared from the Church due to the marginalization of *charisms*.[536] I will elucidate more on that later. For now, we shall look into the sacramental rite of initiation that was modeled after the biblical practice of baptism in the Holy Spirit. It was through the experience of baptism in the Holy Spirit that *charisms* were manifested in the lives of individuals.

Most biblical documentations of baptism in the Holy Spirit of the early Church are found in the Acts of the Apostles (1:4-5; 2:1-11, 38, 10:44-48; 11:15-16; 19:1-6). New

---

[530] Congar, op. cit., 67.

[531] A. von Harnack, 'Cyprian als Enthusiast', *NWZ*, 5 (1902), 177-191; A. d'Ales, *La theologie de S. Cyprien* (Paris, 1922), pp. 77-83. Referenced in Ibid.

[532] Cyprian, *Ep.* LVII, 5 (ed. W. von Hartel, p. 655). Quoted in Congar, I Believe in the Holy Spirit, 67.

[533] Ibid.

[534] Gerhard Lohfink, *Does God Need the Church? Toward a Theology of the People of God.* (Collegeville, Minnesota: The Liturgical Press, A Michael Glazier Book 1999), 59.

[535] McDonnell, and Montague, *Fanning the Flame*, 16.

[536] McDonnell, and Montague, *Christian Initiation and Baptism in the Holy Spirit*, 364.

converts were asked to repent and be baptized in order to receive the Holy Spirit (Act 2:38). However, some biblical texts reveal to us that the Holy Spirit is not confined to a particular mode of operation. The Holy Spirit can descend on a person or people prior to or after water baptism. In the gospel of John 3:8, Jesus alludes to the Spirit as *ruach*, the wind that blows where it wills. You hear the sound but nobody knows where it goes. This brings to mind the unpredictable nature of *ruach* Yahweh, the Spirit of God as we interpreted in chapter two. At times with hands laid on people, they manifest the gifts of the Holy Spirit/ *charisms*. Other times, the laying on of hands may not be needed for the manifestations of the Holy Spirit. Nevertheless, the general biblical norm is water baptism, laying of hands and then manifestations of the Holy Spirit/*charisms* through the outward sign of speaking in tongues (glossolalia). However, as mentioned above, the Holy Spirit is a free agent who acts and manifests God's presence as she wills. There are a few astonishing occurrences where individuals received the Holy Spirit/*charisms*, prior to water baptism. Paul received the Holy Spirit before water baptism (Acts 9:10-19). Another exceptional incident happed in the household of Cornelius:

> *"While Peter was still speaking these things, the Holy Spirit fell upon all who were listening to the word. The circumcised believers who had accompanied Peter were astounded that the gift of the Holy Spirit should have been poured out on the Gentiles also, for they could hear them speaking in tongues and glorifying God. Then Peter responded, "Can anyone withhold the water for baptizing these people, who have received the Holy Spirit even as we have?" He ordered them to be baptized in the name of Jesus Christ"* *(Acts 10:44-48).*[537]

The revelation that Gentiles could receive the Holy Spirit and manifest the gifts/*charisms* shows us that God is willing and ready to minister and use whoever is open to being used for God's salvific mission in the world. Regrettably, there was a Jewish-religious historical bias against nations outside the Jewish state. However, by God's special grace, Luke and Paul modeling after the inclusive ministry of Jesus put an end to that religious bigotry in their writings. I give credit to Luke, the author of Luke/Acts, who creatively reveals the availability of God's gratuitous presence to other nations different from the Jewish state. With this understanding, I believe there should be no hard and fast rules about the required norm for the reception of the gifts of the Holy Spirit. I know there are set principles in the Church, Charismatic prayer groups, and Pentecostal Churches today.

It is my opinion that for a more experiential phenomenon, the Holy Spirit should be given the freedom to minister in whatever form and to whomever she wills to bless. This

---

[537] Senior and Collins, op. cit., 1462.

is not to say that the Holy Spirit has lost her sovereignty but expressing how set rules that defined spiritual policies can hinder both the minister and a people's openness to receive and manifest the gifts of the Holy Spirit.

A close look at Acts 10:1-48: the vision of Cornelius (1-8), the vision of Peter (9-33), Peter's speech (34-43) and the baptism of Cornelius (44-48), expose how the dismantled learned religious prejudice of Peter gave him a new understanding of God as the God of all without favorites. It was the candid truth about the God of all peoples that opened Cornelius and his household to the Holy Spirit and the manifest *charisms*. I believe the axiom of St Thomas Aquinas that says, "Whatever is received is received according to the mode of the receiver,"[538] fits here. However, the receiver is also conditioned by whatever formative knowledge is received. Knowledge, therefore, plays a significant role in creating the atmosphere or a world where the Holy Spirit flourishes. Moreover, baptism in the Holy Spirit is an experience, I believe, God wishes for everyone.

Let us now look at the foundational understanding of baptism in the Holy Spirit. All the evangelists mentioned baptism in the Holy Spirit in their texts. This shows the significant role that the sacramental/spiritual initiatory exercise will play to establish the Church and sustain her mission of proclaiming the good news to all the nations.

3.4 *Baptism in the Holy Spirit in the New Testament*

The word baptism is linked to a group of practices associated with washing with water.[539] Its occasional literal secular Greek usage implies a ritual bath. But with the Jewish cultic provision of purity, baptism is interpreted in the New Testament as a total rebirth of human existence.[540] The Greek word βάπτω (*bapto*) in a secular sense means to dip or to dip into a dye.[541] The word βαπτίζω *(baptizo)*, which is an intensive form of *bapto* and the technical term for baptisms in the New Testament means to dip but also carries the notion of immersion occurs only 4 times, twice in John 13:26, and also in Luke 16:24 and Rev. 19:13.[542] However, the noun *baptism* is not found in the New Testament phrase. It is the verb "baptize" with the Spirit as accompaniment that appears eight times of which four are the promises of John and are

---

[538] Thomas Aquinas, *Summa Theologiae,* 1a, q. 75, a. 5; 3a q. 5. Quoted in Dunstan Robidoux, O.S.B. *Applying a Thomistic Principle: Quidquid recipitur ad modum recipientis recipitur.* The Lonergan Institute. http://lonergan.org/?p=599 Accessed on May 15, 2016.

[539] Brown, op. cit., 143.

[540] Ibid.

[541] Ibid., 143-145. See also Kittel, and Friedrich, op. cit., 529-530

[542] Ibid.

found in all the gospels (Mark 1:8; Matt. 3:11; Luke 3:16; John 1:33).[543] John administers the baptism of repentance for the forgiveness of sins (Mark 1:4), in anticipation of the Messianic baptism with Spirit and fire.[544] He baptizes Jesus, who submits to his baptism in solidarity with sinful humanity. However, the metaphorical sign of the heavens that opens, and the voice of endorsement from above (Matt. 3:17; Mark 1:11; Luke 3:22) shows his empowerment to fulfill the mission of establishing God's kingdom through a new movement that leads to the salvation of the world.[545] The ministry of Jesus is effectively powerful and successful because it is sanctioned from above. During the course of his ministry on earth, Jesus gathered and sent out his disciples at different times to preach about the kingdom of God, through teaching, healing, and casting out demons (Matt. 10:1; Mark 6:7, 12-23; Luke 9:1-10). After his resurrection, Jesus commanded his disciples to baptize (Matt. 28:18-20; Mark 16:15), which they commenced with the name of Jesus following the proclamation of the gospel (Acts 2:38).[546] The disciples preached about repentance and forgiveness of sins, in expectation of the gift of the Holy Spirit on converts.[547] The New Testament and post-biblical periods reveal the practice of baptism in the Holy Spirit even without a clear expression of the term. The practice was discontinued. Fortunately, the Pentecostal movement revived this practice many centuries later and began to associate their membership and experience to that of Christ's followers on the Day of Pentecost, "that is, to be filled with the Holy Spirit in the same manner as those who were filled with the Holy Spirit on that occasion."[548] This makes it look like the Pentecostals invented the term baptism in the Holy Spirit, which is not the case.

As a matter of fact, the expression baptism in the Holy Spirit is not a creation of classical Pentecostals but has its origin in the experiential historical reality of Christian initiation

---

[543] McDonnell, and Montague, *Christian Initiation and Baptism in the Holy Spirit*, 4.

[544] G.R. Beasley-Murray, *Baptism in the NT*, 1962, 31 ff. Referenced in Brown, *The New International Dictionary of New Testament Theology* .

[545] Brown, op. cit., 146.

[546] Ibid.

[547] Ibid.

[548] The Pentecostal Movement's systematic theologian, writing in *The Pentecostal Evangel* (15 January 1961) 11 – cited by F. D. Bruner, *The Doctrine and Experience of the Holy Spirit in Pentecostal Movement and Correspondingly in the New Testament* (Hamburg dissertation 1963) 36; cf. K. Hutton, RGG3 II (1958) 1303 f.; O. Eggenberger, *TZ* 11 (1955) 272, 292; J.T. Nichol, *Pentecostalism* (1966) 1f., 8f. Cited in James, D.G. Dunn, *Baptism in the Holy Spirit: A Re-examination of the New Testament Teaching on the Gift of the Spirit in relation to Pentecostalism today* (Second Edition, Kindle Edition retrieved from Amazon.com). (London, UK: SCM Press 2010), location 1094.

as witnessed by the New Testament and early post-biblical teachers of the Church.[549] Regardless, the Pentecostal movement has helped to revitalize and bring to the forefront of Christianity the gracious tradition that was left untapped by the Catholic Church for centuries.[550] The early Christians experienced the outpouring of the Holy Spirit when new members received water baptism. They also manifested and used the gifts of the Holy Spirit/*charisms*. Nonetheless, the manifestations of the gifts of the Holy Spirit were undermined when the Church later took on a Romanized structure.[551] Consequently, the Holy Spirit became intellectualized, giving rise to more emphasis on sacraments as obvious signs without the visible signs of the gifts of the Holy Spirit/*charisms* as experienced in biblical times and the early Church. There was a definitive shift in understanding. The faithful now understood not to expect manifest signs even when sacramental rites were in process. Sacraments now became signs of invisible presence. In the words of Theodore of Mopsuestia: "Every sacrament points to invisible and ineffable realities by means of signs and symbols."[552] I believe with the intellectualization and spiritualization of *charism*, the physical manifestations become more and more inaccessible. The non-expectation of visible manifestations of spiritual gifts/*charisms* turned out to be the norm for the Church's definition of the sacraments. The manifest reception of the Holy Spirit became estranged from water baptism and the sacrament of confirmation. This separation did not take place until the fifth century.[553] Many commentators still contend that the two sacraments have always flowed into one another and should remain together. The understanding that water baptism follows with the outpouring of the Holy Spirit is clearly expressed in Acts 19:1-7, where Paul asks the Ephesians if they received the Holy Spirit when they were baptized (v. 2). They said they never heard about the Holy Spirit (v. 3). Paul was surprised and wondered how they received baptism without the manifestation of Holy Spirit. They received the baptism of John, which was that of repentance (v. 4). After telling them about Jesus, they believed and were baptized in the name of Jesus and received the Holy Spirit with a visible manifestation of the gifts of tongues and prophecy (vv. 4-7). This experience was common in the early Church.

---

[549] McDonnell, and Montague, *Fanning The Flame,* 14.

[550] Dunn, op. cit., 446-481.

[551] Hahnenberg, op. cit., 61. This was not the only reason as there are other reasons the Church undermined the *charisms*.

[552] Joseph Martos, *Doors to the Sacred: A Historical Introduction to Sacraments in the Catholic Church.* (Liguori, Missouri: Liguori/Triumph 2001), 19.

[553] Ibid., 184.

The experiential encounter of the early Christians made them feel the reality of the living person of the risen Christ in their communities.[554] Their experience was grounded in the fulfillment of the promise of Jesus to his apostles that he will not leave them orphans (John 14:8). They felt the presence of a comforter/helper as Jesus promised them (John 14:16). This life-changing encounter caused by what is known by Luke-Acts as the coming down of the promise of the Father (Luke 24:49; Acts 1:4) radically changed the disciples. Furthermore, the phenomenal encounter of the disciples brought the proclamation of John the Baptist to fruition. They experienced the fire of the Holy Spirit that purified and burnt out fears, doubts, and confusion that had earlier characterized their lives. The four gospels recorded John the baptizer saying: The one coming after me will baptize with the Holy Spirit and fire (Mark 1:8; Matt. 3:11; Luke 3:16; John 1:33).[555] After experiencing the outpouring of the Holy Spirit, Peter said in Acts 2:38: "Repent and be baptized …in the name of Jesus Christ for the forgiveness of your sins, and you will receive the Holy Spirit.[556] The Pentecost Day experience was the disciples' baptism with the Holy Spirit and fire.

In light of treating the Baptism in the Holy Spirit in this chapter, I will sum up the understanding of the different New Testament authors. It is not the same as the treatment of the Spirit in the previous chapter even though there may be points of convergence occasionally.

In Mark's gospel, Jesus experienced baptism in the Holy Spirit and was proclaimed the Son of God (1:9-12). He was endowed with charismatic power to heal and deliver all who were captives of evil spirits (1:21-35; 2:1-12; 3:1-6, 23-35; 5:1-20, 21-42; 6:53-56; 7:31-37; 8:22-26; 9:14-29; 10:46-52).[557] Matthew's gospel also recorded Jesus' experience of baptism in the Holy Spirit in the Jordan and was proclaimed Son and Servant of God (3:3-17), empowered to preach, teach, heal and do works of compassion (8:1-4, 5-13, 14-17; 9:1-13, 18-26, 27-31, 32-34; 12:22-32; 14:34-36, 15:21-28, 29-31; 17:14-21). The Baptismal Trinitarian formula that is modeled after the commission of Jesus in Matthew 28:18-20, initiates converts into the ministry of Jesus and empowers them to continue his mission of preaching and healing (10:1-15; 28:18-20).[558] After his resurrection, Jesus promised to send his disciples the promise of the Father (Luke 24:48). As stated above, Acts 1:5 records that the disciples will receive the promise of the Father and be baptized with the Holy Spirit after which they will be enabled from on high to become witnesses of Christ in Jerusalem,

---

[554] Thomas P. Rausch, *Who is Jesus: An Introduction to Christology.* (Collegeville, Minnesota: Liturgical Press, A Michael Glazier Book 2003), 119.

[555] McDonnell, and Montague, *Christian Initiation and Baptism in the Holy Spirit,* 4.

[556] McDonnell, and Montague, Eds. *Fanning The Flame,* 14ff.

[557] McDonnell, and Montague, *Christian Initiation and Baptism in the Holy Spirit,* 14.

[558] Ibid., 22.

throughout Judea and Samaria, and to the ends of the earth (1:8). In Luke and Acts of the Apostles, Christian initiation involves baptism and the gift of the Holy Spirit were considered to be an essential in the process,[559] and this was a way of incorporating converts into the community of disciples.[560]

In Pauline writings and the letter to the Hebrews, the gifts of the Spirit are believed to be an integral part of Christian initiation (1 Cor. 6:11, 12:13; Gal. 3:1-5).[561] The letter to the Hebrews remotely also connects water baptism to baptism in the Holy Spirit (Hebrews 6:1-5)[562] The author of 1 Peter with his introductory Trinitarian greetings (1:1-3), reflects on the gifts and call of God in baptism (1:3-9), the role of the Holy Spirit (1:11), impresses that baptismal grace is saving and charismatic, attributes Old Testament prophecy to the Spirit of Christ, speaks of an experiential dimension of the new Christian life (2:2-3) and asserts that the varied gifts received by each Christian are for the service of the community (4:10-11).[563] 2 Peter 1:20 speaks of the divine inspiration of authentic prophecy.[564]

In the letter of John, the Holy Spirit was bestowed at the moment of baptism. Members were empowered with the knowledge that is both true and experiential, and these were manifested in the community through prophetic and healing gifts.[565]

Consequently, from our exposure to the different New Testament communities, we can see the varied ways each community experienced the baptism in the Holy Spirit, showing that each community has a different understanding of baptism in the Holy Spirit, which I believe also affects the disposition to receiving the gifts of the Holy Spirit/*charisms*. We shall now look at the different theological understandings of the Baptism of the Holy Spirit by Churches and theologians alike.

3.5. *Varied Understanding of Baptism in the Holy Spirit*

Baptism in the Holy Spirit is a tangible, experiential encounter with the divine through the power of the Holy Spirit upon an individual or community. As we have explored with correlated texts above, Jesus, the disciples, and the early Christians experienced baptism in the Holy Spirit

---

[559] Ibid., 30 & 35.

[560] Ibid., 37.

[561] Ibid., 42-47.

[562] Ibid., 53-55.

[563] Ibid., 56-63.

[564] Ibid., 88.

[565] Ibid., 66-72.

and many Christians have experienced it also in our time. However, certain terms that may create ambiguity have come to be associated with this baptism in the Holy Spirit, which are, "release of the Spirit," "new outpouring of the Spirit," or to "being baptized in the Spirit."[566] Though the term baptism in the Holy Spirit may be expressed differently with nuances in usage and application, they all mean the same thing. The different expressions of the same term create an opening to different theological explanations or exploration of the basis of what happens to a person who experiences the baptism in the Holy Spirit.[567] I think to have an experience and understand that experience calls for different modes of examinations, which probably bring about various explanations. Thus, the interpretation, meaning, understanding, and practice of baptism in the Holy Spirit have different implications to diverse Christian religious traditions, and scriptural theologians. In the Catholic tradition, baptism in the Holy Spirit has an evolutionary understanding because of the emergence of the Charismatic renewal group that has exposed members to an unparalleled experience with the Holy Spirit. To explain this phenomenon and create new meaning without obliterating the traditional understanding of baptism, for example, commentators agree baptism in the Holy Spirit is not a new sacrament but considered an "unreleased" sacrament.[568] The term "unreleased" refers to the dormant gifts of the Holy Spirit in children until they make their confirmation. However, with baptism in the Holy Spirit, and through the conscious openness of an individual to God's grace, all the untapped gifts are released with the outpouring of the Holy Spirit to full manifestation.[569] Some commentators have described this as a "coming alive," "renewal," or "release" of the grace of sacramental baptism and confirmation.[570] This release of the Holy Spirit's gifts here is connected to the sacrament of initiation in Catholic sacramental theology, which sees a connection between baptism and confirmation.[571] More importantly, the understanding here is that the outpouring of the Holy Spirit actualizes and revives whatever dormant *charism*s are in a baptized infant.[572] And in a more metaphorical concrete term, it is "fanning into flame" the gift already received (2

---

[566] Sullivan, op. cit., 59.

[567] Ibid.

[568] Cantalamessa Raniero, *Sober Intoxication of the Spirit: Filled With the Fullness of God* (Kindle Edition, retrieved from Amazon). (Cincinnati, OH: Anthony Messenger Press 2005) 41.

[569] Ibid., 41-42.

[570] *Baptism in the Holy Spirit*: International Catholic Charismatic Renewal Services Doctrinal Commission, 70.

[571] Ibid.

[572] Ibid.

Tim. 1:6) but remained inactive until activated by the Holy Spirit.[573] At whatever stage a person experiences the surge of God's empowerment in the Holy Spirit, I believe baptism in the Holy Spirit is the process through which God releases *charisms* on God's children for ministry with special graces for the purpose of being witnesses in bringing the good news of salvation to the ends of the earth. Nevertheless, different ecclesiastical Church traditions have their different understandings and applications of baptism in the Holy Spirit and its relevance to the universal work of evangelization. We know that whatever understanding we infer from any Christian religious group come from perceived pneumatological worldview. I believe that every theological interpretation that has come to us is still in a process, as no theological position is absolute.

Besides, the New Testament authors did not set out to give us manuals for the religious liturgical rites that took place in their communities. All they wanted to do was lead us into the apparent theological understanding and application of the life, ministry, death and resurrection of Christ as lived out in their communities. However, a close study of documented texts leads to the deduction that there are some sustained practices with developmental enhancements. For example, baptism was initially done in the name of Jesus (Acts 2:38, 8:16, 10:48, 19:5, 22:16); however, the practice evolved with the use a Trinitarian formula (Matt. 28:19). In like manner, all religious liturgical practices have evolutionary twists to them. Consequently, we see different understanding about doctrines and liturgical practices in different Christian denominations today.

Still, my understanding of baptism in the Holy Spirit comes from a close examination of related New Testament texts and post-biblical writings on baptism in the Holy Spirit. I agree with Yves Congar, George Montague, Kilian McDonnell, Cantalamessa Raniero, and some other commentators that baptism in the Holy Spirit was part of Christian initiation.[574] Considering that the term Christian initiation has a Catholic connotation, we can say that baptism in the Spirit was part of the biblical and post-biblical practice of converts being incorporated into the Christian community. This tradition is backed up by biblical texts that have been referenced above on baptism in the Holy Spirit. Subsequently, the synoptic gospels confirmed that the process of baptism in the Spirit started with water baptism when they situated the water baptism of Jesus before the Holy Spirit descending upon him like a dove (Matt. 3:3-17; Mark 1:9-11; Luke 3:21-22). Although John's gospel did not give us the actual baptismal scenario of Jesus like the synoptic gospels, we can, however, deduce that the testimony of John as a witness came from baptizing Jesus. John testified saying,

---

[573] Ibid., 71-72.

[574] Congar, *I Believe in the Holy Spirit*, (vol. 2), 189-198, Raniero, *Sober Intoxication of the Spirit,* 41-52, McDonnell and Montague, *Christian Initiation and Baptism in the Holy Spirit,* 14,37,93,96, McDonnell, and Montague, *Fanning the Flame*, 15-22.

> *I saw the Spirit come down like a dove from the sky and remain upon him
> I did not know him, but the one who sent me to baptize with water told me,
> 'On whomever you see the Spirit come down and remain, he is the one who
> will baptize with the holy Spirit' (1:32-33).*[575]

Furthermore, I believe Peter's response to the people's request on what to do after listening to his first homily on Pentecost Day gives us an opening to the original practice of the early Christians. Peter said to them,

> *Repent and be baptized, every one of you, in the name of Jesus Christ for
> the forgiveness of your sins; and you will receive the gift of the Holy Spirit
> (Acts 2:38).*[576]

Besides, in Pauline and early post-biblical writings, we come across the consecutive documentations of the practice and apparent relationship between water baptism and baptism in the Spirit. Paul sees the life given by the Spirit as life in Christ, which we come to share through faith (Gal. 3:2), and this is expressed and consummated by water-baptism and integration into the death and resurrection of Christ (Rom. 6:3ff; 8:1; Col. 2:2)[577]. And in Paul's theological reflections, he shows that the Spirit is given with water-baptism.[578] Accordingly, in his letter to the Corinthians he affirms this relationship when he wrote:

> *That is what some of you used to be, but now you have had yourselves
> washed, you were sanctified, and you were justified in the name of the Lord
> Jesus Christ and in the Spirit of our God (1 Cor. 6:11).*[579]

In addition, some other New Testament texts reveal the process by which converts are incorporated into the body of Christ, which is (a) "faith in the name of Jesus" (1 Cor. 6:11; Acts 19:1-6); (b) through water baptism, being plunged into water through faith in the death of Jesus leading to the resurrection (Rom. 6:3-4).[580] In the post-biblical period, especially

---

[575] Senior and Collins, *The Catholic Study Bible*, 1405.

[576] Ibid., 1447.

[577] Congar, op. cit., 189

[578] Ibid., 189-190.

[579] Senior and Collins, *The Catholic Study Bible,* 1523. Biblical text referenced in Congar, op. cit., 190.

[580] Ibid.

in the second century, Irenaeus was mentioned repeatedly in this chapter emphasized the unity that existed between water baptism and the gift of the Spirit.[581] The fathers of the Church of both East and West did not see water baptism as divorced from baptism in the Holy Spirit.[582] The fathers view Pentecost not as a past event but as a living reality in the Church.[583] In commenting on the disciples' supposed drunkenness on Pentecost Day who Peter said, they were "filled with new wine" (Acts 2:13), St. Cyril of Jerusalem (c. 318-386), clarified to his catechumens,

> *They were not drunk in the way you think. They are indeed drunk, but with the sober intoxication, which kills sin and gives life to the heart and which is the opposite of physical drunkenness. Drunkenness makes a person forget what he knows; this kind, instead, brings an understanding of things that were not formerly known. They are drunk insofar as they have drunk the wine of that mystical wine, affirms, "I am the vine, you" (John 15:5).[584]*

Consequently, Catechumens in the early Church were taught to expect the gifts of the Holy Spirit during their water baptism because the experience of the Spirit was considered fundamental to water baptism.[585] Furthermore, in his letter to Donatus, St. Cyprian of Carthage (d. 258) testified to the effects of baptismal gifts of the Holy Spirit when he was baptized:

> *I went down into those life-giving waters, and all the stains of my past were washed away. I committed my life to the Lord; he cleansed my heart and filled me with the Holy Spirit. I was born again, a new man. Then in a most marvelous way all my doubts cleared up. I could now see what had been hidden from me before. I found I could do things that had previously been impossible. I saw that as long as I had been living according to my flesh I was at the mercy of sin and my course was set for death, but that by living according to my new birth in the Holy Spirit I had already begun to share God's eternal life ... We do not have to toil and sweat to achieve our own*

---

[581] Ibid

[582] *Baptism in the Holy Spirit*, op. cit., 51.

[583] Ibid.

[584] St. Cyril of Jerusalem, *Catechetical Lectures*, 17.19, quoted in Cantalamessa, *Sober Intoxication of the Spirit,* 2. And also quoted in *Baptism in the Holy Spirit*: International Catholic Charismatic Renewal Services Doctrinal Commission, 51-52.

[585] Ibid.

perfection, nor are money and influence needed to obtain the gift of the Holy Spirit. It is freely given by God, always available for us to use. Just as the sun shines and the day brings light, the stream irrigates the soil and rain waters the earth, so the heavenly Spirit pours himself into us.[586]

The above extract insightfully and strikingly expresses a mystical but also a charismatic and transformational experience of the power of the Holy Spirit imparting a person with the gifts of the Holy Spirit/*charisms* through the process of water baptism. This must have been a common occurrence in the early Church, as many fathers reflecting on baptism in the Spirit, believe in the interrelatedness of water baptism and the baptism in the Holy Spirit.[587] More importantly, the post-biblical Church adopted the biblical teaching of baptism in the Holy Spirit and incorporated it into the public liturgical life of the Church.[588] Besides, baptism in the Holy Spirit was a synonym for Christian initiation in Justin Martyr,[589] Origen,[590] Didymus the Blind,[591] and Cyril of Jerusalem.[592] Conclusively, the testimonies of the above early Christian post-biblical authors have shown clearly that our present understanding of the relationship between Christian initiation/water baptism and baptism in the Holy Spirit is not unfounded. Although baptism in the Holy Spirit vanished from the public liturgical life of the Church, the Catholic Charismatic Renewal group is bringing about a reawakening through the exposition of baptism in the Holy Spirit, which is truly the Church's heritage. This resurgence has pushed the Church for a renewed understanding of baptism in the Holy Spirit. Honestly, Catholic theologians have done a great job at investigating, discovering, and publishing a vast expanse of literature on baptism in the Holy Spirit since the emergence of the Catholic Charismatic Renewal group in 1967. One of the documents that came out to help with the Renewal is the Malines Document, A Theological and Pastoral Orientations

---

[586] *Treatise to Donatus on the Grace of God*, paraphrased by Anne Field in *From Darkness to Light. What It Meant to Become a Christian in the Early Church* (Ann Arbor: Servant, 1978), 190-92. Quoted in *Baptism in the Holy Spirit*: International Catholic Charismatic Renewal Services Doctrinal Commission, 53-54.

[587] St. John Martyr, *Dialogue with Trypho*, 29.1; Origen, *On Jeremiah, Catechetical Lectures*, 17.18. Cited in *Baptism in the Holy Spirit*: International Catholic Charismatic Renewal Services Doctrinal Commission, 52.

[588] McDonnell, and Montague, Eds. *Fanning the Flame,* 15.

[589] *Dialogue with Trypho* 29:1; Patrologia graeca 6:537. Cited in Ibid.

[590] *On Jeremiah* 2:3; Sources Chretiennes 232:244. Cited in McDonnell, and Montague, *Fanning the Flame*, 15.

[591] *On the Trinity* 2:12; PG 39:668, 673. Cited in McDonnell, and Montague, Eds. *Fanning the Flame*, 15.

[592] *Catechetical Lectures* 16:6; Cyril *hierosolymarum archiepiscopi opera quae supersunt Omnia* (2 vols., eds. W. K. Reischl, J. Rupp; Munich: Stahl, 1846-1860) 2:213.

Document on the Catholic Renewal.[593] The document brought out a salient point that helps to dispel shades of confusion among Catholics facing conflicting understanding of initial baptism after experiencing baptism in the Holy Spirit:

> *Within the Catholic Renewal the phrase "baptism in the Holy Spirit" refers to two senses or moments. First, there is the theological sense. In this sense, every member of the Church has been baptized in the Spirit because each has received sacramental initiation. Second, there is the experiential sense. It refers to the moment or the growth process in virtue of which the spirit, given during the celebration of initiation, comes to conscious experience. When those within the Catholic renewal speak of "the baptism in the Holy Spirit" they are referring to this conscious experience, which is the experiential sense.[594]*

Unfortunately, with the immeasurable wealth of literature available today on *charisms* and baptism in the Holy Spirit, some Catholics are still oblivious and set in their uncompromising ways of seeing manifestations of *charisms* as a protestant invention. Furthermore, some non-charismatic commentators have shown a reluctance to speak of a new imparting of the Spirit if it is not linked to the reception of a sacrament, as though this would be irreconcilable with Catholic theology.[595] As mentioned briefly above, different Catholic commentators have employed different terms to explain the replication in the lives of those empowered by the Holy Spirit as experienced on Pentecost Day. Expressions like "release of the Spirit," "new outpouring of the Spirit," or "being baptized in the Spirit,"[596] go a long way to express renewed awareness that Pentecost is open-ended. Kevin and Dorothy Ranaghan have also given a succinct answer to help resolve the theological conflicts many Catholics still face in the renewal group:

> *Baptism in the Holy Spirit is not something replacing baptism and confirmation. Rather it may be seen as an adult re-affirmation and renewal of these sacraments, an opening of ourselves to all their sacramental graces. The gesture of 'laying on of hands', which often accompanies 'baptism in the*

---

[593] Sullivan, op. cit., 62.

[594] *Theological and Pastoral Orientations on the Catholic Charismatic Renewal*, (Michigan: Servant Books, Ann Arbor 1974), 30. Quoted in Ibid.

[595] Ibid.

[596] Ibid., 26.

Holy Spirit', is not a new sacramental rite. It is a fraternal gesture of love and concern, a visible sign of human corporeality.[597]

Contrary to the Catholic church's understanding and teaching on baptism in the Holy Spirit as presented above, Pentecostals mostly maintain that there is a distinction between water baptism (rebirth) and baptism of the Spirit.[598] They believe that water baptism is separate from baptism in the Holy Spirit. James D.G. Dunn is an adherent of this position. He believes that baptism in the Holy Spirit is part of the process of becoming a Christian, with the effective proclamation of the Gospel, and faith in Jesus as Lord.[599] For Dunn also, water baptism in the name of the Lord Jesus was a chief element in conversion-initiation but only those who received the Holy Spirit could be called Christians.[600] However, he strongly believes that water baptism is clearly distinct from Spirit-baptism. He looks at the sacrament of baptism merely as a rite.[601] In refuting this idea, Congar presents baptism as one organic all-inclusive process as expounded above, which includes conversion, the Church, and the action of God through the Holy Spirit who imparts *charisms*.[602] The discharge of the *charisms*, through the baptism of the Holy Spirit, brings about manifestations of the gifts for ministry in the Church. We have examined manifestations of *charisms* in the gospels, Pauline writings, other New Testament letters and early Church. I shall now assess the testimonies of how the demonstrations of the gifts of the Holy Spirit/*charisms* impacted the post-biblical Church. In doing this, I will look into the works of a few reliable figures in the first eight centuries of the Church.

3.6 *The Early Post-Biblical Evidence*

Since this thesis is not exhaustive of the complete works of the post-biblical authors, I have chosen a few of them to study how *charisms* were given, openly received and used for ministry in the different documented Christian communities. As we shall see, the writings provide us with a profound representation of how the post-biblical practice of the use

---

[597] Kevin Ranaghan, and Dorothy Ranaghan, *Catholic Pentecostals*, (Indiana: Deus books, 1969), 20. See also E. O'Connor, *The Pentecostal Movement in the Catholic Church* (Notre Dame, Indiana, 1971), pp. 117, 131ff., especially 136, 215-218. Quoted in Congar, 198

[598] Congar, op. cit., 190. Cited in McDonnell, and Montague, Eds. *Fanning the Flame,* 15.

[599] Dunn, op. cit., 508-523

[600] Ibid.

[601] Congar, op. cit., 194.

[602] Ibid.

of *charism* was in compliance with the mandate of Jesus to his disciples not to begin ministry until they received power from on high (Luke 24:49; Acts 1:4). The rite of Christian initiation, which was synonymous with baptism in the Holy Spirit empowered believers to launch themselves into ministry at this time in Christian history. We shall start with two of the Apostolic Fathers who were the writers that followed after the New Testament period.[603] While the Apostolic Fathers were strictly concerned about inspiration and prophecy,[604] we will unravel other *charisms* in subsequent centuries as our explorations of evidence of the manifestations and use of *charisms* lead us to the first eight centuries of Christianity.

3.7 *Justin Martyr (c. 100-165)*[605]

There is no much historical documentation on the life and works of Justin Martyr as such. What we know of him comes from his writings.[606] Justin Martyr was born into a pagan family in Flavia Neapolis (ancient Shechem in Judea/Palestine, modern-day Nablus).[607] He was educated as a philosopher; however, his search for truth eventually brought him to Christianity,[608] which he confessed as "true philosophy.[609] His travels took him to different parts of the known world, but he finally settled in Rome[610] where he wrote his apologies. Regrettably, Emperor Markus Aurelius martyred him about 165.[611]

Justin Martyr was the most prominent Christian apologist of his time, defending the faith against opponents of the Christianity, Judaism or paganism alike.[612] He believed Christ, whose divinity is universal is the Logos of God and on this, he based his Christian claim to true philosophy.[613] He had to tackle the problem by explaining the distinctive role of Christ in the universe;

---

[603] Burns, and Fagin, op. cit., 17.

[604] Ibid.

[605] Burns, and Fagin, op. cit., 26.

[606] Burgess, op. cit., 17.

[607] Ibid.

[608] Burns, and Fagin, op. cit., 26.

[609] Burgess, op. cit., 17.

[610] Ibid.

[611] Ibid., See also Burns, and Fagin, op. cit., 26.

[612] Ibid.

[613] Burns, and Fagin, op. cit., 26.

however, his answer does not give a clear distinction between the divine Word dwelling in Christ and the Spirit.[614] His attempt to define the relationship between members of the Trinity was plausible during his time but later declared unsatisfactory by Trinitarians because he seems to subordinate the Son to the Father and the Holy Spirit to the Son.[615] However, in developing his argument to give more credibility to Christianity against the assertions of his Jewish challengers, he pointed out in his dialogue with Trypho that the gifts of prophecy were no more in existence among Jewish people but noticeable among Christians of his day.[616] His studies of Isaiah 11 and 1 Corinthians 12 underscored that the gifts formerly enjoyed by Old Testament community had been transferred to Christian believers.[617] Justin believed that believers in Christ received prophetic gifts because the coming of Christ facilitated the cessation of the prophetic gifts among the Jews. He asserted that the Spirit that inspired Old Testament prophets ceased in order to rest on Christ who gave prophetic gifts to believers. This was possible because of the ascension of Christ into heaven as it was prophesied, "He ascended on high; he led captivity captive; he gave gifts to the sons of men" (Ps. 68:18). Furthermore, it is said in another prophecy: "And it shall be after these things that I will pour out my Spirit upon all flesh, and upon men-servants and upon maid-servants, and they shall prophesy" (Joel 2:28).[618]

Justin Martyr's Dialogues open us to the initial early post-biblical understanding of *charisms* as he sought to find the relationship between Old Testament prophets and prophecy in the Christian group. Interestingly, he leads us into the mystery of the Christ being the fulfillment of the prophecies of Old. Christ is the one with the fullness of prophetic spirit, who after his resurrection breathed the same prophetic spirit into his disciples to carry out their charismatic salvific mission in the world.

3.8 Irenaeus (c.130-200)[619]

There is no clear documentation of the birth time and death of Irenaeus as commentators dispute those dates. What we know about him are conjectures from his writings, bringing

---

[614] Ibid.

[615] Burgess, op. cit., 18.

[616] Sullivan, op. cit., 111.

[617] Burgess, op. cit., 18.

[618] Ibid., 19.

[619] Burns, and Fagin, op. cit., 31.

about conflicting data about his life.[620] However, many commentators believe Irenaeus was a native of Asia Minor and claimed as a youth to have listened to Polycarp, Bishop of Smyrna who testified about the Apostle John.[621] Irenaeus' writings refuted the errors of the Gnostics and saved the Catholic Faith from the danger of being infiltrated by the doctrines of heretics.[622]

His studies took him to Rome where he also taught before going to Lyons. He is believed to be the most influential of all early Church fathers who provided early Christians with the first systematic exposition of its beliefs.[623] Irenaeus defended the Church against many erroneous teachings such as, (a) Gnostics perception of the spirit and matter as opposites through special or secret knowledge, (b) the emanation of the Son and the Spirit from God, (c) Gnostic teaching that Jesus only appeared to take the human flesh and (d) Gnostics "spiritual elitism" to which he responded, "the redemptive act is for all those who have faith in Christ as savior and is not reserved for those who claim a higher calling, a special gift of knowledge, or other spiritual gifts.[624] He recognized the ongoing working of the Holy Spirit in the Church of his day by reporting the continued operations of charismatic gifts, including prophecy, among believers in his church. The heart of his theology is Paul's doctrine of the "recapitulation of all things in Christ." "Through communion with Christ in the Holy Spirit humans are made incorruptible and through redemption are made like God."[625]

Irenaeus makes clear in two passages in *Against Heresies* that the gifts of the Holy Spirit exists in the Church:

> ... *for which cause also his [Christ's] true disciples having received grace from him use it in his name for the benefit of the rest of men, even as each has received the gift from him. For some drive out demons with certainty and truth, so that often those who have themselves been cleansed from the evil spirits believe and are in the church, and some have foreknowledge of things to be, and visions and prophetic speech, and others cure the sick by the laying on of hands and make them whole, and even as we have said, the dead have been raised and remained with us for many years. And why should*

---

[620] Ronald A.N., Kydd, *Charismatic Gifts in the Early Church: The Gifts of the Spirit in the First 300 Years*. (eBook edition). (Peabody, Massachusetts: Hendrickson Publishers Marketing, LLC 2015), loc. 903.

[621] Burns, and Fagin, op. cit., 31.

[622] Catholic Online http://www.catholic.org/saints/saint.php?saint_id=291 Accessed July 29, 2016.

[623] Burgess, op. cit., 20.

[624] Ibid.

[625] Ibid., 21.

I say more? It is not possible to tell the number of the gifts which the church throughout the whole world, having received them from God in the name of Jesus Christ, who was crucified under Pontius Pilate, uses each day for the benefit of the heathen, deceiving none and making profit from none. For as it received freely from God, it ministers also freely Church.[626]

Against Heresies, 5, 6: 1 is our second reference from Irenaeus:

Just as also we hear many brethren in the church who have gifts of prophecy, and who speak through the Spirit with all manner of tongues, and who bring the hidden things of men into the clearness for the common good and expound the mysteries of God.[627]

From the above quotes, the lists of Irenaeus spiritual gifts include such gifts as the ability to cast out demons, knowledge about the future, visions, and prophetic speech. However, we see a striking parallel with Paul's list in 1 Corinthians 12. They both wrote about prophecy, healing and the control of evil spirits. While Paul used the ability to distinguish spirits, Irenaeus, on the other hand, uses exorcism.[628] Irenaeus seeks to demonstrate and establish that the miraculous power of God was still operative in the Church through the use of *charisms*.

3.9 *Tertullian (c 160-225)*[629]

Our knowledge of Tertullian is a construction from the writings of people who lived more than a century after him and from vague references in his works. With this declaration, scholars have repeatedly disputed most accounts about the life of Tertullian.[630] However, there is a general consensus among commentators that he was one of the early fathers of

---

[626] The text from Irenaeus as quoted by Eusebius in his Ecclesiastical History, 5, 7: 3– 5, Kirsopp Lake (Loeb Classical Library), 1: 453 and 455. The Greek text was chosen here and in the next quotation because of the relative weakness of the Latin text, which was edited by W. W. Harvey (1852). Quoted in Kydd, op. cit., loc. 947-950.

[627] Irenaeus as quoted by Eusebius in Ecclesiastical History, 5, 7: 6, Kirsopp Lake (Loeb Classical Library), 1: 455. Quoted in Kydd, op. cit., loc.1053-1054.

[628] Kydd, op. cit., loc. 958-959.

[629] Burgess, op. cit., 30.

[630] Robert L. Wilken, *Tertullian Christian Theologian*, https://www.britannica.com/biography/Tertullian Accessed September 18, 2016.

the Church, notably early Christian apologist, born in the city of Carthage in North Africa. His parents were both Pagan, and his father was a centurion.[631] Tertullian may have been educated in Rome, where he was educated in philosophy, history, science, and 'antiquarian' wisdom.[632] It was in Rome he became interested in the Christian movement but was converted to Christianity when he returned to Carthage toward the end of the 2nd century. There was a documented account of his conversion experience, "but in his early works, Ad martyras ("To the Martyrs"), Ad nationes ("To the Nations"), and Apologeticum ("Defense"), he indicated that he was impressed by certain Christian attitudes and beliefs: the courage and determination of martyrs, moral rigorism, and an uncompromising belief in one God."[633]

Many commentators believe that Tertullian left the Orthodox Church before 210 to join the Montanists, which had spread from Asia Minor to Africa at the time. He was unsatisfied with the permissiveness of Christians who did not see the urgency for any moral reformation because of the imminent end of the world. For Tertullian, Montanism refused to compromise with the ways of the world and thereby gave his service to the new movement as its most eloquent spokesperson.[634] However, toward the end of his life, Tertullian felt Montanism was too moderate for him. He left and founded an even more radical group, the Tertullianists.[635] Though the time of Tertullian's death is disputed, many commentators believe that he must have died between AD 220 and 225.[636] Most Christians of ancient times never forgave Tertullian for his apostasy, which warranted his negative portrayal in many Christian writings. But some writers reluctantly acknowledged his gifts and insightful intelligence.[637] As modern scholarship has unraveled the historical religious bias that repressed the creative intellectual ingenuity of Tertullian through his works that have been widely read and studied, he is now considered one of those who shaped Christian thought in the West.[638] It is now clearer that Tertullian undeniably created a succinct language of Western

---

[631] Gerald Bray, *Tertullian and the Early Church*. http://www.theopedia.com/tertullian Accessed September 21, 2016.

[632] Burgess, op. cit., 30.

[633] Wilken, op. cit.

[634] Ibid.

[635] Burgess, op. cit., 30.

[636] Ibid.

[637] Wilken, op. cit.

[638] Ibid.

theology.[639] Tertullian's first use of the term *Trinitas* (Trinity) to describe the Godhead, paved the way for the development of Trinitarian and Christological doctrines.[640] Tertullian's charismatic experience of the actions of the Holy Spirit[641] also gave him the authority to speak of the Holy Spirit in a variety of contexts.[642] He believed the gift of prophecy flourished in his community because they were open to receive and acknowledge the spiritual gifts.[643] The community also believed that the spiritual gifts were valuable parts of the Church's culture as experienced by the early Christians in fulfillment of the teaching of Apostle Paul.[644] The gift of prophecy was highly placed in Tertullian's community as expressed in the following:

> *We recognize and honor the prophecies and the recent visions, which had been promised equally. We also regard the rest of the powers of the Holy Spirit as tools of the Church to whom the Spirit was sent, administering all the outstandingly impressive gifts to everyone just as the Lord distributes to each.*[645]

The above text from Tertullian confirms once again that he gave credibility to the prophecies of the controversial prophetesses, Maximilla, and Priscilla[646] as already mentioned above. Though some early Christian writers opposed the incorporation of the charismatic spirituality of Montanism into Tertullian's community, I think that only some of their prophetic utterances were genuine but not all. Furthermore, I believe that one of the gifts of the Holy Spirit we explored in Chapter three; the discernment of spirits, can be used to judge what is of God and what is not. I agree with the author of 1 John 4:1 when he advised: "Beloved, do not trust every spirit but test the spirits to see whether they belong to God,

---

[639] Patrick J. Hamell, *Handbook of Patrology: A concise, authoritative guide to the life and works of the Fathers of the Church*. (New York: Alba House, 1968), 71.

[640] Burgess, op. cit., 30.

[641] Ibid.

[642] Burns, and Fagin, op. cit., 47.

[643] *Tertullian, De Anima,* 9, (Corpus Christianorum, 2, part 2), p. 792, Kydd's translation. Cited in Kydd, op. cit., loc. 1464.

[644] *Tertullian,* op. cit., 793. Cited in Ibid.

[645] *Tertullian, Passion S. Perpetuae (Martyrdom of St. Perpetuae),* 1. Ed. J.A. Robinson (Text and Studies 1, 2 Cambridge, 1891), p. 62. Kydd's translation. Cited Kydd, op. cit., 1479.

[646] Kydd, op. cit., loc. 1485.

because many false prophets have gone out into the world."[647] However, one cannot properly be engaged in the spiritual exercises of discernment of spirits if an individual is intellectually or spiritually biased. The depth of the Holy Spirit is inexhaustible, and the Holy Spirit remains unpredictable in the offering of gifts for the evangelization of different eras. On the other hand, the Holy Spirit cannot impose herself on anyone. Therefore, anyone who wishes to receive and manifest the gifts of the Holy Spirit has to be open. Tertullian understood this perfectly when at the end of the treatise *On Baptism* he encouraged the neophytes:

> *"Therefore, you blessed ones, for whom the grace of God is waiting, when you come up from the most sacred bath of the new birth, when you spread out your hands for the first time in your mother's house with your brethren, ask your Father, ask your Lord, for the special gift of his inheritance, the distributed charisms, which from an additional, underlying feature (of baptism). Ask, he says, and you shall receive. In fact, you have sought, and you have found: you have knocked, and it has been opened to you."[648]*

The above text also reveals the hidden treasures of how *charisms* were released to flow into new believers' lives in the context of the sacramental rite of Christian Initiation in Tertullian's community. As the neophytes went through the sacramental-liturgical rite of incorporation into the ecclesial community, prayers of invocation, petitions were said and hands were laid on them for the impartation of the gifts of the Holy Spirit. This ancient sacramental liturgical practice unfolds for us anew that baptism in the Holy Spirit is integral to the Church life.[649]

3.10 *Origen (c. 185-254)*[650]

Origen was born in Alexandria to Christian parents. His father Leonidas was martyred in AD 202.[651] He is one of the most exceptional philosophical and theological minds in

---

[647] Senior, and Collins, op. cit., 1660.

[648] *OB* 20: SC 35:96. Translated by Montague and cited in McDonnell, and Montague, *Christian Initiation and Baptism in the Holy Spirit,* 108. See also A.G. Ph. Borleffs. Ed. (Corpus Christianorum, Series Latina, 1, part 2) (Turnholt: Brepols, 1954), p. 295. Cited in Kydd, op. cit., 1489.

[649] McDonnell, and Montague, *Christian Initiation and Baptism in the Holy Spirit,* 115.

[650] Burns, and Fagin, op. cit., 68.

[651] Ibid.

the history of the Church.[652] Origen was an extraordinarily gifted man who was a "cate-chist, exegete, theologian, apologist, mystic, spiritual master, churchman, schoolman, creative scholar of prodigious output, and an undoubted man of genius."[653] Unfortunately for Origen, his trustworthiness in the Church has diminished because of his controversial doctrinal positions. Nevertheless, he still goes in history as one of the bravest, courageous and thought-provoking theologians in Christian history. Eusebius, the historian, believed that Origen's response to the accusation that Christians' refusal to serve in the military failed the test of good citizenship. He wrote, "We who by our prayers destroy all demons which stir up wars, violate oaths, and disturb the peace are of more help to the emperors than those who seem to be doing the fighting."[654] However, his statement did not go well with the authorities under Emperor Decius who had Origen imprisoned and tortured. He was kept alive to see if he would renounce his faith. Unfortunately, his captor, emperor Decius died, and Origen was set free but died three years after his release in AD 254.[655]

In my opinion, Origen was a committed and devoted religious man, though he was declared a heretic posthumously at the Second Council of Constantinople in AD 553.[656] Although probably the greatest scholar of his time who believed that all of Scripture has spiritual meaning, he fell victim to the literal interpretation of Matthew 19:12, which inspired his self-castration according to Eusebius, the historian.[657] As a consequence, we have an insight into Origen's intense devotion and asceticism. He was contaminated by fanaticism and his philosophy also corrupted his theology, giving birth to some of his flawed teachings.[658] For instance, Origen subordinated "the Son to the Father and the Spirit to the Son. Only the Father is fully God: the Son and Spirit are lesser divine beings."[659] Origen propounded the erroneous doctrine of *subordinationism*, which was condemned with Arianism in AD 381. But his experience and references to *charisms* in his works, *Against Celsius*,[660] are benefi-

---

[652] Kydd, op. cit., loc. 1641.

[653] McDonnell, and Montague, *Christian Initiation and Baptism in the Holy Spirit,* 133.

[654] Origen, *Biblical scholar and philosopher*
http://www.christianitytoday.com/history/people/scholarsandscientists/origen.html

[655] Ibid.

[656] Burns, and Fagin, op. cit., 69.

[657] Burgess, op. cit., 41.

[658] Kydd, op. cit., loc. 1646.

[659] Burns, and Fagin, op. cit., 69.

[660] Kydd, op. cit., loc. 1673-1674.

cial to our exploration of the manifestations and use of *charisms* in the first eight centuries of the Church. In Against Celsus, 1, 2, Origen sought to establish that the Gospel is still valid because the miracles that happened in the apostolic age still endure when he wrote:

> *This more divine demonstration the apostle calls a "demonstration of spirit and of power" – of spirit because of the prophecies and especially those which refer to Christ, which are capable of convincing anyone who reads them; of power because of the prodigious miracles which may be proved to have happened by this argument among many others, that traces of them still remain among those who live according to the will of the Logos.*[661]

Origen continued in *Against Celsus*, 1, 46 to talk about the miracles in the ministry of Jesus as they still happened in the early Church:

> *Traces of that Holy Spirit who appeared in the form of a dove are still preserved among Christians. They charm demons away and perform many cures and perceive certain things about the future according to the will of the Logos.*[662]

To further buttress his point about the presence and manifestation of *charisms* in his day, Origen introduced an argument about the absence of prophets among the Jews after the birth of Jesus:

> *They no longer have any prophets or wonders, though traces of these are to be found to a considerable extent among Christians. Indeed, some works are even greater; and if our word may be trusted, we also have seen them.*[663]

In the above text, Origen testified to having personally experienced miracles, in his words, "some works ... even greater." I believe this was in fulfillment of the words of Jesus in the Gospel of John 14:12: "Amen, amen, I say to you, whoever believes in me will do the works that I do, and will do greater ones than these, because I am going to the Father."[664]

---

[661] Origen, *Against Celsus*, 1, 2, trans. Henry Chadwick (Cambridge: At the University Press), p. 8. Quoted in Kydd, op.cit., loc. 1684.

[662] Ibid., 1, 46, Chadwick, p. 42. Quoted in Kydd, op. cit., loc. 1690.

[663] Ibid., 2, 8, Chadwick, p. 72. Quoted in Kydd, op. cit., loc. 1696.

[664] Senior, and Collins, op. cit., 1430.

Origen continued to reiterate his point about the manifestation and use of the gifts of the Holy Spirit during his time. However, *Against Celsus* 7, 8, he noted that though the presence of the Spirit was observable "in a few people," it was not as common as it used to be.[665] He captured this in these words:

> *But signs of the Holy Spirit were manifested at the beginning when Jesus was teaching, and after his ascension there were many more, though later they became less numerous. Nevertheless, even to this day there are traces of him in a few people whose souls have been purified by the Logos and by the actions, which follow his teaching.[666]*

To summarize, Origen believed that the Holy Spirit came upon the baptized and poured out on them *charisms*. For him, baptism was the principle and source of the *charisms* as listed in 1 Corinthian 12.[667] Without prejudice to this position, I wish to point out as we have discussed above that baptism is not the only source of the *charisms* but one of the sources. The Holy Spirit has the sovereignty to use whatever channel to bestow *charisms,* through or without sacramental baptism. To some extent, we have dealt with how the Holy Spirit also confers *charisms* on people who were not even baptized, like Gentiles, the household of Cornelius in Acts 10:44-48. Origen experienced the manifestation and use of *charisms* in his day and ministry but noted it was gradually disappearing.

3.11 *Hilary of Poitiers (c.315-367)[668]*

We don't know much about the early life of Hilary of Poitiers. However, some consensus exists that he was born of pagan parents.[669] He was a convert from Neoplatonism, baptized as an adult, and became bishop of Poitiers in AD 353.[670] He went on exile to Phrygia (modern Turkey) in AD 356, because of his opposition to Arianism and while in exile he composed the twelve books *On the Trinity*, which gained him a reputation as the leading

---

[665] Kydd, op. cit., loc. 1720.

[666] Origen, op. cit. cit., 7, 8, pp. 401f. Quoted in Kydd, op. cit., loc. 1696

[667] McDonnell, and Montague, *Christian Initiation and Baptism in the Holy Spirit,* 143.

[668] Burns, and Fagin, op. cit., 110.

[669] McDonnell, and Montague, *Christian Initiation and Baptism in the Holy Spirit,* 155.

[670] Burns, and Fagin, op. cit., 110.

Latin theologian of his time before his death in AD 367.[671] For Hilary, the same Spirit that imparted Jesus at his baptism at the river Jordan imparts us and makes us God's sons and daughters. The same anointing that came upon Jesus as he came out of the water comes upon us too enabling us to be baptized in the Holy Spirit.[672] Therefore, he linked the impartation of *charisms* to being baptized in the Holy Spirit.[673] It was a common occurrence that during the rites of Christian initiation that all present experienced the stirring of the grace of the Spirit that filled all with joy.[674] This is made clearer in the words of Montague:

> *"Hilary and the other neophytes experienced intense joy, and the charisms manifest themselves: words of understanding and wisdom, prophecy, healing, and exorcism. Christians are endowed with charisms as indeed Jesus was at the beginning of his public ministry."*[675]

The chrisms that Christians receive at their baptism are for the proclamation of the gospel through the ministry of individual recipients; they should not be left dormant or hidden as if the Spirit were absent in the Church.[676] Hilary enjoined believers to effectively and profitably use the *charisms* that have been generously given to us for the glory of God in the Church.[677] The *charisms* are not just for adornment or self-glorification but also for ministry in service to others.[678]

In summary, Hilary's image of the Spirit as the river of God that flows within each believer, overflowing its banks, overwhelming with *charisms*, are not unconnected but are precisely gifts belonging to the Church to make a difference in the world profitably for God's glory.[679]

---

[671] Ibid.

[672] McDonnell, and Montague, *Christian Initiation and Baptism in the Holy Spirit*, 175.

[673] Ibid.

[674] Ibid., 189.

[675] Ibid.

[676] Ibid., 178.

[677] Ibid., 179.

[678] Ibid., 186-187.

[679] Ibid., 189.

3.12 *Cyril of Jerusalem (c. 315-386)*[680]

Cyril of Jerusalem was a contemporary of Hilary and may have been born in the same year with him.[681] Some commentators speculate that he was probably born in Palestine and educated in Jerusalem, ordained a deacon in AD 325, and a priest by Maximus II around AD 345.[682] He is popularly known for his twenty-four catechetical lectures, which may have been delivered after he became a bishop in AD 348.[683] Cyril held that Christian baptism is "an imitation as in an icon" of Christ's baptism.[684] The baptism of Jesus is the determinant model for our baptismal ritual expression of the imparting of the Spirit. As Christ was anointed with the Holy Spirit as he came out of the River Jordan, likewise candidates are anointed with oil on their foreheads and on the organs of sense after they come out of the pool of the sacred streams.[685]

Charisms are received at baptism and are not restricted to bishops, priests or deacons.[686] *Charisms* are given to each, because the Spirit knows what each says, or thinks, or believes.[687] Cyril taught that candidates should always enter the sacred stream and come out with expectant, enthusiastic and open to receive "the heavenly *charisms*."[688] Everyone receives the same Spirit but experiences differ because of each person's dispositions.[689] The Spirit is not frugal and neither is she a reluctant giver of the gifts but pours them out "profusely" to people of different races and nations.[690] For Cyril, baptism and *charisms* are intertwined, one flows from the other.

---

[680] Burns, and Fagin, op. cit., 92.

[681] McDonnell, and Montague, *Christian Initiation and Baptism in the Holy Spirit,* 191.

[682] Hamell, op. cit., 99.

[683] Burns, and Fagin, op. cit., 92.

[684] McDonnell, and Montague, *Christian Initiation and Baptism in the Holy Spirit,* 210.

[685] Ibid.

[686] Ibid., 213.

[687] Ibid.

[688] Ibid.

[689] Ibid.

[690] Ibid.

He believes Christian initiation is also "baptism in the Holy Spirit" because the same living tradition flows from Justin Martyr,[691] Origen,[692] and Didymus the Blind.[693]

Conclusively, Cyril did not give a complete list of the *charisms* but believes that all the *charisms* are present in the church. However, he wished that candidates should not be concerned about worthiness because God will make them worthy and the Spirit pours out prophetic *charisms* on both poor and rich.[694] Consequently, whatever the Spirit touches, the Spirit transforms.[695] Openness and enthusiastic expectation are all the requirements for the outpouring of the *charisms*.

3.13 *John Chrysostom (c. 347-407)*

John Chrysostom was born into a noble Christian family in Antioch about AD 347, grew up and had his education there, and was ordained a priest in AD 386.[696] He exercised his priestly ministry mostly in Antioch, and his office also prepared catechumens for baptism until AD 398 when he became the patriarch of Constantinople.[697] John Chrysostom is one of the greatest preachers of all times whose creative and oratorical skills drew huge crowds each time to listen to his sermons.[698] Regrettably for Chrysostom, his frequent admonishment of the Empress Eudoxia and outspokenness of the abuses in the Church and society led to his exile to Comana where he died in AD 407.[699] His bones were brought back to Constantinople some years later, and his name was engraved and revered with those of

---

[691] Justin Martyr, *Dialogue with Trypho,* 29:1; PG 6:537. Cited in McDonnell, and Montague, *Christian Initiation and Baptism in the Holy Spirit,* 216.

[692] Origen, *On Jeremiah*, 2:3; SC 232:244. Cited in McDonnell, and Montague, *Christian Initiation and Baptism in the Holy Spirit,* 216.

[693] Didymus the Blind, *On the Trinity*, 2:12; PG 39:668, 673. Cited in McDonnell, and Montague, *Christian Initiation and Baptism in the Holy Spirit,* 216.

[694] McDonnell, and Montague, *Christian Initiation and Baptism in the Holy Spirit,* 217

[695] Ibid., 220.

[696] Ibid., 260.

[697] Ibid., 260-261.

[698] John F. Thornton, and Katharine Washburn, Eds. *The Times: Greatest Sermons of the Last 2000 Years, Tongues of Angels, Tongues of Men.* London: Harper Collins Publishers, 1999), 99.

[699] Ibid. See also Burns, and Fagin, op. cit., 156.

other early saints of the Church.[700] He believed the Holy Spirit that worked in the gospels and Acts of the Apostles was still present in his day, working among the people of God.[701]

However, John Chrysostom's ministry of teaching and preaching focused within the framework of the Syrian ecclesiastical tradition, whose biblical understanding of the baptism of Jesus was central to the model of Christian baptism.[702] Consequently for Chrysostom, "The baptism of Jesus is the model for Christian baptism." [703] At his baptism, Jesus was anointed with the Spirit and declared the Beloved Son, so those wishing to become Christians go down into the waters, and are also anointed to receive the Spirit thereby becoming God's adopted daughters and sons.[704] Through the baptismal experiential encounter of Jesus in the Jordan, he received all the *charisms* needed to fulfill his mission of healing, deliverance and prophetic ministry for the salvation of the world.[705] At the Jordan, Jesus experienced the transformational abiding presence of the Holy Spirit that empowered him for all the miracles he performed.[706] Similarly, the apostles and early Christians who went through the same process of initiation as Jesus did were empowered from on high and given *charisms* to function as God's instrumental presence to bless the world through their ministry. Subsequently following this tradition, many *charisms* existed in Chrysostom's community Tongues and prophecy were not as prominent as they were in the early Church though. He taught about *charisms* but since tongues and prophecy were not manifested in his community, he did not expect them during the initiation ceremonies. [707] Chrysostom grieved over the disappearance of the *charisms* that were implicitly part of ecclesial life during the apostolic days.[708] He lamented the complacency of the Church of his day that was content with not having the manifestations of the *charisms* of the apostolic era and was not even expectant, because they were no more part of the normal life of the Christian community.[709] He noted that during

---

[700] Ibid.

[701] Burns, and Fagin, op. cit., 157.

[702] McDonnell, and Montague, *Christian Initiation and Baptism in the Holy Spirit,* 279.

[703] Ibid.

[704] Ibid.

[705] Ibid., 280.

[706] Ibid.

[707] Ibid., 287.

[708] Ibid., 288.

[709] Ibid., 297.

the initiation of the earliest Christian communities, they prayed for the coming of the Holy Spirit (in the water-bath) with the laying on of the hand, and finally manifested the *charisms*, prophecy, tongues, wisdom, knowledge, healing, miracles and raising the dead.[710] Kilian McDonnell captures Chrysostom's pains in these words:

> *The church of his day is like a woman who wants to display her jewels, but when she opens the coffer it is empty. The Church of tokens looks back to the apostolic age, when all was "heavenly.*[711]

However, Chrysostom with his creative ingenuity found a way of explaining the lack of continuity of the power and glory of the apostolic age into the present age.[712] He created a mental connection between the apostolic days and his days because of his belief that the church cannot exist if the apostolic community is not "the goal and measure of the Christian life"[713] For him, the structures of ecclesial life in the apostolic age had prophetic-charismatic characteristics. Therefore, determinations have to be made to validate the apostolic nature of the Church of his day by claiming the presence of the same charisms that existed in the apostolic era.[714] To accomplish his intellectual insight of building a bridge between the past and present, Chrysostom employed internalization and spiritualization of the charisms.[715] He declared in one of his Pentecost homilies that the absence of the prophetic charisms did not mean that the charismatic dimension of the Church had been ended. That which was formally visible could be accomplished in an unseen manner and grasped by faith.[716] Consequently, Chrysostom fashioned a spiritualization and intellectualization of charisms in the absence of their manifestations.

---

[710] Ibid., 298.

[711] Ibid.

[712] Ibid., 290-291.

[713] A. M. Ritter, *Charisma im Verstandnis des Joannes Chrysostomos und seiner Zeit* (Gottingen: Vandenhoeck & Ruprecht, 1972) 34. Quoted in Ibid., 291.

[714] McDonnell, and Montague, *Christian Initiation and Baptism in the Holy Spirit,* 291.

[715] Ibid.

[716] Ibid.

3.14 *Philoxenus Of Mabbug (c. 440-523)*[717]

Philoxenus was born into a Christian Aramaic family and may have studied the Old and New Testament and Syriac masters.[718] Philoxenus' academic studies focused on biblical interpretation, using literary, philosophical, lexical, and historical tools.[719] His education in the teachings of the theological school of Edessa may have influenced his attachment to the Monophysite faction that opposed the Antiochian Christological school of thought, thereby separating himself from a good number of his generations with like minds.[720] He was a hermit.[721] He became the bishop of Mabbug, and used his position as a shepherd to strengthen Monophysite Christology.[722] As a staunch adherent of Monophysitism and a bishop, he continued his attack on the decrees of Chalcedon.[723] Philoxenus enjoyed the favor of Emperor Anastasius 1, who swapped Orthodox bishops with Monophysite bishops.[724] However, his quest to spread Monophysitism was short lived when Anastasius died in AD 518, and an Orthodox Emperor Justin 1 came in and banished him and fifty-three other Monophysites.[725] Philoxenus continued his polemical and ascetical writings while he was in exile but must have died a tragic death.[726]

Like John Chrysostom, Philoxenus also observed the discrepancy between the apostolic church and the church of his day.[727] However, his idea that the prophetic *charisms* that manifested in the apostolic era were also the gifts believers received at their initiation changed.[728] He abandoned the idea that at baptism believers are given the same *charisms* that Christians

---

[717] Ibid.

[718] Ibid., 302.

[719] Ibid., 303.

[720] Ibid.

[721] Ibid.

[722] Ibid.

[723] http://www.newadvent.org/cathen/12040a.htm Accessed October 6, 2016

[724] https://www.britannica.com/biography/Philoxenus-of-Mabbug Accessed October 6, 2016.

[725] Ibid.

[726] Ibid.

[727] McDonnell, and Montague, *Christian Initiation and Baptism in the Holy Spirit,* 324.

[728] Ibid.

in the apostolic era received. Since he was a man who gave himself to ascetical living and cut himself off from others, he made the *charisms* exclusive only to hermits who had abandoned the world into the way of the rules of the spiritual life. He wrote:

> *"Now again, the Holy Spirit is given by baptism to those who are baptized and they really receive it (the Spirit), like the first believers. However in one of them, does it (the Spirit) manifest its (the Spirit's) work visibly. Even though it (the Spirit) is in them, it (the Spirit) remains hidden there. Unless one leaves the world to enter into the way of the rules of the Spiritual life observing all the commandments Jesus has given, walking with wisdom and perseverance in the narrow way of the Gospel, the work of the Spirit received in baptism does reveal itself.*[729]

Philoxenus insisted that *charisms* would only manifest in those who have totally renounced the world for the monastic life. Consequently, he monasticized *charisms* by restricting the gifts of the Holy Spirit to hermits alone. [730] Philoxenus and some Syrian monastic theologians like Jacob of Serugh (c. 451-521),[731] John of Apamea,[732] Theodoret of Cyrrhus (c. 393–406),[733] Severus of Antioch (c. 465 – 538),[734] Joseph Hazzaya (born c. 710-13),[735] excluded other Christians from the experience of *charisms* as experienced in the apostolic era. To validate their position, they introduced a second baptism, which they believed was for the unfolding, the full flowering of the reality given in the first baptism.[736] The second baptism came from their creation of a two-way baptismal structure based on the distinction between believers who live in the world and those who renounced everything including marriage.[737]

---

[729] *Letter to Patricius*, 120; Patrologia Orientalis, 30:861,863. Quoted in Ibid., 324.

[730] McDonnell, and Montague, *Christian Initiation and Baptism in the Holy Spirit,* 321.

[731] Ibid., 326.

[732] Ibid., 327.

[733] Ibid., 328.

[734] Ibid., 331.

[735] Ibid., 333.

[736] Ibid., 347.

[737] Ibid., 347-348.

Conclusively, as we draw this session to a close we see that in both the West and the East respectively, the manifestation and use of *charisms* gradually moved from the believers generally to residing in hermits but at different times and with a different understanding. While the West struggled to understand the reason for the disappearance of the *charisms* as manifested in the apostolic era and finding a theological explanation as started by John Chrysostom, the East was struggling with different heresies and corruption in the Church that gave birth to Monasticism.

3.15 *Benedict (c. 480 – 547)*[738]

There is no established historical documentation of the life of Benedict. Legends have obscured what we know about him.[739] However, Pope Gregory the Great's earliest biographer wrote that he was born into a noble family of Nursia, at about AD 480.[740] He was sent to Rome to study and while he was in Rome, the vice and corruption he found there disgusted him. He renounced his inheritance and desiring a life of solitude, retired to a cave near Subiaco where he resided for three years.[741] Benedict founded the monastery of Monte Cassino in about AD 529 and created the Rule of Benedict that provided an organizational way of life, work, and worship in the communal monastic setting.[742] Beyond creating the most important plans for the monastic life in the Middle Ages and the whole of Europe, Benedict is also known for the many miracles that are attributed to him.[743] His ministry was not limited to the confines of the monastery alone. He ministered to the sick, cast out demons and he is said to have raised the dead.[744] Benedict was believed to have manifested the *charisms* of knowledge and prophecy. He knew about his death, told his disciples to dig his grave six days before he passed and died standing with his hands raised

---

[738] Eddie L. Hyatt, *2000 Years of Charismatic Christianity: A 21st Century Look at Church History from a Pentecostal/Charismatic Perspective* (Kindle Edition). (Charisma House, Lake Mary, Florida: A Strang Company 2002), Loc. 433. Retrieved from Amazon.com

[739] Richard Woods, *Christian Spirituality: God's Presence Through the Ages*. Allen, Texas: Thomas More Publishing, 1996), 124.

[740] Ibid.

[741] Ibid.

[742] Hyatt, op. cit., loc. 436.

[743] Ibid.

[744] Ibid.

toward heaven in the chapel.[745] Many scholars today question the credibility of some of the miracles attributed to Benedict. However, beyond the excesses of embellishments, which authors may have used in telling their stories of the saints, Benedict remains a man who manifested the *charisms* at a time the gifts of the Holy Spirit found a home in the monasteries. Considering also that many commentators now live at a time when miracles are not readily available, they tend to be skeptical about the recorded miracles of Benedict. Whatever happens, it is a verifiable fact that miracles have always occurred in the history of the Church. Though we do not have many authors testifying to the miracles of Benedict, Gregory the Great who happened to be an ardent believer in miracles recorded for our spiritual nourishment the miracles of Benedict.

3.16 *Gregory The Great (c. 540–604)*[746]

Gregory the Great was born around AD 540 into an affluent family and had a noble education.[747] He was made the prefect of Rome in AD 570, a prestigious position.[748] At the death of his father, Gregory gave up his fortune, made his home on the Coelian Hill a monastery and founded six other monasteries in Sicily.[749] He was named deacon to Pope Pelagius, and in AD 579 Gregory was sent to Constantinople as papal nuncio but continued his monastic life.[750] At the death of Pope Pelagius, he was elected Pope in AD 590, thereby, becoming the first monk to become a pope[751] and he reigned for 14 years.[752]

Gregory the Great's pontificate (c. 590 604) marked a turning point in the lives of the Italian people. He profoundly committed himself to the temporal and eternal welfare of Italy during a hard time of devastation, famine, pestilence and the invasion of the Lombards.[753] He exhibited an incredible administrative skill in the civil administration and the military

---

[745] Ibid.

[746] Ibid., loc. 445.

[747] Ibid.

[748] Ibid.

[749] Jordan Aumann, *Christian Spirituality in Catholic Tradition*. (San Francisco: Ignatius Press 1985), 74.

[750] Ibid.

[751] Ibid.

[752] F.H. Dudden, *Gregory the Great: His Place in History and Thought*, Russel and Russel, New York, N.Y., 2 vols., 1967. Cited in Aumann, J., op. cit., 74.

[753] Burgess, op. cit., 71.

defenses of Italy.[754] Gregory defended the sovereignty of the Roman See and rejected the claim of the Patriarch of Constantinople's claim of preeminence.[755] Under his pontificate, Pope Gregory the Great introduced the mission to England, and later to Canterbury, with 40 monks from St. Andrews.[756] His pastoral passion created a remarkable expansion of Christianity throughout Europe.[757] He was not only pastorally minded but also socially and spiritually concerned about the wellbeing of his people. He never forgot his contemplative life in the midst of the social and spiritual turmoil Italy faced at a time. He thought that the Holy Spirit, whom Christ sent to his disciples, perfected the work of man's salvation.[758] For him, the Holy Spirit is the best gift to Christianity and works through the *charisms*.[759] "And when the Holy Spirit works in the soul through his gifts, whereby man is led successively from fear to wisdom, the soul is able to enjoy union with God through contemplation."[760] Subsequently, the contemplative life seems to have helped Gregory the Great to receive the *charisms* because, in his *Dialogues*, he testified to personal miracles and even the experience of raising the dead.[761]

Gregory also believed that the miracles performed by those with the *charisms* as recorded in his *Dialogues* reflected a fulfillment of what Jesus said in Mark 11:23, "If anyone says to this mountain, 'Go, throw yourself into the sea,' and does not doubt in his heart but believes what he says will happen, it will be done for him" (NIV).[762] He absolutely believed that miracles were to continue throughout the history of the church and emphasized that holy men of God performed miracles.[763]

Conclusively, our historical exploits of the manifestations and the use of *charisms* in the first eight centuries in this chapter has brought us to how the *charisms* were spiritualized, intellectualized and eventually institutionalized in the mystics and monks who lived holy

---

[754] Ibid.

[755] Ibid., 72.

[756] Ibid.

[757] Aumann, op. cit.,77.

[758] Ibid.

[759] Ibid.

[760] Cf. *Hom. in Ezech*,. 77; *Moralia*, 18, 81. Cited in Aumann, op. cit., 77.

[761] Hyatt, op. cit., loc. 445.

[762] Ibid., 448.

[763] Ibid., 459.

lives. Consequently, during the middle ages, miracles became the sole possession of those who withdrew themselves from the world to live the ascetical solitary lifestyle. Conversely, the ascetic way of life, which arose from a desire for an experiential encounter with the presence of Christ gradually became engrossed with excessive devotion to religious formulas and spiritual pride took over.[764] For this reason, there was a decline in what many commentators believe as genuine miracles and the ultimate disappearance of *charisms* as manifested in the early Church.

3.17 *The Use of Charisms Disappeared and the Reasons for Disappearance*

From our study so far, we know that the disappearance of *charisms* did not happen precipitously. It took years of misunderstanding and suppression to finally obliterate the use and manifestations of *charisms*. As early as the second century, Origen already lamented about the demise of *charisms*. Furthermore, Augustine wrote about cessations of *charisms*, which he later recanted after experiencing some miracles in his ministry. We also have seen above how John Chrysostom creatively spiritualized and intellectualized *charisms* because his community did not experience some *charisms* as they were in the apostolic era. Finally, we unraveled how the monasticization of *charisms* by Philoxenus found expression and credence in Benedict and Gregory. In summary, let us look at how the *charisms* vanished.

Many scholars have speculated about the reasons for the disappearance of the manifestation and utilization of *charisms* in the Church. Edward P. Hahnenberg beautifully articulates his findings thus:

> *For about three hundred years following Paul's letters to the church at Corinth, charisms maintained a place in preaching and baptismal liturgies as a normal and expected dimension of the Christian life. But in subsequent history, charisms moved from the center of church life to the ecclesial margins. So important to Paul's ecclesiology, charisms virtually disappeared from Catholic reflection on ministry.*[765]

He further buttresses his points by reiterating John Haughey's reasons for disappearance of *charisms* as follows; (a) the prohibition of *Montanism*, (b) the authority of the charismatics became a threat to Episcopal authority and the Church order, (c) the conversion of Constantine and the Edict of Milan in AD 313, which made legitimization of Christianity possible, and paved the way for the declaration of Christianity as universal religion of the

---

[764] Ibid., 471.

[765] Hahnenberg, op. cit., 61.

Roman Empire by Theodosius in AD, and (d) the spread of infant baptism and the separation of confirmation from the rite of baptism.[766]

(a) Montanism

Montanism was believed to be a heresy by the Church, developed by the Montanists, a late second-century charismatic group founded by Montanus, whose method of prophecy was different from traditional methods and was condemned by the Church.[767] The group was an enthusiastic and apocalyptic movement that gave much attention to the *charisms*.[768] Adherents of the group manifested and used particularly the gifts of tongues, prophecy, and knowledge. They lived in hope of a fresh outpouring of the Holy Spirit on the Church.[769] I have briefly referred to Montanism above but will recap quickly why the total obliteration of the Montanist group contributed to the disappearance of the manifestation and the use of *charisms* in the Church. As described above many commentators believe that the ban on Montanism was a costly mistake the early Church made. The Church was apprehensive about the exhibited prophetic style of ecstasy, and unintelligible utterances of the Montanist group.[770] The Church believed that the manifested characteristics of the Montanists style of prophecy were pagan even though the practices were also the expressions seen in mainstream Christianity at that time.[771] Many commentators believe that the texts of the Montanists prophecies reflect that the spiritual gifts of tongues and prophecy, which were prominent in the New Testament Church, continued to be part of the early Christians' experience in the second half of the second century.[772] One of the writings of Origen, 'Against Celsus' gives us an idea of the manifestations of the gifts of the Holy Spirit among certain religious groups of people at a time. While Origen was set out to refute Celsus

---

[766] John C. Haughey, "Connecting Vatican II's Call to Holiness with Public Life," *Proceedings of the* CTSA 55 (2000): 8-9. See also Kilian McDonnell and George T. Montague, *Christian Initiation and Baptism in the Holy Spirit: Evidence from the First Eight Centuries* (Collegeville, Minn.: Liturgical Press, 1991), 83-342. Cited in Hahnenberg, op. cit., 61.

[767] Burgess, op. cit., 25.

[768] McDonnell, and Montague, *Christian Initiation and Baptism in the Holy Spirit,* 116.

[769] Ibid.

[770] Kydd, op. cit., loc. 753.

[771] Ibid., 753-759.

[772] Ibid.

on his attempt to discredit the Christians, the text below, however, gives us an insight into how Christians of the second century used *charisms*.

Against Celsus, 7, 9:

> *There are many, he says, who become enraptured and prophesy very easily on any grounds, both in temples and outside of temples, and there are some who—begging and visiting cities and camps periodically—are gesticulating and posturing as if they are prophesying. And it is convenient and customary for each one to say, "I am God, or a son of God, or a divine spirit. And I have come. For the world is already perishing, and you, O men, are dying because of wickedness. But I want to save you. And you shall see me returning hereafter with heavenly power. Blessed is he who has now worshiped me. Upon all others, I shall cast eternal fire, on both cities and country regions. And men who do not know their penalties shall repent and groan in vain. But I shall preserve eternally those who believe in me." … To these things which were held up before men were added unheard of raving and entirely unknown speech, the meaning of which no rational man was able to determine; for being obscure and meaningless they allow any irrational person or cheat to make of the words whatever he wishes.*[773]

In as much as the above text did not name the group that Celsus observed, it reveals the exhibited expressions of the Montanist group that was condemned by the Church. Celsus' observation shows that the use of prophecy and tongues were prominent during this time. His misunderstanding of the manifestations of the *charisms*, however, was foreshadowed by Paul in 1 Corinthians 14:23: "So if the whole Church meets in one place and everyone speaks in tongues, and then uninstructed people or unbelievers should come in, will they not say that you are out of your minds?"[774]

I believe that Celsus's problem of not understanding the prophetic mannerisms, tongues and the Holy Spirit's embodiment of individuals who spoke in the voices of the divine persons were also the dilemmas of some Church leaders who vigorously condemned the Montanists as noted above. They condemned what they did not understand. The Montanists may have had some excesses in their declarations; however, I do not think there was anything heretical about their ecstatic prophetic mannerisms or tongues or the divine persons

---

[773] P. Koetschau, Ed. *Die griechischen christlichen Schriftsteller*, 4 (Leipzig: J.C. Hindrich, 1899), p.160. Kydd's translation. Quoted in Kydd, op. cit., Loc. 770-777.

[774] Senior, and Collins, op. cit., 1535. Quoted in Ibid., Loc. 810.

using them at different times for God's divine purposes. The content of their prophecy was in line with what the Church professed at that time. On the other hand, I believe Church could not deal with the problem of the Montanists excesses because the gifts of the Holy Spirit, especially, the gift of discernment was beginning to decline. Consequently, the Church became only concerned about the exertion of authority, which she thought was slipping away because of the acceptance of the Montanists by many people at this time.

(b) The Charismatic Threat to the Episcopal Authority and the Church Order

The Montanist charismatic group grew rapidly and enjoyed the admiration of many because the group expressed the Spirit's freedom to use humans for God's work, including women.[775] As mentioned above, their teachings, prophetic utterances, and the inclusion of women for ministry drew Tertullian to the group. Tertullian under the influence of the Montanist differentiated the Church of bishops from a prophetic Spirit-filled Church.[776] As the Montanists thrived, the early mainstream Christian community felt the group's appeal to the Spirit's initiative was a threat to episcopal authority and church order.[777] However, some commentators believe that the excessive claims of the Montanists also contributed to a marginalization of "prophetic persons in the mainstream Church. The prophetic function had to be assessed and authenticated by bishops.[778] The only problem I have with a bishop's assessment of the authenticity of a prophetic person is, not all bishops are spirit-filled with the grace of discernment to determine what is of God and what is not of God. The manifestations and use of the *charisms* are a threat to some bishops, who are not connected to what the Holy Spirit is doing among God's children in the Church. They just clamp down on users of the gifts as was done in the early Church with the Montanists.

(c) Legitimization of Christianity

The conversion of Constantine was great news for the Church that had suffered severe persecution under different emperors who were hostile to Christianity. Providentially, Emperor Constantine was converted in AD 312 and enacted the Edict of Milan in AD 313,

---

[775] Hahnenberg, op. cit., 61

[776] Prusak., op. cit., 126.

[777] Hahnenberg, op. cit., 61.

[778] James L. Ash, "The Decline of Ecstatic Prophecy in the Early Church," *Theological Studies* 37 (1976), pp. 227-52; Bernard Sesbouè, "Ministères et structure de l'Église: Re exion théologique à partir du Nouveau Testament," in J. Delorme, *Le ministére et les ministéres...*, pp. 413-17; von Campenhausen, *Ecclesiastical Authority and Spiritual Power*, pp. 187-92. Cited in Prusak., op. cit., 126.

which ended the persecution of the Christians and legitimized Christianity.[779] With this action, Constantine became personally involved in the business of the Church; thus, creating the platform for the integration of the powers of the Church and state.[780] In AD 325, Constantine convoked the first General Council of the Christian church, which involved Bishops from all parts of the Roman Empire in Nicea, a city in Asia Minor.[781] He presided over the first session and interfered in subsequent sessions even though he did not have any theological knowledge and had not received baptism at the time.[782] The merger of the Church and State marked the beginning of the Church's rise to raw power and the systematic end of the manifestation and use of the *charisms* in the Church.[783] The Church took on the imperial structure of the Roman Empire. Accordingly, the universalization of Christianity by Theodosius in AD 380 finally sealed the process of institutionalization of Christianity, which played a vital role in the steady disappearance of *charisms*. I agree with A.J. Gordon, Baptist pastor and founder of Gordon College in Boston, when he said:

> *It is not altogether strange that when the Church forgot her citizenship in heaven and began to establish herself in luxury and splendor on earth, she should cease to exhibit the supernatural gifts of heaven.*[784]

In conclusion, the Church started losing that which she flourished as the beacon of hope and salvation of the world when she unknowingly yielded to a merger with the state, thereby forsaking the power from above, the *charisms* to minister to a broken world. Unfortunately, the Church that was supposed to be a nurturer of the *charisms* became dominant, worldly, dismissive and oppressive of bearers of the gifts of the Holy Spirit.

(d) Infant Baptism and Severing of Confirmation from the Rite of Baptism[785]

The promotion and practice of infant baptism and the separation of confirmation from baptismal rite also contributed to an estrangement of *charism* from baptism, and ultimately

---

[779] Hyatt, op. cit., loc. 33.

[780] Ibid.

[781] Ibid.

[782] Ibid., loc. 34.

[783] Ibid.

[784] A.J. Gordon, *The Ministry of Healing* (Harrisburg, PA: Christian Publ., 1961), 64. Quoted in Hyatt, op. cit., 36.

[785] Hahnenberg, op. cit., 61.

a divorce of *charism* from the life of the baptized person.[786] As our study has shown so far, from the baptism of Jesus, through the apostolic era to the post-early biblical time, the reception of the Holy Spirit was part of the baptismal rite. In the early Church, converts received the *charisms* during water baptism and the laying on of hands. The rite of Christian initiation was for adults who made a conscious choice of being the followers of the Christian way of life. The *charisms* through the Holy Spirit were expected to come down on the newly baptized with the celebration of the sacraments. "Baptism was, then a sign that those who had accepted the message of Christ had also received the Spirit of God."[787] It was not clear at what time people received the Holy Spirit during baptism during their initiation as Christians. Nonetheless, all the Fathers of the Church agree that by the completion of the ceremony Christians had received the Spirit, either during the baptismal washing, during the anointing or the imposition of hands.[788] Children were not part of Christian initiation.

The idea of infant baptism evolved when some people in the third century took the doctrine of the necessity of baptism to mean that children who died without baptism would not have the opportunity for everlasting life.[789] The theological question arose about the rationale for the baptism of babies of which Cyprian of Carthage gave the answer–"the sin of Adam."[790] Cyprian's argument was from Romans 5:12-21:

> *Therefore, just as through one person sin entered the world, and through sin, death, and thus death came to all, inasmuch as all sinned for up to the time of the law, sin was in the world, though sin is not accounted when there is no law. But death reigned from Adam to Moses, even over those who did not sin after the pattern of the trespass of Adam, who is the type of the one who was to come. Grace and Life through Christ. But the gift is not like the transgression. For if by that one person's transgression the many died, how much more did the grace of God and the gracious gift of the one person Jesus Christ overflow for the many. And the gift is not like the result of the one person's sinning. For after one sin there was the judgment that brought condemnation; but the gift, after many transgressions, brought acquittal. For if by the transgression of one person, death came to reign through that one, how much more will those who receive the abundance of grace and of the gift of*

---

[786] Ibid., 61-62.

[787] Martos, op. cit., 186-187.

[788] Ibid. 190.

[789] Ibid. 156.

[790] Ibid.

justification come to reign in life through the one person Jesus Christ. In con-clusion, just as through one transgression condemnation came upon all, so through one righteous act acquittal and life came to all. For just as through the disobedience of one person the many were made sinners, so through the obedience of one the many will be made righteous. The law entered in so that transgression might increase but, where sin increased, grace overflowed all the more, so that, as sin reigned in death, grace also might reign through justification for eternal life through Jesus Christ our Lord.[791]

Cyprian reinforced his point that the Church urged parents to baptize their infants because baptism wiped away the guilt acquired by the human race in Adam's fall.[792] Cyprian's idea was acceptable, but it raised the question of how the descendants of Adam could inherit his sin.[793] Augustine resolved this question a hundred and fifty years later in answer to Pelagius. Pelagius believed that people were born with the state of "original grace" and as such children who were born innocent did not need to have baptism.[794] In response to Pelagius, Augustine adopted Cyprian's conception that all are born with the sin of Adam and deformed in their soul, and so everyone needs to be fashioned into the image of Christ by receiving the baptismal seal.[795] By the end of the sixth century, infant baptism became universal in the Church and the idea of confirmation evolved, thereby separating the *charisms* from Christian initiation. The Church moved from the process of Christian initiation that was experiential and unlocked believers to the *charisms* for ministry in the church and world, to a ritual ceremony that only offers a rational explanation of what they receive.

3.18 *Conclusion*

In conclusion, we can infer that the inheriting of the theological thought pattern of John Chrysostom and Philoxenus by bishops and theologians boosted the spiritualization of *charisms* and gradually detached *charisms* from ordinary ministry in the Church. I believe the normalization of the spiritualization of *charisms* is one of the most stifling of all the reasons as it ties *charisms* to the past, making it unrealistically possible to be appropriated

---

[791] New American Bible, Revised Edition 2011 (Kindle Locations: 55515-55529). Kindle Edition. Accessed October 15, 2016. Cited in Martos, op. cit., 156.

[792] Martos, op. cit., 156.

[793] Ibid., 156-157.

[794] Ibid.

[795] Ibid., 157-158.

and experienced today. However, the good news is, since we have established that *charisms* were traditionally part of the Church's life and as such, the Church's heritage, I believe that they can be recovered and restored for ministry in the Church today. The positive proof we have about the possibility of recovery and restoration of *charism* in the Catholic Church is in 100 years for of Pentecostal and charismatic renewal in the world. Millions of Christians all over the world have an experiential encounter with the Holy Spirit and have been able to access their *charisms* for their churches and the good of humanity.

The rapid growth of Pentecostal and charismatic churches in the world is a testimony of why the Church needs an introspective openness to retrieve buried treasures that I consider *charisms* of the Holy Spirit and allow them to blossom to full manifestations for ministry in the world today. Interestingly, many founders of Pentecostal and charismatic churches were Catholics or members of some other mainstream churches. Many commentators assert that some of them left their churches because they could not express their *charisms*/gifts because practically, the clergy has the full manifestations and use of *charisms*. Furthermore, most leaders do not want the change and surprises bearers of these gifts bring to their churches. Francis A. Sullivan recorded that "the initial reaction of the governing bodies of the Protestant churches in the United States was negative to the outbreak of the Pentecostal movement among clergy and faithful."[796] To reinforce his point, he asserts that in some cases, pastors were removed or forced to resign as a result of their involvement with the movement.[797] Unfortunately, this negative attitude to the Pentecostal or charismatic group in not a thing of the past, many lay people and pastors are still subject to oppression in the Catholic Church in different parts of the world as a result of their involvement in the charismatic renewal group. Consequently, many leave the Church. Nevertheless, we can see from their apparent ministerial success outside the Church, that the charismatic wealth of the Church endures in baptized members of the Church. I am convinced that everyone incorporated into the Church through sacramental baptism remains God's chosen vessel to bless the world through the use of his or her *charisms*. I believe that through the power of the Holy Spirit, we can unravel the hidden *charisms* in all members of the Church. However, there has to be a change in understanding and attitude towards *charisms* and bearers of the gifts. I am convinced that it is only through the restoration of the *charisms* that the Church may regain her real distinctiveness.

---

[796] Sullivan, op. cit., 55.

[797] Ibid.

Chapter Four

Charisms Can Be Retrieved

4.1 *Introduction*

We have seen from our study so far that *charisms* are the Church's heritage. Nevertheless, it is strange that many Church leaders seem unacquainted with this fact. This study is a quest to continue the discussion started already by some theologians and Church historians who have established through their inquiries that for the Church to continue to be effectually relevant, she will forever need a persistent use of *charisms* as manifested in the early Church. The enduring presence of God made manifest in the workings of the Holy Spirit's *charisms* in the early Church, was not meant to disappear with each age, but to remain constant with evolving twists in each epoch's understanding and openness to the actions of the Holy Spirit. However, there has been a flawed inherited theological tradition in each era that has stifled the openness of religious adherents to the actions of the Holy Spirit. Undoubtedly, this is because whatever a people of each era were taught and understood, reflected their attitudes and dispositions to perceived new knowledge.

Consequently, most members of diverse Christian groups oppose new teaching/interpretations on the ground of tradition. But, I believe anyone who opposes the manifestations and use of charismatic gifts is ignorant of the actual traditions of the early Church. "History helps us understand our past so that we can better understand who we are. History provides inspiration for the present and hope for the future."[798] Thus, this study was my attempt to urge the Church to return to her Pentecostal and charismatic roots. I believe the Church runs the risk of being extinct if she does not tap into her charismatic historical treasure, which

---

[798] Roberts Liardon, *The Azusa Street Revival: When the Fire Fell, An In-Depth Look at the People, Teachings, and Lessons*. (PA, Shippensburg: Destiny Image Publishers Inc., 2006), 9.

147

is the soul of her existence and why she came into being. She is an instrument of healing and blessing to the world.

In addition, I do not want the Church to become a museum or an ancient institution that exists only for study purposes. Regrettably, it is happening already in Europe. Magnificent Catholic cathedrals and churches have become Lecture Halls, Clubs, and Restaurants. Some cathedrals welcome tourists on weekdays but not for worship on Sundays. In the United States of America, some dioceses are merging, and closing parishes. Sunday attendance has also dropped significantly, while Pentecostal and charismatic churches continue to thrive. It is apparent from what is going on around the world that the Catholic Church cannot survive for long, insisting on dogma and tradition alone without its charismatic or Pentecostal dimension. Karl Rahner once alleged that the Church's emphasis on adherence to doctrine and dogma has contributed to Christians neglecting the deeper dimension of faith for a purely intellectual observance to the propositional content of faith.[799] There is an urgent need to recover the *charisms*, which I believe is the dynamic, invigorating power of the Church. People everywhere are hungry for the divine; they want a touch of God on earth. I know this is possible in an enabling atmosphere in our churches. The Church's leaders need to perpetually nurture a new attitude that embraces a genuine openness to the newness and surprises of the future,[800] which, only the Holy Spirit makes possible. It is not enough to repeatedly profess faith in the Holy Spirit as the giver of life without bearing the fruits of this belief. The Church has to be open to receiving the newness of the wonders of the Holy Spirit. Beyond the dogmas and theologies of the Holy Spirit, I believe the Church has to take ownership of the gifts of the Holy Spirit, *charisms* as her genetic inheritance.

4.2 *The Baptism of Jesus as the Root of Charisms for Ministry*

The ritual of baptism, followed by openness for the reception of the Holy Spirit who gives *charisms* for ministry started with Jesus in the River Jordan where the Holy Spirit descended and anointed him for ministry. Luke captures the unction upon Jesus to function as God's instrument of salvation in the world:

> *The Spirit of the Lord is upon me, because he has anointed me to bring*
> *glad tidings to the poor. He has sent me to proclaim liberty to captives and*

---

[799] Robert J. Wicks, Ed. *Handbook of Spirituality for Ministers* Vol. 1. New York and Mahwah: Paulist Press, 1998), 134.

[800] Prusak, op. cit., 5.

recovery of sight to the blind, to let the oppressed go free, and to proclaim a year acceptable to the Lord (4:18-19).[801]

The above text is not self-explanatory that Luke was referring to what happened to Jesus at his baptism. However, some commentators agree that it was a confirmation of what happened then.[802]

After all the people had been baptized and Jesus also had been baptized was praying, heaven was opened and the Holy Spirit descended upon him in bodily form like a dove. And a voice came from heaven, "You are my beloved Son; with you I am well pleased (3:21-22).[803]

I agree with John Chrysostom that the baptism of Jesus is the standard for Christian baptism, and just as Jesus was anointed with the Spirit and declared God's beloved Son, those baptized are also anointed to receive the Spirit thereby becoming God's adopted daughters and sons.[804] I think metaphorically being God's adopted children is certainly an empowerment with *charisms* for ministry.

The ministry of God's healing and saving grace also did not to end with Jesus but continued through his disciples and the early Christians and should proceed with all ministers of the good news today and in the future. I believe that the *charisms* flow out of the Holy Spirit on a person or a group when they are predisposed to receive the gifts of the Holy Spirit. The disciples and the early Christians were enthusiastically open to receive and actively use the *charisms*, and they did before they eventually disappeared. The call for the reclamation of the *charisms* here is not necessarily the repetition of rituals but the resultant effects that are the theology of *charisms* received during Christian initiation.

4.3 *The World Needs the Charismatic Gifts*

Retrieving and restoring *charisms* as manifested in the early Church does not mean recreating and reliving the socio-economic-political condition of the early Church. We live in the 21st century, and our socio-economic-political conditions are definitely different from that of more than 2000 years ago. However, the human spiritual needs of each period remain

---

[801] Senior, and Collins, op. cit., 1360.

[802] McDonnell, and Montague, *Christian Initiation and Baptism in the Holy Spirit*, 25.

[803] Ibid., 1358.

[804] McDonnell, and Montague, *Christian Initiation and Baptism in the Holy Spirit*, 279.

the same. Beyond the sensible cravings of the human person is the unquenchable thirst and longing for love, joy, and peace, which can only be fulfilled by the divine alone. Saint Augustine captured this hunger of the human heart in his Confession when he wrote, *Thou hast formed us for Thyself, and our hearts are restless till they find rest in Thee.*[805] This restlessness makes the human person long for a union with the transcendent one, which we call God. Karl Rahner called God the *incomprehensible mystery*,[806] "the ineffable and unfathomable one, the silent yet near one" who is imageless but gratuitously communicates Godself to humanity.[807] Our Christian faith reveals to us through the Scriptures that, "No one has ever seen God. The only Son of God, who is at the Father's side, has revealed him."[808] Paul affirms Jesus as, "The image of the invisible God, the firstborn of all creation."[809] Thus, in Jesus, we see the hidden God, a God who cannot be seen. It is still a mystery that God became human and dwelt among us (Matthew 1:23; John 1:14). Nonetheless, this mystery could not conceal God's unconditional love in Jesus. Even though the people then did not know Jesus as God, they saw and experienced in him everything they ever wished for, and that was why they could not get enough of him. His life and ministry reflected the unconditional love, mercy, compassion, forgiveness, gratuitousness, and the inclusiveness of God's salvific grace for all peoples. For three years a disenfranchised people were attached to Jesus because of what he personified. Peter experienced first hand in a vision that God is the God of all peoples after the Holy Spirit enlightened his prejudiced mind (Acts 10:15). He preached concerning,

> *How God anointed Jesus of Nazareth with the Holy Spirit and power. He went about doing good and healing all those oppressed by the devil, for God was with him. We are witnesses of all that he did both in the country of the Jews and in Jerusalem. They put him to death by hanging him on a tree. This man God raised on the third day and granted that he be visible.*[810]

---

[805] Philip Schaff, Ed., Marcus Dods, Trans. *The Complete Works of Saint Augustine: The Confessions, On Grace and Free Will, The City of God, On Christian Doctrine, Expositions on the Book Of Psalms,...* (Kindle Edition 2013), Location 28927. Accessed October 26, 2016.

[806] Declan Marmion, and Mary E. Hines, *The Cambridge Companion to Karl Rahner.* (Cambridge: Cambridge University Press 2007), 78.

[807] Ibid., 25.

[808] Collins and Senior, op. cit., 1404.

[809] Ibid., 1587.

[810] Ibid., 1461.

The visibility of Jesus after his resurrection also made the testimony of his rising from the dead more valuable. His followers were sad as soldiers took Jesus to Calvary for execution. They watched with helplessness the one who epitomized the fulfillment of the human heart's desire crucified on the cross. Though they were distraught and despondent, their mourning was turned into dancing, and their sadness into joy (Ps. 30:11). Peter testified that God raised Jesus from the dead. Different scriptural texts attest to the disciples' joy when they heard that Jesus was alive (Luke 24:40, John 20:20). They gladly went about proclaiming to everyone who was open to hearing the good news that the crucified one was, and is alive. Furthermore, their joy was whole when they received the Holy Spirit on Pentecost Day. The disciples became God's instrumental presence to give healing, mercy, forgiveness and salvation to a sick world.

Apparently, the first-century world certainly needed healing and the mercy they could get from the ministration of the disciples of Jesus. But 21st needs the charismatic gifts more than ever. More importantly, a hunger for a holistic world, free of sin, sickness, oppression, racism, hate, injustice and open to God's salvific healing grace, make people of different Christian faith traditions continually seek the restoration of the Pentecostal experience of the early Christian era.

4.4 *The Resurgence of the Charismatic Gifts*

For more than two thousand years of Christian history, there have been renewals, revivals, and reforms at different times that helped the Church not drift completely into dead ritualism and eventual irrelevance.[811] However, these reforms have not had the revolutionary consequence that we saw in the last one hundred years with the resurgence of Pentecostal and charismatic movements across different Christian denominations. Vinson Synan, in his *The Century of the Holy Spirit: One Hundred Years of Pentecostal and Charismatic Renewal*, gives a well-articulated exhaustive account of the extraordinary beginnings and spread of the Pentecostal and charismatic movement in the US and around the world.[812]

Many commentators also acknowledge that Charles Fox Parham (1873-1929) was the architect of Pentecostal doctrine and the theological founder of the movement.[813] The Azusa revival of 1906 and creation of the world Pentecostal movement was a result of his doctrine

---

[811] Vinson Synan, *The Century of the Holy Spirit: 100 Years of Pentecostal and Charismatic Renewal.* (Nashville: Thomas Nelson 2001), 15.

[812] Ibid.

[813] James R. Goff, Jr. *Fields White Unto Harvest* (Fayetteville, Ark.: Univ. of Arkansas Press. Cited in Synan, op. cit., 42.

of tongues as the "Bible evidence" of the baptism in the Holy Spirit.[814] Parham is credited as the one who started the theological argument that tongues are always the preliminary evidence of anyone receiving the baptism with the Holy Spirit and should be expected and seen as part of every Christian's experience, and standard at Church services.[815] His moment of illumination came toward the end of 1900 when he proposed a question to his Bethel Bible students in Topeka Kansas: "What is the scriptural sign of a true baptism in the Holy Ghost?" The students unanimously concluded that it was tongues considering the accounts of Pentecost (Acts 2:1-12), the Holy Spirit's baptism of the household of Cornelius (Acts 10:44-48), and also Paul's laying of hands on some Christians in Ephesus (19:1-7).[816] The Bible School of about 30 residents experienced a surge of excitement that led them into constant prayers for several days and nights. One of the students, Agnes Ozman asked Parham to lay his hands on her head on January 1, 1901, and as he did, she experienced "baptism in the Spirit" and started speaking in tongues.[817] Parham and all the students had a similar experience in a few days, giving birth to all Pentecostals view that the experience of the first disciples on the day of Pentecost was the usual experience of all believers in the early Church and all believers should be allowed to and should sincerely seek a similar experience.[818] Armed with his newly discovered glossolalia pneumatology, Parham traveled everywhere for revivals. In 1905, he went back to Bryan Hall in Houston, Texas where he conducted a successful revival campaign. A local newspaper reported that many healings and other charismatic phenomena occurred in the meetings.[819] To further spread the fruits of his revelation and train people to carry the Pentecostal message everywhere in South Texas, Parham started a short-term Bible school,[820] where William Joseph Seymour was drawn to his theory of "initial evidence" that receiving the baptism of the Holy Spirit was first accompanied by glossolalia.[821]

---

[814] Synan, op. cit., 42.

[815] Ibid., 43.

[816] Sulivan, op. cit., 52. See also Synan, op. cit., 43.

[817] Ibid., 52-53.

[818] Ibid., 52.

[819] Hyatt, op. cit., loc. 143.

[820] Ibid.

[821] Martha Simmons, and Frank A. Thomas, Eds. *Preaching with Sacred Fire: An Anthology of African American Sermons, 1750 to the Present.* (New York, London: W.W. Norton & Company, 2010), 373.

Parham may have been the one who introduced the doctrine of tongues as the "Bible evidence" of the baptism in the Holy Spirit, and coined the term, "Pentecostal movement."[822] However, William Joseph Seymour (1870-1922)[823] was the one who made Pentecostalism an American and international phenomenon. Parham created a little fire through the seed of knowledge planted, while Seymour stirred it into flame and created an outburst of a new Pentecost.[824]

It happened that Seymour learned about Parham's Bible school in Houston. So he enrolled and Parham's doctrine of tongues as evidence of baptism in the Holy Spirit enthralled him. After his encounter and interaction with Parham at his Bible school, Seymour received an invitation to pastor a newly formed Holiness congregation in Los Angeles. He went, and made tongues the primary object of his sermons on his mission.[825] "He preached that unless a person spoke in tongues, he/she had not experienced the true baptism with the Holy Spirit."[826] But the Holiness congregation's leaders rejected his message and locked him out of the Church. He found sympathizers who helped him with accommodation and he had services in their homes.[827]

Seymour had his first teaching meeting at the home of Owen "Irish" Lee until it could not accommodate the people who attended.[828] Providentially, Seymour was invited to start holding prayer meetings and worship services in the home of Richard and Ruth Asberry, at 214 North Bonnie Brae Street in Los Angeles, which he accepted.[829] On April 9, 1906, something spectacular happened after several weeks of prayer meetings. Seymour, the Asberry family, and the people in attendance were filled with the Holy Spirit and the revival spread into the streets until the home could not accommodate the crowds that gathered.[830] Synan notes that the incident was so exceptional that it became legendary but cites one eyewitness account:

---

[822] Synan, op. cit., 44-45.

[823] Simmons, and Thomas, op. cit., 372.

[824] Liardon, op. cit., Loc. 63.

[825] Hyatt, op. cit., loc. 144.

[826] Synan, op. cit., 47.

[827] Ibid.

[828] Ibid.

[829] Ibid.

[830] Simmons, and Thomas, op. cit., Loc. 374.

They shouted three days and nights. It was Easter season. The people came from everywhere. By the next morning there was no way of getting near the house. As people came in they would fall under God's power; and the whole city was stirred. They shouted until the foundation of the house gave way but no one was hurt.[831]

The foundation of the house collapsed because it could not hold the infinite numbers of people who were inside and around it. In a search for an elaborate venue to cater for all who were hungry for the new move of God, they found an abandoned two-story building that was originally the Steven African Methodist Episcopal (AME) Church on 312 Azusa Street in Los Angeles.[832] They quickly cleaned it up and commenced their first meeting on April 14, 1906. The Holy Spirit continued the work of unlocking tongues and healing people who were hungry for God's touch, and there was an explosion of revival in Los Angeles that spread to the rest of the world.[833] The Azusa marvels were beyond human comprehension. The simplistic minds of journalists could not process what they saw that took place at Azusa Street. In the story about the event, *The Los Angeles Times* called it weird, fanatical, irreverent, mad, and wild.[834] Frank Bartleman, an eyewitness, thought that *The Los Angeles Times'* coverage of the Azusa Street was shameful. But quickly noted that the negative coverage only drew more crowds. Below is an excerpt from Bartleman's account:

The services ran almost continuously … The meetings were controlled by the Spirit, from the throne … Someone might be speaking. Suddenly the Spirit would fall upon the congregation. God Himself would give the altar call. Men would fall all over the house, like the slain in battle, or rush for the altar en masse to seek God. The scene often resembled a forest of fallen trees. Such a scene cannot be imitated … The whole place was steeped in prayer … The presence of the Lord was so real.[835]

I am familiar with the above description of the Azusa Street phenomenon. I have also seen the Holy Spirit take absolute control and move in a miraculous way at different prayer

---

[831] *Pentecostal Evangel*, vol. 6, no. 4 (1946): 6, as quoted in Hollenweger, *The Pentecostals*, 23. Quoted in Synan, op. cit., 49.

[832] Synan, op. cit., 50. See also, Simmons, and Thomas, op. cit., Loc. 238.

[833] Synan, op. cit., 58.

[834] Ibid.

[835] Frank Bartleman, Azuza Street (Shippensburg, PA: Destiny Image, 2006. Quoted in Liardon, op. cit., 99-101.

conferences, healing and setting all who are in bondage free. For a spectator, it may be chaotic because of the struggles of people who are taken by surprise. The experience of losing control terrifies some people, and they moan, scream and cry. However, some people unassumingly yield to the power of the Holy Spirit and slump to the floor or their chairs. Some Pentecostal commentators have called this phenomenon 'being slain in the Spirit.' Catholics like Cardinal Josef Suenens and Robert DeGrandis call it 'resting in the Spirit.' At the end of the day, those readily disposed experience peace, joy, hope, healing, and freedom from the oppressive powers of negative forces.

Also, contrary to the views of observers who are undiscerning to the miraculous moves of God, I believe Azusa was truly an event God orchestrated. It was not necessarily because of the many recorded miracles of physical healings[836] and the many tongues[837] that people spoke but the fact that the "educated, uneducated, rich, poor, African-Americans, Asians, Hispanics, whites, men, women, native-born, recent immigrants, and foreign visitors"[838] could come together and worship God under a ramshackle house. It is surely fascinating to read about how people of more than twenty different nationalities came together in loving harmony.[839] Bartleman articulated this as the melting of the races and the breaking down of racial prejudice and later wrote that the blood of Jesus washed away the color line.[840] Unquestionably, we need a world of mutual honor and respect, a world free of racism and religious bigotry, the world where our humanness reminds us of our common inheritance in God. I am confident that an authentic Christian practice can realize this world and it is only the Holy Spirit that can help us see one another the way God sees each of us. Paul articulated this in his Letter to the Galatians 3:26-28:

> *For through faith you are all children of God in Christ Jesus. For all of you who were baptized in Christ have clothed yourselves with Christ. There is neither Jew nor Greek, there is neither slave nor free person, there is not male and female; for you are all one in Christ Jesus.*[841]

---

[836] Liardon, op. cit., 131.

[837] Ibid., 134-135.

[838] Synan, op. cit., 54.

[839] Liardon, op. cit.,103.

[840] Ibid., I03-104.

[841] Collins, and Senior, op. cit., 1566-1567.

I think the hallmark of a Spirit-filled community is the love and harmony in the group. One of the fruits of the Holy Spirit in Galatians 5:22 is love, which can also be a determinant factor if an event is of God. We have seen from Pentecost Day and the early Christians' experience of mutual love and concern for one another. It was really the authenticity of their lives that earned us the term Christians (Acts 11:19-26). What a wonderful world we will have if all Christians should live in harmony. Some Christian Churches experience unity but it is not very common. However, Patty Gallagher Mansfield testified to the experience of unity when the Holy Spirit came upon her group in 1967:

> *That night the Lord brought the whole group into the chapel. ... The professor then laid hands on some of the students but most of us received the baptism in the Spirit while kneeling before the Blessed Sacrament in prayer. Some of us started speaking in tongues; others received gifts of discernment, prophecy and wisdom. But the most important gift was the fruit of love, which bound the whole community together. In the Lord's Spirit we found a unity we had long tried to achieve on our own.*[842]

Patty Gallagher Mansfield was one of the 25 Catholics who gathered at a retreat house north of Pittsburgh, Pennsylvania on February 18, 1967, when the Holy Spirit fell on them.[843] The event, now known as the "Duquesne Weekend" gave birth to the Charismatic Catholic Renewal,[844] but it did not happen by chance. Though those who had the initial experience of the Holy Spirit never planned to have a Holy Spirit encounter, God had set things in motion historically to lead to this remarkable event among Catholics. Many commentators believe that the Charismatic Catholic Renewal was an answer to the prayer of Pope John XXIII for a new Pentecost before the convocation of the Second Vatican Council in 1965.[845]

It all started with the Pope John XXIII's perception that only the Holy Spirit would bring about the renewal desperately needed in the Church at a time of tremendous socio-political and technological change in the world. As a newly elected Pope, he called for an ecumenical council and prayed in 1962 for "a new Pentecost."[846] As part of the planning for the Second Vatican Council, he prayed to God,

---

[842] Patty G. Mansfield, *As by A New Pentecost: The Dramatic Beginning of the Catholic Charismatic Renewal* (Steubenville, Ohio: Steubenville Univ. Press, 1992), 5-29. Quoted in Synan, op. cit., 209-210.

[843] Synan, op. cit., 209.

[844] Ibid., 209-210.

[845] Ibid., 212.

[846] http://vatican2voice.org/91docs/convoke.htm Accessed Nov. 2, 2016.

"Renew your wonders in this our day, as by a new Pentecost. Grant to Your Church that, being of one mind and steadfast in prayer with Mary, the Mother of Jesus, and following the lead of blessed Peter, it may advance the reign of our Divine Savior, the reign of truth and justice, the reign of love and peace. Amen."[847]

The Church actually experienced a new Pentecost when the Catholic Charismatic Renewal came into being. However, many commentators also believe the preparation for the 20th-century revival of the Church actually began with Elena Guerra (1835-1914). She was an Italian nun and a passionate devotee to the Holy Spirit whose persuasion of Pope Leo XIII led to a universal declaration of the novena to the Holy Spirit in 1897[848] for every Catholic Church in preparation for Pentecost.[849] Things do not always work in isolation. There are always spiritual webs of relationships that inspire people to bring something good into being. John XXIII must have been inspired also by the Pentecost novenas that Catholics recited every year before Pentecost. As mentioned above, the Pope spoke clearly of "a new Pentecost." It was to be an ecumenical council marked by dialogue, openness, reconciliation and unity."[850] I believe the four Catholic faculty members at Duquesne University also played a decisive role in activating the Charismatic Catholic Renewal to coming into existence. After reading *The Cross and the Switchblade* by David Wilkerson, they attended a charismatic meeting led by a Presbyterian woman, Flo Dodge, where two young Catholic professors, Ralph Keifer and Bill Storey, were prayed over for baptism in the Spirit.[851] Providentially, I think this is in fulfillment of the Pope's desire for an ecumenical dialogue with more groundbreaking implication. The two professors' profound experience of being baptized in the Holy Spirit led them to focus the Duquesne retreat weekend on the Holy Spirit. The retreat reached a peak with an intense experience of the Holy Spirit by many who were present. Most of them spoke in tongues, and some received other gifts.[852] Subsequently, the two professors visited Notre Dame, shared their experiences, and prayed over some of

---

[847] http://www.resurrectionparish.ca/files/docs/Papal_Quotes.pdf Accessed Nov. 3, 2016.

[848] Synan, op. cit., 212.

[849] Edward O'Connor, in *New Covenant*. Cited in Synan, op. cit., 213.

[850] Oscar Andres Rodriguez Maradiaga, *The council revealed John XXIII's hope for dialogue*. A New Pentecost. October 8, 2012 Issue. http://www.americamagazine.org/issue/5153/article/new-pentecost Accessed Nov. 12, 2016.

[851] Synan, op. cit., 211.

[852] http://www.nsc-chariscenter.org/article/what-we-have-seen-and-heard/ Accessed November 2, 2016.

the students who were also filled with the Holy Spirit. The students' excitement spread like wildfire and this marked the beginning of the Charismatic Renewal at Notre Dame and from there, Ann Arbor. It quickly spread across the United States and the world.[853]

4.5 *The Charismatic Catholic Renewal*

Different epochs have witnessed revivals at various times, but there has never been anything like the 20th century when an explosion of charismatic gifts occurred as was manifested in the early Church. We know that the Catholic Church and other Christian faith traditions have had individuals who had the *charisms* and were sources of blessings to their communities. However, the re-emergence of the Pentecostal and charismatic renewal feels like the first centuries of Christianity. I am convinced that the reappearance of the charismatic gifts is a wake-up call for the Church to actualize her full potentials as the agent of God's healing and salvific presence in the world. Also, God wanted this reawakening to start from inside. By inside I mean faithful Catholics who knew deep down their spirits that they want something more. Like many Catholics across the world, they were hungry for an experience of God. They wanted to meet the God who engages all aspects of the human person, intellectually and emotionally. People crave for a tangible experience of God, a touch from God and to be touched by God. Karl Rahner envisaged this many years ago when he wrote, *The Christian of the future will be a mystic, or he will not exist at all.*[854] Mysticism, he wrote, is *"a genuine experience of God emerging from the very heart of our existence."*[855] The doubting disciple Thomas was mocked for centuries for his incredulity about the resurrected Jesus until he was able to see Christ for himself. However, Christians seeking ways of an experiential encounter with God have now elevated him to the position of patron Saint of experiential desirous Christians today. From the look of things, Christians of the future may not believe because of what they learn in class, but because Christ has revealed himself to them in deeply moving ways.[856] Nobody experiences Christ and remains the same. The experience of Christ carries enthusiasm to share what one has experienced.

All the Popes after John XXIII and most theologians in recent memory have endorsed the Charismatic Catholic Renewal and also testified to its relevance in the Church today. There is something unique about the Renewal because of the immediate acceptance and recognition by the Church leadership. Like the deer that yearns for running streams, Catholics

---

[853] Ibid.

[854] Karl Rahner, *The Spirituality of the Secular Priest*, TI XIX, 115. Quoted in Wicks 134.

[855] Ibid.

[856] Wicks, 134.

welcomed the Renewal with open hearts. Catholic theologians rose up to the task of finding Scriptural resonance in the manifested activities of the charismatics especially, tongues and prophecies, thereby giving credibility to the Renewal. As I mentioned earlier, we now have a wealth of literature published already from Catholic perspectives on evolving charismatic spirituality, especially baptism in the Holy Spirit and *charisms*. The Renewal has recorded a tremendous success across the Catholic world within 50 years of its existence. There are numerous parish charismatic prayer ministries, Diocesan, National and International Service teams, established to help accelerate the promotion of the Renewal, especially baptism in the Holy Spirit. The recorded progress of the renewal so far is good, but I think it is a tip of the iceberg compared to what could happen when the Church leadership restores baptism in the Holy Spirit as part of Christian initiation.

Baptism in the Holy Spirit belongs intrinsically to Christian initiation as established by the works of Kilian McDonnell and George Montague.[857] It is possible to restore baptism in the Holy Spirit as part of the Church's sacramental life through the ground tool of the charismatic renewal in the Church today. The endorsement of the Charismatic Catholic Renewal by all the Popes after Vatican II is a good sign that the Church leadership is abreast with the urgency that the Church needs to, incorporate the *charisms* into the Church's sacramental and liturgical life.

4.6 *The Popes and Charismatic Renewal*[858]

The Church leadership has had a long tradition of discerning and defining doctrines for the unity of the Church. All preachers and teachers of the Church must comply with the set-theoretical principles to remain in good standing with the Church. The Roman Curia has different offices to handle various causes in the Church, and for any evolving religious groups to be credible; the Church has to endorse it. When the Charismatic Renewal started spreading with many Catholics receiving baptism in the Spirit, some commentators were skeptical about the hierarchy of the Church giving approval. Well, never underestimate what God can do to effect a remarkable change to a system. When God is ready for transformation, God strategically uses the most unlikely people. Cardinal Leo Jozef Suenens (1904–1996)[859] was an unlikely person to carry the banner for the Charismatic Catholic Renewal. Cardinal Danneels pointed out that he was reserved, shy and almost overly intellectual, and captures this seamlessly at the homily he preached at Suenens funeral in 1996:

---

[857] McDonnell, and Montague, *Christian Initiation and Baptism in the Holy Spirit*, 86.

[858] McDonnell, *Open the Window: The Popes and the Renewal*, i.

[859] http://sites.jcu.edu/suenens/pages/cardinal-suenens/ (Accessed Nov. 11, 2016).

How could a cardinal with a face that did not show many emotions, with a straight and immobile stature, with a grave and steady voice, find himself at ease in the midst of a crowd that sang, danced, clapped hands and spoke in tongues? Was it a late life conversion to fantasy and imagination in a man who had been until then too rational and responsible? No. Rather, he perceived in this revival a return to the church of the Acts of the Apostles about which he had always dreamed – with a taste for the Scriptures, spontaneous prayer, joy, a sense of community, the stirrings of the Spirit, the proliferation of charisms. The renewal gave the legitimate role of the heart and the body back to the spiritual life of Christians.[860]

Suenens was also one of the most significant and impressive figures of the Second Vatican Council. Many commentators believe that his leadership at the Council made him a major architect of 20th century Roman Catholicism.[861] Suenens was a man of great faith and deep confidence in the functioning of the Holy Spirit in history. Those who knew him talked about his impressive intelligence, fearless courage and unshakable fidelity to the Church.[862]

In 1972, Veronica O'Brien encouraged Suenens to visit the United States concerning the Renewal. He went and was impressed by Catholics who had received the baptism in the Holy Spirit, including some members of the hierarchy. He became enthusiastic from that moment and desired to see the Church flourish in a new Pentecost through the work of the Holy Spirit. He took it upon himself to promote the Renewal.[863] He became a forefront theologian for the Renewal. He dialogued with the leaders of the Renewal–Ralph Martin, Steve Clark, Kevin Ranaghan, and Father Jim Ferry–in the United States and Europe.[864] With the cardinal's persuasive recommendation to Pope Paul VI, the Renewal was invited to have its world congress at Rome on Pentecost during the Holy Year. "The Charismatic Renewal was unwaveringly accepted into the Catholic Church when Pope Paul endorsed it in St. Peter's Basilica on Pentecost Sunday."[865] The Church gradually appropriated and

---

[860] Donnelly, op. cit., 164.

[861] http://sites.jcu.edu/suenens/pages/cardinal-suenens/ (Accessed Nov. 11, 2016).

[862] Ibid.

[863] http://www.sfspirit.com/renewal-history.html (Accessed Nov. 11, 2016).
Cardinal William J. Levada, *Pentecostal Catholics – A History of the Catholic Charismatic Renewal*. A keynote address of May 31, 1996, delivered at the Cleveland symposium from which the foregoing was condensed, see Origins, CNS Documentary Service, June 20, 1996, Vol.26: No.5, The Charism of Cardinal.

[864] Ibid.

[865] Ibid.

identified that the phenomena expressed and lived out by the Charismatic Renewal was historically part of the Church's liturgical life. Consequently, all the Popes since the inception of the Renewal have communicated with representatives of the charismatic renewal on several occasions, and formally and informally spoken about the significance of the renewal.[866] However, Killian McDonnell notes that the popes have not considered the question of the centrality of the renewal to the life of the Church, nor the prominence of the baptism in the Holy Spirit.[867] For a Church that has more than 2000 years of tradition, change comes slowly. We hope that the leadership of the Church will soon consider overhauling the general structure of the sacraments of initiation and fit in baptism in the Holy Spirit in the Church today. Before the change arrives, let the Renewal continue the work of helping Catholics experience baptism in the Holy Spirit.

With regards to the Renewal's endorsement, Pope Paul VI was impressed by the exciting news about the fruits of the renewal around the world. He did not miss the opportunity to let the leaders of the Renewal know that their ministry around the world was appreciated. This is an excerpt from 1973 address of Pope Paul VI to the First International Leader's Conference of the Catholic Charismatic Renewal:

> *We rejoice with you, dear friends, at the renewal of the spiritual life manifested in the church today, in different forms and in various environments. Certain common notes appear in this renewal: the taste for deep prayer, personal and in groups, a return to contemplation and on emphasis on praise of God, the desire to devote oneself completely to Christ, a great availability for the calls of the Holy Spirit, more assiduous reading of the Scriptures, generous brotherly devotion, the will to make a contribution to the service of the church. In all that, we can recognize the mysteries and discreet work of the Spirit, who is the soul of the church.*[868]

In the following year, 1974, Pope Paul VI reflected on the abiding presence of the Holy Spirit in the Church and insightfully told the Synod of Bishops that the Holy Spirit is the one who perpetually renews the Church. Below is an excerpt from his statement:

> *The Holy Spirit was sent on the day of Pentecost in order that He might forever sanctify the church, and thus all believers would have access to the Father through Christ in one Spirit (cf. Eph.2: 18). He is the Spirit of life …*

---

[866] McDonnell, *Open the Window: The Popes and the Renewal* ix.

[867] Ibid.

[868] Ibid., 4

The Spirit dwells in the church and in the hearts of the faithful as in a temple (cf. 1 Cor. 3:16; 6:19). In them he prays and bears witness to the fact that they are adopted sons (cf. Gal. 4:6; Rom. 8:15-16,26). The Spirit guides the church in the fullness of truth (cf. John 16:13) and gives her a unity of fellowship and service. He furnishes and directs her with various gifts, both hierarchical and charismatic, and adorns her with the fruits of his grace (cf. Eph. 4:11-12; 1 Cor. 12:4; Gal. 5:22). By the power of the gospel he makes the church grow, perpetually renews her" (Lumen Gentium, 4).[869]

Pope John Paul II, the successor of Paul VI, continued in the footsteps of his predecessor by his openness to the Renewal. He was excited to identify with the Renewal personally. At the International Council of the Charismatic Renewal on December 11, 1979, John Paul II had a special audience with Cardinal Suenens, Bishop Alfonso Uribe, and the members of the Council. In his informal interaction with them, he talked about the charismatic aspect of his life and asserted that the charismatic renewal is a renewal tool for the Church and a response to materialism. He went to speak to the larger group saying:

I have always belonged to this renewal in the Holy Spirit. My own experience is very interesting. When I was in school, at the age of 12 or 13, sometimes I had difficulties in my studies, in particular with mathematics. My father gave me a book on prayer. He opened it to a page and said to me: 'Here you have the prayer to the Holy Spirit. You must say this prayer every day of your life.' I have remained obedient to this order that my father gave 50 years ago. I am convinced that this movement is a sign of his action. The world is much in need of this action of the Holy Spirit, and it needs many instruments for this action. The situation in the world is dangerous, very dangerous. Materialism is opposed to the true dimension of human power, and there are many different kinds of materialism. Materialism is the negation of the Holy Spirit. Now I see this movement, this activity everywhere … Consequently, I am convinced in the total renewal of the church, in this spiritual renewal of the church.[870]

At another occasion on January 22, 1987, John Paul II had an audience with the bishops of Northern France. One of the subjects he addressed was the Charismatic Renewal. He assured the bishops that his interest and satisfaction in the Renewal grew with discernment

---

[869] Ibid., 7.

[870] Ibid., 25-25.

and after going through the process, he declared the Renewal as a grace for the Church.[871] Below is an excerpt from his address to the bishops of Northern France:

> *Nowadays, there exists another possibility: that of prayer groups which have multiplied in the Catholic Church as in other church communities, and this spontaneously, in an unexpected manner. Prayer can be developed here in a classic way. It can also seek the support of the more exuberant manifestations. Some pastors have received this movement with restraint. And, in fact, it is necessary to keep watch always so that an authentic doctrine inspires this type of prayer, and the ecclesial character of the sacramental ministers may be well respected, and that the tasks of charity and justice are not abandoned. On the other hand, the dynamism and generosity of these groups should not impede other initiatives animating the life of parish communities. However, with all necessary discernment, it is possible to speak of a grace directed to sanctify the church, to renew in her the taste for prayer, to rediscover, with the Holy Spirit, the sense of gratuitousness, of joyful praise, of confidence in intercession, and to be converted into a new fountain of evangelization.[872]*

I was one of the participants at the Ninth Leaders' Conference of Fiuggi, 30 October 1998 and in our audience with Pope John Paul II, he said,

> *The Catholic Charismatic Renewal has helped many Christians to rediscover the presence and power of the Holy Spirit in their lives, in the life of the Church and in the world, and this rediscovery has awakened in them a faith in Christ filled with joy, a great love of the Church and a generous dedication to her evangelizing mission. In this year of the Holy Spirit, I join you in praise of God for the precious fruits, which he has wished to bring to maturity in your communities and, through them, in the particular Churches.[873]*

It was gratifying to see the excitement in members of the conference chanting, "Viva Papa, Viva Papa." Listening to the Holy Father, John Paul II and his moving testimony of

---

[871] Ibid., 59.

[872] Ibid., 59-60.

[873] http://www.iccrs.org/it/10th-international-event-iccrs-leaders-conference-fiuggi-italy/ (Accessed November 16, 2016).

the Holy Spirit in the lives of many Catholic Christians filled all present with joy. Many shed tears of joy.

On October 31, 2008, Pope Benedict XVI addressed the Catholic Fraternity of Charismatic Covenant Communities and Fellowships and affirmed that the *charisms* that were manifested in the early Church were not meant to die with the past but be re-experienced. Furthermore, he said:

> *What we learn in the New Testament on charism, which appeared as visible signs of the coming of the Holy Spirit, is not a historical event of the past, but a reality ever alive. It is the same divine Spirit, the soul of the Church, that acts in every age and those mysterious and effective interventions of the Spirit are manifest in our time in a providential way. The Movements and New Communities are like an outpouring of the Holy Spirit in the Church and in contemporary society. We can, therefore, rightly say that one of the positive elements and aspects of the Community of the Catholic Charismatic Renewal is precisely their emphasis on the charisms or gifts of the Holy Spirit and their merit lies in having recalled their topicality in the Church.*[874]

In his address at Saint Peter's Square on July 3, 2015, to members of the Renewal of the Holy Spirit and those present in Rome for their 38th annual Convocation, Pope Francis publicly recounted and recognized those who helped bring the Renewal to the Church's hierarchy's attention.[875] Cardinal Léon-Joseph Suenens said the Pope recalled and appreciated the extraordinary role of Veronica O'Brien who enjoyed the trust and affection of Pope Paul VI. The Cardinal's visit exposed him to the Charismatic Renewal, which he described as a "flow of grace" and he played a significant role in maintaining the Renewal in the Church.[876] "At the Mass on Pentecost Monday in 1975, Pope Paul VI thanked him with these words: "In the name of the Lord I thank you for having brought the Charismatic Renewal into the heart of the Church."[877] Pope Francis reiterated the thoughts of some theologians when he repeated the quotes of Cardinal Suenens:

---

[874] https://w2.vatican.va/content/benedict-xvi/en/speeches/2008/october/documents/hf_ben-xvi_spe_20081031_carismatici.html Accessed November 11, 2016.

[875] http://w2.vatican.va/content/francesco/en/speeches/2015/july/documents/papa-francesco_20150703_movimento-rinnovamento-spirito.html Accessed November 11, 2016.

[876] Ibid.

[877] Ibid.

The first error that must be avoided is including the Charismatic Renewal in the category of a Movement. It is not a specific Movement; the Renewal is not a Movement in the common sociological sense; it does not have founders, it is not homogeneous and it includes a great variety of realities; it is a current of grace, a renewing breath of the Spirit for all members of the Church, laity, religious, priests and bishops. It is a challenge for us all. One does not form part of the Renewal; rather, the Renewal becomes a part of us provided that we accept the grace it offers us.[878]

I agree with Heribert Mühlen, who goes further to say, "Movements arise from the fact that individuals or groups set themselves certain goals of reform and attempt with their ideas to influence or change society or the Church."[879] Nevertheless, Charismatic Renewal is a new historical form of the *basic Christian experience*, and it is from the latter that all special formations emerge from the very beginning."[880] For whatever reasons, many theologians and Church leaders still maintain that the Charismatic Renewal is a movement. I think there is the need to repeatedly stress that the Charismatic Renewal is not the idea of an individual or a group of people but the initiative of the Holy Spirit to reinstate the missing aspects of the Church's life, which are *charisms* for full-animated existence. I believe that the rebirth of the charismatic renewal in the Church is an urgent call to retrace herself to her charismatic roots. I also think that a full dynamically efficient Church is the one with all parts of her body functioning for her wellbeing and the salvation of the world.

The Church has been in existence for more than 2000 years, and like the universe that is still in an evolutionary process, the Church in like manner is also still evolving into attaining the full prominence that God has designed for her from all eternity. The Church may not reach her full status in glory if her suppressed treasured wealth, which I call *charisms*/gifts, are not recovered and restored. However, the task of beginning the recovery and restoration of the *charisms* for ministry in the Church today must start now with a paradigm shift in understanding the charismatic renewal and the mission of the Holy Spirit. We have seen how shifts in understanding at different times have shaped various eras of Church history. It is my understanding that the Church in collaboration with the people, theologians, and the Holy Spirit can also shape the Church for the future. We shall continue to unravel how the manifest *charisms* in the early Church can be recovered and restored in the Church today. As has been noted, this study is a call for the renewal of a religious tradition of Christian initiation that opens candidates to the Holy Spirit for *charisms*. It is my opinion that baptism

---

[878] Ibid.

[879] Mühlen, op. cit., 15-16.

[880] Ibid.

in the Holy Spirit helps to unlock the latent *charisms* in Christians who do not manifest the gifts yet, what Paul calls 'fanning into flame' (2 Tim. 1:6). The early Christians believed that baptism in the Holy Spirit is a key to living the Christian life to the full; it is vital to reawakening the Christian experience.[881] To engage in a Church ministerial work without the *charisms* is as good as participating in a social function without power from above.

4.7 *The Relevance and the Use of Charisms in the Church Today*

All through biblical history, God's self-revelation has always been transformational but interpreted to take different forms and manifestations. As was articulated in chapter one, the Jews believed that certain people received God's revolutionary Spirit, which empowered them to carry out specific tasks. In the NT, the early Christians experienced and articulated that the same Spirit of God that was operational in the OT is the third person of the Blessed Trinity, the Holy Spirit. It was this life-changing presence revealed as the advocate, the comforter, and helper (John 14:16; 27) that rested on the disciples on Pentecost Day and empowered them with gifts/*charisms* for ministry in the world. Their empowerment did not happen by chance. They were told to wait in prayerful preparation, which they did. The disciples, Mary, the mother of Jesus and some of his relatives were all gathered in one accord at the upper Room in Jerusalem for Pentecost (Acts 1:14). Jesus had told his disciples not to depart from Jerusalem until they received the promise of the Father, the Holy Spirit (Luke 24:49). By implication, to be a witness in the world, a Christian needs to prepare. The preparation of a witness requires is openness and reception of the Holy Spirit who empowers Christians with the *charism* for ministry in the world.

The only way the disciples and early Christians prepared for the mission of being witnesses was by waiting prayerfully. They were open to receiving baptism in the Holy Spirit, which unlocked the graces in each person for ministry. The evolution of Christian history in the NT testifies that the disciples were fruitful in their mission because they operated in the Spirit of God. I think the yardstick to measure fruitfulness here is their ability to create an atmosphere of love among people. They lived in love and harmony, sharing all that they had in common as God's children (Acts 4:32-47). The testimony of their mutual love inspired the word Christians (Act 11:19-26). People are bound to live in harmony when they allow the Holy Spirit to teach and inspire them. That was why the disciples lived in fulfillment of the words of Jesus: *This is how all will know that you are my disciples if you have love for one another* [882](John 13:35). From the Azusa Street and Duquesne Weekend testimonies of mutual love, we can trust that love, one of the fruits of the Holy Spirit (Gal. 5:22), manifests

---

[881] McDonnell, and Montague, Eds. Fanning The Flame, 9.

[882] Senior, and Collins, op. cit., 1429.

when people are open to receive and share it. The world certainly needs love at this time of global socio-religious-political confusion. The Church is required more than ever to explore and use more than human intellectual constructs to resolve the issues of humanity today. I am not in any way downplaying the role of natural talents in confronting and addressing our global malaise today. It is my opinion that we will be better off if we tap into the supernatural for God's help and that is why we need to be empowered from above for a restoration of *charisms* as tools for ministry in the Church for the good of the world today.

It is truly through the power of the Holy Spirit in our lives and in the life of the Church that we can bring about the transformational change in the world for God's glory. We can reactivate the graces of the supernatural gifts we received at our baptism and confirmation through the experience of baptism in the Holy Spirit. We cannot minister in emptiness or the flesh. Jesus said in John 6: 63, *It is the spirit that gives life, while the flesh is of no avail. The words I have spoken to you are spirit and life.*[883] For us to effectively minister God's grace in the world, the Holy Spirit must flow through us to build the Church and God's kingdom in this world.[884] When we are open to the Holy Spirit, in expectant prayer, we receive *charisms* for ministry.

Charisms are gifts of the Holy Spirit, which prepare people for the roles, and ministries, they undertake in the Church and the world.[885] In addition, they are some of the various ways God pours out God's gracious power on individuals called for specific but effective ministry in the world.[886] The *charisms* will come from openness to baptism in the Holy Spirit, which leads to a tangible experiential encounter with God, who assures each Christian of the relevance to be a positive agent of blessing in the world. I am not writing about an intellectual appropriation or presumption of having *charisms* because we belong to a particular faith designation but an experience with the presence of God that propels one to pray, praise and act and live in God's gratuitous love. It is always heartwarming to see Christians, who have been baptized in the Holy Spirit, experience a manifestation of charismatic gifts that create urgency in their hearts for ministry in the world. I am convinced that if *charisms* are recovered and restored, and used, we will experience a functional body of Christ where each part is enthusiastically engaged in graced functions for the glory of God. This is what will keep the Church ever young and new. Without the application of "*charisms*, the ecclesiastical ministry would be impoverished and sterile"[887]

---

[883] Senior, and Collins, op. cit., 1416.

[884] George Montague, *Holy Spirit, Make Your Home in Me, Biblical Meditations on Receiving the Gift of the Spirit*. (Maryland: The Word Among Us Press, 2008), 204.

[885] Sullivan, op. cit., 10.

[886] Ibid., 18.

[887] Sullivan, op. cit., 11.

4.8 *Charisms and Evil*

The problem of evil has always been in the world. It does not matter a person's religious affiliation or socio-political orientation; evil is what everyone has to deal with in life. As a missionary priest who has ministered in different parts of the world, I have seen godly and ungodly people alike suffer the misfortune of evil. I know the problem of evil is as real and old as known human history. However, schools of thoughts differ on the origin and solution to the problem of evil; I won't go into that. I wish to concern myself with how Jesus dealt with the manifestations of the power of darkness in people's lives and how the empowerment of Christians can also help relieve the pains caused by the evil presence in our lives or the world.

Being a Christian does not exempt one from suffering. In fact, the mark of true discipleship is the cross (Matthew 16:24; Mark 8:34; Luke 9:23). I believe the cross is the suffering that comes to the Christian because of virtuous living. I have heard people say, they were doing pretty well until they started taking their faith more seriously and doing more good in the world. Some give up doing good because they cannot stand the onslaught of the devil. However, this does not mean that the Christian should sit back and relax; suffering must be fought with every material and spiritual gift we have. To delight in suffering, as God's permissive will is to misinterpret the ploy of the devil, which comes to steal, kill and destroy. But Jesus came that we may have abundant life (John 10:10). We have to always fight back for healing and deliverance through love and spiritual warfare prayers. In the gospel of John 16:33 we read, "In the world, you will have trouble, but take courage, I have conquered the world."[888] By his death and resurrection, Jesus overcame the "prince of this world" (John 14:30) and won victory for us once and for all by casting out the prince of this world (John 12:31; Rev 12:10).[889]

Preachers and religious teachers in the Church have been trying to understand why Christians must continue to suffer and fight a battle that was already won by Jesus on the cross. I think Saint Paul could not also comprehend why he must suffer and that was why he talked about suffering for what was lacking in the sufferings of Christ (Colossians 1:24). On the other hand, the author to the Hebrews said, "For by one offering he has made perfect forever those who are being consecrated" (10:14).[890] I believe that Paul, like every person of faith, was seeking to understand the reason for his continued suffering. Many holy individuals in the Catholic Church pray for suffering. I think it is a misconstrued spirituality. Nobody needs to pray for suffering. Suffering strikes good people and that is why

---

[888] Collins and Senior, op. cit., 1433.

[889] *Catechism of the Catholic Church*, 2nd ed., 2853.

[890] Collins and Senior, op. cit., 1630.

excruciating pains at times plagued many saints. However, I believe that a person's faith and spirituality also determines how quickly suffering may gain access into their lives. God wants us to live in good health of mind and body, and that was why Jesus spent three years of his earthly ministry healing and delivering captives. On his physical departure from this world, he empowered his disciples to do the same.

The ministry of Jesus started with a battle with the powers of darkness. In his temptations, which he defeated the devil by the persistent choice he made to follow God's will and purpose (Matthew 4:1-11; Mark 1:12-13; Luke 4:1-13), Jesus showed clearly that part of his mission was to set captives free. Peter articulated this when he said, "How God anointed Jesus of Nazareth with the Holy Spirit and power. He went about doing good and healing all those oppressed by the devil, for God was with him."[891] This same idea we see expressed in 1John 3:3, "Indeed, the Son of God was revealed to destroy the works of the devil."[892]

From the moment of his baptism, Jesus received power with the charismatic gifts for his ministry, he preached, healed the sick and cast out demons. Luke 4: 18-19 shows clearly the manifesto of Jesus:

> *The Spirit of the Lord is upon me because he has anointed me to bring glad tidings to the poor. He has sent me to proclaim liberty to captives and recovery of sight to the blind, to let the oppressed go free, and to proclaim a year acceptable to the Lord.*[893]

The Holy Spirit is the giver of *charisms* for ministry, and Jesus testified from the above text that it was the Holy Spirit that empowered him for his mission. Well, Jesus' task of preaching, teaching, healing and deliverance did not end with Jesus; his disciples were to continue his work of healing and deliverance of all in bondage. That was why he commissioned the disciples to heal the sick and cast out demons (Matthew 10:1; Mark 6:7; Luke 9:1), and in Luke 10:1-12 he commissioned seventy-two disciples. In Luke 10:17, the seventy-two came back with joy and reported, "Lord, even the demons are subject to us when we used your name."[894] Jesus said in v.19, "Behold, I have given you the power 'to tread upon serpents' and scorpions and upon the full force of the enemy and nothing will harm you."[895]

---

[891] Ibid.,1461.

[892] Ibid., 1659.

[893] Ibid., 1360.

[894] Ibid., 1374.

[895] Ibid.

The devil is not a physical entity, nor readily visible to the eyes. However, we see and experience the negative presence of the influences of evil all around us. Christians are to live by faith and not by sight (1 Cor. 5:7). We have the power as Christians to defeat the schemes and lies of the devil. The sight of the havoc perpetrated by the evil one can be intimidating to Christians at times. Nonetheless, we must not give up, "for the weapons of our battle are not of flesh but enormously powerful, capable of destroying fortresses."[896] Christians have the power to exercise authority over the devil, in the name of Jesus. One of the miraculous graces of believers and especially those with charismatic gifts is the power to cast out devil, the power of evil forces. The NT calls the influence of the devil by different names. Mark concludes his gospel by saying,

These signs will accompany those who believe: in my name they will drive out demons, they will speak new languages. They will pick up serpents with their hands, and if they drink any deadly thing, it will not harm them. They will lay their hands on the sick, and they will recover.[897]

The experience of baptism in the Holy Spirit makes some feel the power of the presence of Jesus to act in his name. Jesus' promise to the disciples that they will receive power when the Holy Spirit comes upon them (Acts 1:8) is fulfilled in the life of those open to empowerment from above.[898] McDonnell testifies that members of the renewal have helped many people to receive deliverance.[899] However, he warns that an excessive fixation with the demonic and an undiscerning exercise of deliverance ministries will be a misrepresentation of the biblical evidence, which can be pastorally harmful.[900] I agree with McDonnell as many people in bondage have also been liberated through my deliverance ministry. I have also seen many lay people exercise their charismatic gifts in a way that has been beneficial to many people in the Church. Linda Schubert, the author of Miracle Hour, is a devout Catholic woman who has helped many people all over the world through her healing and deliverance ministry. I met her at the 10th International Charismatic Leaders Conference in Fiuggi, Italy in October 1998.

---

[896] Ibid., 1554.

[897] Ibid., 1348.

[898] McDonnell, *Presence Power Praise*, 32.

[899] Ibid., 59.

[900] Ibid., 60.

4.9 *How Charisms Can Be Recovered and Restored*

In conclusion, I will propose ways that I believe can make the Church more holistic in dispensing God's treasured graces that I call *charisms*. I use the word holistic because the Church has functioned for decades without fully engaging the different parts of its body. The clergy was the sole functionary and dispenser of God's precious gifts to the world, which may account for the fact that we have more canonized saints among the priests and religious. I think that is quite unfortunate. The priest was the sole evangelical overseer of all the ministries of the Church at a time, which made people in different parts of the Catholic world refer to the parish as, "Father's church" i.e. the priest's church. All thanks to Vatican II that recognizes the Church as the people of God. It is no more the work of the clergy alone, but God's work using human instruments among the clergy and lay people altogether. The following are the fruits of my theological reflection.

(a) *The Body of Christ Includes Every Baptized Christian*

In the statement on the Charismatic Catholic Renewal issued by the Bishops of Antilles Episcopal Conference at their annual meeting in Belize, Central America in November 1976, they recognized that the Renewal had made a positive impact on the Church. The conference affirmed the teaching of the Second Vatican Council.

> *It is not only through the sacraments and the ministrations of the Church that the Holy Spirit makes holy the people, leads them and enriches them with his virtues. Allotting his gifts according as he wills (Cf. 1 Cor. 12:11), he also distributes special graces among the faithful of every rank. By these gifts he makes them fit and ready to undertake various tasks and offices for the renewal and building of the Church, as it is written, 'the manifestation of the Spirit is given to everyone for profit' (1 Cor. 12:7).[901]*

Before Vatican II, ministry in the Church was the work of the ordained ministers. Other members of the Church were either spectators or helpers of the clergy and not collaborators in the work of Christ. Consequently, Vatican II's new vision of the *Church as People of God* recognized that the laity shares in the ministerial priesthood of Christ.[902] *You are a chosen race, a royal priesthood, a holy nation, a people of his own, so that you may announce the*

---

[901] *Lumen Gentium* No. 12 Cited in http://www.aecrc.org/documents/aecstatement_ccr.pdf (Accessed Nov. 15, 2016).

[902] Ibid.

praises of him who called you out of darkness into his wonderful light (1 Pet. 2:9).[903] The Council affirmed that every baptized person shares in the priestly, kingly and prophetic ministry of Christ. Each baptized person is part of the body of Christ. If the Holy Spirit offers gifts/*charisms* to each as she wills and empowers for various undertakings for the good and building of the Church, the exclusion of some, therefore, means the partial function of the body of Christ. I believe that the active involvement of all members of the Church with their *charisms* make the Church healthier in her function and ministry in the world.

(b) *The Charismatic Renewal as a Revived Missing Part of the Church*

The Charismatic Renewal is not a movement. I believe that it is the revived missing part of the Church. In chapter four I stated some reasons for the loss of the *charisms* in the Church. The disappearance of *charisms* deprived the Church of her wholeness. It is my contention that the Church operated for years but was deficient. Deficiency is a lack or deprivation of that which belongs to the whole by nature. Paul wrote about the Church as the body of Christ. He used a human analogy to explain the interconnectedness of the human body. Though there are different parts, it is still one body (1 Cor. 12:12-31). Knowing what we know about human physiology today, we can say that for the body to be healthy, every part has to go through a routine exercise. If one part is dead or inactive, it affects the whole. Paul strengthened this point in verse 26 when he wrote: *If one part suffers, all the parts suffer with it: if one part is honored, all the parts share its joy.*[904] The Spirit and the *charisms* are not additions to an already existing Church but an integral part of the Church, which is the body of Christ.[905] The Church cannot be whole without the Spirit and the *charisms*.[906]

Accordingly, the Spirit and charisms belong to the Christian also. For Paul, the Christian is a person of who possesses the Spirit of Christ, and without that, a person does not belong to Christ (Rom. 8:9).[907] It is the sacrament of initiation through which a person becomes part of the body of Christ. *For in one Spirit, we are all baptized into one body, whether Jews or Greeks, slaves or free persons, and we were all given to drink of the one Spirit.*[908] The

---

[903] Senior, and Collins, op. cit., 1647, cited in Ibid.

[904] Senior, and Collins, op. cit., 1533.

[905] Kilian McDonnell, Ed. *Presence Power Praise: Documents on the Charismatic Renewal.* Vol. III. (Collegeville, Minnesota: The Liturgical Press, 1980), 4.

[906] Ibid.

[907] Ibid.

[908] Ibid. See also Senior, and Collins, op. cit., 1532.

process of Christian initiation involved baptism, confirmation and the Eucharist and candidates expected to receive the Holy Spirit, who empowered them with *charisms* since it was the standard practice.[909] Becoming a Christian meant receiving the perceivable outpouring of the Holy Spirit. The experience of knowing that one has received the gifts of the Holy Spirit compels one to the action of commitment to truly be a functional part of the body of Christ.

(c) *Baptism in the Holy Spirit as Part of Faith Formation and Parish Life.*

Part of the faith formation for candidates for the sacrament of initiation should include baptism in the Holy Spirit and the use of *charisms* and should also be part of each parish standard life. A parish life in the Spirit seminar that leads to baptism in the Holy Spirit brings out the hidden treasures in the parishioners. The hidden treasures are *charisms,* and people are filled with joy and enthusiasm to work for the Church when they begin to manifest the gifts. I believe that for any institution to remain relevant in the future, there is always the need for constant reevaluation, updating, and upgrading of knowledge. Considering what we know of our Catholic Pentecostal and charismatic heritage, I think a revision of the curriculum of the Church's catechesis is necessary. A review should include the origin of baptism in the Holy Spirit and the use and manifestations of *charism* in the early Church. Consequently, baptism in the Holy Spirit should resume as an integral part of the sacraments of initiation as done in the early Church.

Baptism in the Spirit also helps to bring about the release of *charisms,* especially the "spiritual gifts" as listed in 1 Corinthians 12: 8-12 and manifested in the Corinthian community.[910]The Second Vatican Council eloquently acknowledged that the charismatic gifts are appropriate for the needs of the Church today. We can see the profound change in the lives of those who have experienced baptism in the Holy Spirit. Their experience with the Holy Spirit, Lord, and giver of life is revolutionary, which makes them bear fruits that are visible, as seen love for prayer life, a love for Sacred Scripture, a devotion to the Eucharist, a burning zeal, a heart for evangelization, and an ongoing response to conversion and a life of holiness. Every parish should be excited to have passionate people for the reign of God's kingdom.

(d) *Balance the Intellectual and Experiential Dimension of the Manifestations of*
   the Holy Spirit

The Catechism of the Catholic Church states that in matters of discernment of *charisms,* "No *charism* is exempt from being referred and submitted to the Church's shepherds. Their

---

[909] Ibid.,5.

[910] *Baptism in the Holy Spirit*, op. cit., 20.

office is not indeed to extinguish the Spirit, but to test all things and hold fast to what is good, so that all the diverse and complementary *charisms* work together 'for the common good.'"[911] The Church enjoins those in leadership positions to help the faithful in discerning what is appropriate and promote the good of the Church. However, the clergy cannot discern, lead or guard a people with *charisms* without first of all having an experience with the Holy Spirit. The experience here is not acquired knowledge through studies but an encounter with the transforming presence of the Holy Spirit, the Lord, the giver of life. Hence, there is a need for an ongoing formation of the faithful through catechesis, teaching, and preaching. A Latin adage says, *"Nemo dat quod non habet"* meaning *"no one can give what he does not have,"*[912] is ad rem here. Those in leadership positions cannot teach what they have not learned. In my opinion, everyone in leadership positions should go through a process of Life in the Spirit Seminar as already established by the Charismatic Catholic Renewal for baptism in the Holy Spirit.

(e) *My Experience and the Quest for Charismatic Spirituality*

In June of 1998, the youths of the Diocese of Gaborone had their annual convention at my parish, Saint Gabriel Catholic Church, Serowe-Botswana. The leadership of the youths asked me to give a talk, and have an altar call on the last night of their convention, called, (Tsosoloso) revival. It was a Saturday night. The youths were excited. The night was electrifying as the presence of the Holy Spirit filled the gathering. Many signs, unexpected and new in my priestly experience began to happen. Some people cried for joy while others writhe in pain; others fell and rolled on the floor as we sang and prayed. As the night drew to an end, there was calm and happiness. Many people experienced physical and emotional healing.

Though I had no theological understanding or explanation of what took place during the night session of the revival, I was, however, happy that many people were healed. I felt that my parishioners would benefit from the prayers of their children from different parts of Botswana who had their *charisms* revived during the previous night's ministration. So, I invited a few of the leaders that I felt had received the *charisms* to join me at the altar to lay hands on those who needed prayers after Sunday Mass. After the Mass with my parishioners on that Sunday morning, I asked the congregation to sing a song that was common among the people.

> *Ntate, Ntate kea go rapela kea le utlwa letsogo la gago Amen fa ke khubama,*
> *ka mangole, ke rapela kea le utlwa letsogo la gago Amen*

---

[911] *Catechism of the Catholic Church*, 2nd ed., 801.

[912] http://definitions.uslegal.com/n/nemo-dat-quod-non-habet/ (Accessed November. 15, 2016).

Father, Father I pray unto you, I feel your hand upon me, Amen. When I kneel down and pray I feel your hand upon me, Amen.[913]

As the whole congregation sang the song, I can say with my current understanding and reflection on what happened that morning that all present felt the power of God. Nobody was in doubt about the presence of God in the place. There were shouts of excitement and cries of anguish. People were dropping on the floor as they approached the altar. The phenomenon was overwhelming and yet confusing to me. Those standing and singing also slumped on their pews. The sight was frightening and yet a delight as it was indeed a display of what the Holy Spirit can do when people are hungry and open to God as He moves them. I believe the whole experience was to teach me that the Holy Spirit acts through simple ordinary human beings who are open to and be ready to be used by Him. Although I did not understand everything that happened, I moved from obscurity into notoriety. The children went back to their different parishes and talked about what had happened at St. Gabriel Catholic Church, Serowe-Botswana. I received invitations from pastors across the country to preach and pray in their Churches. Since I was still new to the experience of the working of the Spirit and wanted to learn more about it, I started searching the scriptures and charismatic magazines for educational help.

My search led me to visit and spend three days in Pretoria with Fr. Eugene Clarkson, M.S.C, who was at that time the chaplain of the Charismatic Renewal in South Africa. I explained my experiences and bewilderment to him. He was delighted to give me the following books to read: *The Power to Heal* by Francis MacNutt, *Deliverance Prayer* by Mathew and Dennis Linn, and *Resting in the Spirit* by Robert DeGrandis. These books have enlightened and armed me with a better understanding of the manifestations of the gifts of the Holy Spirit.

I returned to Botswana prepared to give some explanation to whoever needed to know more about the marvels in the prayer events. I did not know that when the news reached the Bishop, I would not have an opportunity to explain what had happened at the prayer sessions in my parish. Contrary to the views of some that I was destroying the Catholic faith, my parish was packed each Sunday even with people from other Church denominations. The news of what happened in my Church in June of 1998 spread like wildfire all over the Central District. The Council of Barutis (Pastors of the Central District) met and unanimously voted that I should preach at the Christians Annual Ecumenical Convention, which took place at the United Congregational Church of Southern Africa (UCCSA) in Serowe. The huge Church was bursting to its capacity. There were over 23 ministers and five bishops from different denominations in attendance

It was on Pentecost Day, July 31, 1998. I preached on Unity in Diversity. Before I preached the word, I asked the congregation in collaboration with my parishioners who at this time

---

[913] *Botswana Church folklore song*, translated by Oanthata Lebeko.

175

followed me everywhere to sing 'Come Holy Spirit' in Setswana (Tla Moya O Boithepo). The Church was full of expectation and liveliness. As they sang, people started speaking in tongues, and there were shouts and what looked like confusion in the gathering. Since I did not know what to do, I allowed it to go on for about 10 minutes, after which, I prayed, "Let there be calm in the name of Jesus," and there was an instant peace. I delivered my message, and as I preached, there was what seemed like commotion again, people speaking and praying in tongues and there were also shouts of affliction and joy. The pastor of the Church was weeping uncontrollably on the altar. At the end of the conference, many people testified that it was the most powerful Christian gathering they ever attended. I believed them because of the many healing testimonies that were given by those in attendance.

I gave retreats and revivals all over Botswana. I had the privilege of attending the 10th International Leadership Conference of the Charismatic Catholic Renewal at Fiuggi, Italy between October 26 and 31, 1998. During the Congress, I met Linda Schubert, Ralph Martin and some other leaders from other parts of the world. The conference affirmed my experiences as regular occurrences at Pentecostal and charismatic gatherings. I wanted to know more about the Holy Spirit and the *charisms* in the Church, and if those manifestations were at odds with the spirituality of the Catholic Church.

I was shocked and confused when in late January 1999, the then Superior General of the Missionary Society of Saint Paul, Rev. Felix Elosi, informed me that the Bishop of Gaborone, Boniface Tshosa Setlalekgosi, wanted me withdrawn from his Diocese. The bishop's reason: he would not permit my kind of spirituality in his diocese.

Prior to this, some expatriate parish nuns and the chairperson of the Church Council in my parish had reported to the Bishop that my spirituality was strange and not Catholic. They complained that I caused people to scream and fall in Church and that I was destroying the Catholic faith with my brand of spirituality. To my consternation, the bishop, and his counselors did not have the courtesy to ask me about those occurrences in prayer sessions across the country. My ordeal in Gaborone Diocese, in my opinion, played into the historical narrative of how the hierarchy, clergy, and people in the pew are reckless, critical and condemnatory of what they do not understand. I contend that if the hierarchical and clerical arm of the Church had a good understanding of charismatic spirituality, it would prevent the anti-charismatic tendencies that cause the seeming death of *charisms* that we experience in our Church today. It was this nonchalant and the 'holier-than-thou' attitude among the hierarchy and the clergy that caused my painful withdrawal from Botswana, thereby depriving the people of the blessing and the use of my *charisms*.

When this chapter in my ministry came to a sad end, I decided to learn more about charism and the ministration of the Holy Spirit. My quest led me to search the history of Christian spirituality. I found different spiritualties; I did not find anything on charismatic spirituality. I wondered why a Church that professes faith in the Holy Spirit as "the Lord, the giver of life,"[914] established on Pentecost Day[915] and founded on Pentecostal and charismatic spirituality does not have a Pentecostal or charismatic spirituality. After many years of search, I discovered that the *charisms* are the Church's heritage. I think it is time to incorporate charismatic spirituality into the academic curriculum of the seminaries. It will help ministers in the Church to enrich and give historical and theological understanding to their experience of baptism in the Holy Spirit if they have had one. Furthermore, a grounded study in charismatic spirituality will help priests properly discern the different manifestations of the *charisms* among their parishioners. It will also assist them in having a doctrinal appreciation of what is operative in the lives of those who readily use their gifts.

(f) *Expectant Spirituality*

The early Christians learned to be expectant of the *charisms*. In the early Church on the night of Christian initiation, converts were excited and hopeful of what God was going to do in their lives through the transformational empowerment of the Holy Spirit. Tertullian encouraged the neophytes as they came up from the water to raise their hands and pray with insistence that they may receive the special part of the inheritance, the bounty of *charisms*, which was normal.[916] I believe that if candidates for the sacraments of initiation are taught to expect the *charisms* at the baptism or confirmation, they will receive the gifts. I have first-hand experience of preparing some candidates for Confirmation in the Diocese of Gaborone in Botswana in 1997. I taught them to expect the experience of the Holy Spirit in a tangible way when the bishop anointed them and said, "receive the Holy Spirit." It happened that they were all filled with inexpressible joy and some of them spoke in tongues. The experience of the first disciples on the day of Pentecost was the usual experience of all believers in the early Church. All believers should be taught and prepared to seek a similar experience sincerely.

4.10 *Conclusion*

We have explored why and how the manifest *charisms* in the early Church disappeared. Also, we studied how the *charisms* can be recovered and restored. I think it is now incumbent on the Church leadership to review the relevance of the *charisms* in the Church today and reestablish the *charisms* as fundamental to the Church's well-being and for the good of the world.

---

[914] John Paul II, *Dominum et Vivicantem: Encyclical Letter – On The Holy Spirit in the Life of the Church and the World*. (Rome: Pontifical Vatican Press 1986), 3.

[915] Ibid., 26.

[916] McDonnell and Montague, *Christian Initiation and Baptism in the Holy Spirit*, 114.

Chapter Five

Work Yet to Be Done

———————— ❧ ————————

This study is not exhaustive; in the sense that it has not covered everything we need to know about *charisms* as manifested in the early Church, Pentecostal, and Charismatic Churches today. It does not claim to be all-encompassing in its coverage of the ramifications of the *charisms* with reference to 1 Corinthians 12:8-11 and Romans 12:6-8. As already stated in chapter 4, the inspiration behind my pursuit of the study on *charisms* was to find out whether the manifestations and use of charismatic gifts in the early church are congruent with the phenomena I experienced in my ministry as a priest. Consequently, this study focused on *charisms* as manifested in the early Church, why and how the tradition of the use of the *charisms* seemed to have disappeared and how it could be restored, because, in my opinion, the world craves for an experiential spirituality today.

However, this book did not consider the following: (a) the theological understanding or the worldview of the people at a time, and how that affects openness to the *charisms*. Does one's socio-religious orientation influence one's disposition to receive the *charisms*? (b) How does a person know he or she has *charisms*? Are there physical signs to identify different *charisms*? (c) What are the concrete ways the *charisms* can be applied in a structured Church today? (d) In implementing the *charism* of prophecy there has to be an ongoing evolutionary understanding of God's word and God. (e) What are the significance and implication in the life of the recipient of the phenomena of resting in the Spirit? (f) Are the *charisms* limited to what has manifested in the Scriptures alone or can there be new charisms to deal with the sophistication of our scientific generation?

5.1 *Worldview and Charisms*

I am of the opinion that when anyone goes through the process of baptism in the Holy Spirit, his or her *charisms* are activated. Nevertheless, everyone does not experience or manifest the same *charism* equally. Since everything we know and perceive comes to us through our senses, we can begin to discern if we have *charisms* when we become observant to our sensory organs. Different bodily sensations reveal different charismatic gifts. As many as there are people who go through the process so do, the experiences differ. Are there concrete ways the charismatic gifts can be discovered? I know from giving conferences and through praying with people and discerning, through series of questions on what happened during praying over people, that it is possible to know one's *charisms*. (i) Some of the gifts are discernible through the experience of physical signs during and after prayer sessions. The sweaty or soothing sensation on the palms reveals gift of healing. The experience of electroshock sensation through the body shows power, a gift of miracles. (ii) The gift of knowledge can be revealed in different ways. Knowledge here is not an intellectual knowledge but the revelation of what God is doing in the life of a person or people. Knowledge comes through dreams, visions, intuition or innate and assurance of things that have not manifested physically. (iii) For those with the gifts of intercession/counseling, people always ask them for prayers or advice. I think the above and more could also enhance this area of study.

5.2 *Concrete Ways to Apply the Charisms in the Church.*

The Catholic Church has been in a process of structural evolution for the past 2000 years. However, she has an enduring liturgical structure. Since the dissertation proposed how to retrieve and restore the *charisms*, what are the concrete ways members with charismatic gifts can serve in the Church?

5.3 *An Ongoing Theological Development of Understanding of the Idea of God.*

In the exercise of *charisms*, people are inspired to speak for God in charismatic meetings or conferences. We know that God does not change, but our understanding of God has continued to evolve and improve. We are aware today that God is the God of all nations and all religions. However, since messages come to people who are open to the Holy Spirit, what if a person has an erroneous view of God? The message will be distorted since every message that a prophet receives is presented from the messenger's mode of understanding of God. For example, there are prophetic-charismatic ministers in different religious groups who claim to have the *charisms*, and they look believable, but their messages are not consistent with what we know of God today. Consequently, prophetic words are discernible if they are about love, forgiveness, mercy, and unity and not about war, destruction of other races or people's religions. There can also be an examination of the relationship between what is known of God and the prophetic messages from God in this study.

5.4 *The Phenomenon of Resting in the Spirit*

A study of the manifestations and use of charismatic gifts in the early Church, Pentecostal and charismatic Churches today show that 'resting in the Spirit' is a common phenomenon. However, its meaning and significance are still ambiguous and scary. I know that different people have varied experiences that are beneficial. What are the consequences of people who yield to the power of God by resting in the Spirit?

5.5 *Are the Charisms Limited to what was Manifested in the Scriptures Alone?*

Can there be *charisms* suitable for each period, locality, or Church? I am of the opinion that everything will depend on the formation and openness of people to let God be God. All through history God inspires and empowers people with *charisms* to minister to the needs of the period. I think in a Globalized world like ours there should be *charisms* that break through the barriers of ethnic-religious backgrounds to ministering to people. An examination of the possibility of new *charisms* may expose us to the unlimited power of God to reach out to a convoluted world. We never can tell what happens when we explore the depths of God.

5.6 *The Art of Discernment in the Seminaries*

Pope Francis urged that discernment should be studied in the seminaries. A further study of how baptism of the Holy Spirit can help seminarians learn the spiritual art of discernment can broaden the scope of this study. Furthermore, what are the ramifications of the *charisms* being shared by ministers in the peripheries as suggested by Pope Francis? I believe that a study of how people on the margins of society open up to the charismatic gifts will further give credence to the idea of God's gratuitousness on everyone who is disposed to receive from God.

5.7 *Conclusion*

Nobody can predict or totally comprehend God or the workings of God in the universe. From the beginning of creation, God has demonstrated His majesty and omnipotence through various ways to bless the world. The earth as we know it is still unfolding. God uses human beings, elements, and *charisms* to invite God's people to participate in the work of evolving creation. However, in our context of looking at the *charisms* as tools for blessing, we fall short. As finite human beings, we are only exposed to a small part of God's infinite possessions, the manifestations and use of the charismatic gifts. Whatever gifts we have are from God's gratuitousness to us and we should apply them in continued gratitude for service. Our effectiveness in whatever we do depends on our openness to allowing God to use us for God's work.

Resources and Bibliography

Abbott-Smith, G. (1977). *A Manual Greek Lexicon of the New Testament*. Edinburgh: T&T Clark.

Aland, B., Aland, K., Karavidopoulos, J., Martini, M. C., and Metzger, B. (Eds). (2014). *The Greek New Testament*. (Fifth Revised Edition). Deutsche Bibel Gesellschaft, American Bible Society, United Bible Society.

Aland, K. (1972). *Synopsis of the Four Gospels: Greek-English Edition of the Synopsis Quattuor Evangeliorum with the Text of the Revised Standard Version*. Stuttgart: United Bible Societies.

Aridas, C. & Boucher, J. (1990). *Bringing Prayer Meetings to Life*. Pecos, New Mexico: Dove Publications.

Aumann, J. (1985). *Christian Spirituality in Catholic Tradition*. San Francisco: Ignatius Press.

Barton, J. & Muddiman, J. (Eds.). (2000). *The Oxford Bible Commentary*. New York: Oxford University Press.

Bauer, W. (1979). *A Greek-English Lexicon of the New Testament and Other Early Christian Literature*, 2nd ed., trans. Arndt, W. F. and F. W. Gingrich, Chicago/London: The University of Chicago Press.

Beker, J. C. (1980). *Paul the Apostle: The Triumph of God in Life and Thought*. Minneapolis: Fortress Press.

Bercot, D. W. (1998). *A Dictionary of Early Christian Beliefs: A Reference Guide to More than 700 Topics Discussed by the Early Church Fathers*. Peabody Massachusetts: Hendrickson Publishers.

Black, M. (1954). *An Aramaic Approach to the Gospels and Acts* (2nd Edition ed.). Oxford: Oxford at the Clarendon Press.

Boadt, L. (1984). *Reading the Old Testament: An Introduction*. New York, N.Y/Mahwah, N.J: Paulist Press.

Bokenkotter, T. (2005). *A Concise History of the Catholic Church*. New York, London, Toronto, Sydney, Auckland: Image Books Doubleday.

Boucher, J. & Boucher, T. (2004). *An Introduction to the Catholic Charismatic Renewal*. Cincinnati: St Anthony Messenger Press.

Brown, C. (Ed). (1986). *The New International Dictionary of New Testament Theology* (English language ed.). Grand Rapids, Michigan: Zondervan and Exeter, Devon, U.K: The Paternoster Press Ltd.

Brown, E. R., S. S., Fitzmyer, A. J., S.J., & Murphy, E. R., O.CARM. (Eds). (1990). *The New Jerome Biblical Commentary*. Upper Saddle River, New Jersey: Prentice Hall.

Bullinger, W. E. (1999). *A Critical Lexicon and Concordance to the English and Greek New Testament*. Grand Rapids, MI: Kregel Publications.

Burgess, M. S. (2011). *Christian Peoples of the Spirit: A Documentary History of Pentecostal Spirituality from the Early Church to the Present*. New York and London: New York University Press.

Burns, P. J. & Fagin, M. G. (2002). *The Holy Spirit*. Eugene, Oregon: Wipf & Stock Publishers.

Cantalamessa, R. (2005). *Sober Intoxication of the Spirit: Filled With the Fullness of God* (Kindle Edition). Cincinnati, OH: Anthony Messenger Press. Retrieved from Amazon.com

Chamberlain, W. D. (1984). *An Exegetical Grammar of the Greek New Testament*. Grand Rapids, MI: Baker Book House.

Christenson, L. (Ed.). (1987). *Welcome Holy Spirit: A Study of Charismatic Renewal in the Church*. Minneapolis: Augsburg Publishing House.

Clark, R. (2007). *There is More! Reclaiming the Power of Impartation*. Mechanicsburg, PA: Global Awakening.

Clark, R. (2005). *The Essential Guide to the Power of the Holy Spirit* (Kindle Edition). Shippensburg, PA: Destiny Image Publishers, Inc. Retrieved from Amazon.com

Clark, B. S. (2004). *Charismatic Spirituality: The Work of the Holy Spirit in Scripture and Practice*. Cincinnati, Ohio: Servant Books.

Clement, O. (2000). *On Human Being: Spirituality Anthropology*. London, New York, Manila: New City Press.

Collins, F.R. (Ed.). (1995). *First Corinthians*. Minnesota: The Liturgical Press.

Congar, Y. (2006). *I believe in the Holy Spirit: The Complete Three-Volume Work in One Volume*. New York: A Herder & Herder Book.

Cunningham, S. L. & Egan, J. K. (1996). *Christian Spirituality: Themes from the Tradition*. New York, Mahwah, N.J: Paulist Press.

Cremer, H. (1977). *Biblico-Theological Lexicon of New Testament Greek*. Edinburgh: T&T Clark.

Csordas, J. T. (2001). *Contemporary Anthropology of Religion: Language, Charisma, and Creativity, Ritual Life in the Catholic Charismatic Renewal*. New York: Palgrave, Macmillan.

Declan, M., and Mary, E. H. (Eds). (2007). *The Cambridge Companion to Karl Rahner.* Cambridge: Cambridge University Press.

Doles, J. (2008). *Miracles & Manifestations of the Holy Spirit in the History of the Church* (Kindle Edition). Seffner, FL: Walking Barefoot Ministries. Retrieved from Amazon.com

Donnelly, D. (Ed.). (1999). *Retrieving Charisms for the Twenty-First Century.* Collegeville, Minnesota: The Liturgical Press.

Downey, M. (Ed.). (1993). *The New Dictionary of Catholic Spirituality.* Collegeville, Minnesota: The Liturgical Press.

Dufour-Leon, X. (Ed) (1988). *Dictionary of Biblical Theology* (2nd ed.). Frederick, Maryland: The Word Among US Press.

Dunbar, E. E. (2009). *Teaching and Understanding Pnematology & Spiritual Gifts: Exegetes and Apologetes Emphatically on Leadership and Ministry, an Interdisciplinary Text* (Kindle Edition). Xlibris Corporation. Retrieved from Amazon.com

Dunn, D. G. J. (2010). *Baptism in the Holy Spirit: A Re-examination of the New Testament Teaching on the Gift of the Spirit in relation to Pentecostalism today* (Second Edition, Kindle Edition). SCM Press. Retrieved from Amazon.com

Durken, D. O.S.B. (Ed) (2009). *The New Collegeville Bible Commentary: New Testament.* Collegeville, Minnesota: Liturgical Press.

Dreyer, E. (1990). *Manifestations of Grace.* Collegeville, Minnesota: The Liturgical Press.

Edwards, D. (2004). *Breath of Life: A Theology of the Creator Spirit.* Maryknoll, New York' Orbis Books.

Egan, D. H. (1991). *An Anthology of Christian Mysticism.* Collegeville, Minnesota: A Pueblo Book, The Liturgical Press.

Farmer, W. R. (Ed.). (1998). *The International Bible Commentary: A Catholic and Ecumenical Commentary for the Twenty-First Century*. Collegeville, Minnesota: The Liturgical Press.

Fitzyman, J. (2008). *First Corinthians: A New Translation with Introduction and Commentary*. New Haven University Press.

Flannery, A. (Ed.). (2004). *Vatican Council I: The Conciliar and Post Conciliar Documents*. New Revised Edition. Northport, NY: Costello Publication Company.

Gelpi, L. D. (1971). *Pentecostalism: A Theological Viewpoint*. New York/Paramus/ Toronto: Paulist Press.

Hahnenberg, P. E. (2003). *Ministries: A Relational Approach*. New York: A Herder & Herder Book, The Crossroad Publishing Company.

Hamell, J. P. (1968). *Handbook of Patrology: A concise, authoritative guide to the life and works of the Fathers of the Church*. New York: Alba House.

Hawthorne, F. G., Martin, P. R., & Reid, G. D., (Eds). (1993). *Dictionary of Paul and his Letters*. Downer Grove, Illinois: InterVarsity Press.

Hill, R. B. (1995). *Exploring Catholic Theology: God, Jesus, Church, and Sacraments. Mystic*. Connecticut: Twenty–Third Publications.

Hummel, C. E. (1993). *Fire in the Fireplace: Charismatic Renewal in the Nineties*. Downers Grove: Intervarsity Press.

Hyatt, L.E. (2002). *2000 Years of Charismatic Christianity: A 21st Century Look at Church History from a Pentecostal/Charismatic Perspective* (Kindle Edition). Charisma House, Lake Mary, Florida: A Strang Company. Retrieved from Amazon.com

Johnston, W. (1995). *Mystical Theology: The Science of Love*. Maryknoll, New York: Orbis Books.

Johnson, T. L. (1999). *The Writings of The New Testament: An Interpretation* (Revised Edition). Minneapolis, MN: Fortress Press

Karkkainen, V-M. (2002). *Pneumatology: The Holy Spirit in Ecumenical International, and Contextual Perspective*. Grand Rapids, Michigan: Baker Academic a division of Baker Publishing Group.

Kittel, G. & Friedrich, G. (Eds). (2006). *Theological Dictionary of the New Testament*. 10 vols. Grand Rapids, MI: Wm. B. Eerdmans Publishings.

Kydd, N.A.R. (2015). *Charismatic Gifts in the Early Church: The Gifts of the Spirit in the First 300 Years*. (eBook edition). Peabody, Massachusetts: Hendrickson Publishers Marketing, LLC.

Levison, R. J. (2009). *Filled with the Spirit*. Grand Rapids, Michigan/ Cambridge, U.K: William B. Eerdmans Publishing Company.

Liardon, R. (2006). *The Azusa Street Revival: When the Fire Fell, An In-Depth Look at the People, Teachings, and Lessons*. PA, Shippensburg: Destiny Image Publishers Inc.

Lohfink, G. (1999). *Does God Need the Church? Toward a Theology of the People of God*. Collegeville, Minnesota: The Liturgical Press, A Michael Glazier Book.

MacArthur, J.F. (1992). *Charismatic Chaos*. Grand Rapids, Michigan: Zondervan Publishing House, Academic and Professional Books.

MacNutt, F. (2006). *The Healing Reawakening: Reclaiming our Lost Inheritance* (Kindle Edition). Grand Rapids, Michigan: Chosen. Retrieved from Amazon.

MacNutt, F. (1977). *The Power to Heal* (Kindle Edition). Grand Rapids, Michigan: Notre Dame, Indiana: Ave Maria Press. Retrieved from Amazon.

MacNutt, F. (1999). *Healing* (Kindle Edition). Grand Rapids, Michigan: Notre Dame, Indiana: Ave Maria Press. Retrieved from Amazon.

Mansfield, P.T. (2016). *As a New Pentecost: The Dramatic Beginning of the Catholic Charismatic Renewal*. Phoenix, AZ: Amor Deus Publishing.

Martos, J. (2001). *Doors to the Sacred: A Historical Introduction to Sacraments in the Catholic Church*. Liguori, Missouri: Liguori/Triumph.

McDonnell, K. & Montague, T. G. (Eds.). (1991). *Fanning The Flame: What Does Baptism in the Holy Spirit Have to Do with Christian Initiation?* Collegeville, Minnesota: The Liturgical Press.

McDonnell, K. & Montague, T. G. (1994). *Christian Initiation and Baptism in the Holy Spirit: Evidence from the First Eight Centuries* (2nd ed.). Collegeville, Minnesota: The Liturgical Press.

McDonnell, K. (Ed.). (1989). *Open The Windows: The Popes and Charismatic Renewal.* South Bend, Indiana: Greenlawn Press.

McDonnell, K. (Ed.). (1980). *Presence, Power, Praise: Documents on the Charismatic Renewal.* Volume I – Continental, National, and Regional Documents, Numbers 1 to 37, 1960-1974. Collegeville, Minnesota: The Liturgical Press.

McDonnell, K. (Ed.). (1980). *Presence, Power, Praise: Documents on the Charismatic Renewal.* Volume II – Continental, National, and Regional Documents, Numbers 38 to 80, 1975-1979. Collegeville, Minnesota: The Liturgical Press.

McDonnell, K. (Ed.). (1980). *Presence, Power, Praise: Documents on the Charismatic Renewal.* Volume III – Continental, National, and Regional Documents, Numbers 1 to 11, 1973-1980. Collegeville, Minnesota: The Liturgical Press.

McGrath, E. A. (2011). *Christian Spirituality: An Introduction.* Malden, MA: Blackwell Publishing.

McKenzie, L. J. (Ed.). (1995). *Dictionary of the Bible.* (First Touchstone Edition). New York. London. Toronto. Sydney: A Touchstone Book. Published by Simon & Schuster.

Meeks, A.W. & Fitzgerald, T.J. (Eds). (2007). *The Writings of St. Paul; A Norton Critical Edition* (2nd ed). New York. London: W.W. Norton & Company, Inc.

Montague, T. G. (2008). *Holy Spirit: Make your Home in Me, Biblical Meditations on Receiving the Gift of the Spirit.* Maryland: The Word Among Us Press.

Montague, T. G. (2006). *The Holy Spirit: The Growth of a Biblical Tradition.* Eugene, Oregon: Wipf & Stock Publishers.

Mounce, D. W. (1993). *The Analytical Lexicon to the Greek New Testament: Zondervan Greek Reference Series*. Grand Rapids, Michigan: Zondervan.

Muhlen, H. (1978). *A Charismatic Theology: Initiation in the Spirit*. New York/Ramsey, NJ. Toronto: Burns & Oates. London/Paulist Press.

Njiru, K.P. (2002). *Charisms and the Holy Spirit's Activity in the Body of Christ: An Exegetical-Theological Study of 1 Corinthians 12,4-11 and Romans 12,6-8)*. Rome: Editrice Pontificia Universuta Gregoriana.

Nwachukwu, A. O. (2011). *Keeping Human Relationships Together: Self Guide to Healthy Living (Studies in Spiritual Psychology vis-à-vis Human Values)*, Bloomington, IN: iUniverse Publishers.

O'Collins, G. & Farrugia, E. G. (Eds.). (2000). *A Concise Dictionary of Theology*. New York/Mahwah, N.J.: Paulist Press.

O'Connor, D. E. (1971). *The Pentecostal Movement in the Catholic Church: The Definitive Study of A Dynamic Spiritual Rebirth From the Standpoint of Catholic Theology …Its Significance in Catholic Life and Thought Today*. Notre Dame, Indiana: Ave Maria Press.

Rahner, K. Morland, D. (Trans). (1983). *Theological Investigations: Vol. XVI Experience Of The Spirit: Source of Theology*. New York: Crossroad,

Ranaghan, D., & Ranaghan, V. (1969). *Catholic Pentecostals*. Paramus, N.J., New York, Toronto, Ont: Paulist Press Deus Books.

Rausch P.T. (2003). *Who is Jesus: An Introduction to Christology*. Collegeville, Minnesota: Liturgical Press, A Michael Glazier Book

Pelikan, J. (1975). *The Christian Tradition: A History of the Development of Doctrine, 1, The Emergence of the Catholic Tradition (100-600)*. Chicago and London: The University of Chicago Press.

Prusak, P. B. (2004). *The Church Unfinished: Ecclesiology through the Centuries*. New York/Mahwah/N.J.: Paulist Press.

Senior, D. & Collins, J. J. (Ed.). (2006). *The Catholic Study Bible*. Oxford: New York: Oxford UP.

Schaff, P. (Ed). & Dods, M., (Trans). (2013). *The Complete Works of Saint Augustine: The Confessions, On Grace and Free Will, The City of God, On Christian Doctrine, Expositions on the Book Of Psalms*, ...(Kindle Edition). Accessed October 26, 2016.

Schreck, A. (2013). *The Gift: Discovering the Holy Spirit in Catholic Tradition*. Brewster, Massachusetts: Paraclete Press.

Schreck, A. (1995). *Your Life in the Holy Spirit: What Every Catholic Needs to Know and Experience*. Ann Arbor, Michigan: Servant Publications.

Silva, M. (Ed). (2014). *New Dictionary of New Testament Theology And Exegesis* (2nd ed). Grand Rapids, Michigan: Zondervan

Stronstad, R. (2012). *The Charismatic Theology of St. Luke: Trajectories from the Old Testament to Luke-Acts*. Grand Rapids, Michigan: Baker Academic, a division of Baker Publishing Group.

Suenens, C. L-J. (1987). *A Controversial Phenomenon: Resting in the Spirit*. Dublin: Veritas Publications.

Sullivan, A. F. (2004). *Charisms and Charismatic Renewal: A Biblical and Theological Study*. Eugene, Oregon: Wipf & Stock Publishers.

Synan, V. (1987). *The Twentieth-Century Pentecostal Explosion: The Exciting Growth of Pentecostal Churches and Charismatic Movements*. Altamonte Springs, Florida: Creation House.

Synan, V. (2001). *The Century of the Holy Spirit: 100 Years of Pentecostal and Charismatic Renewal*. Nashville: Thomas Nelson.

Teasdale, W. (1999). *The Mystic Heart: Discovering a Universal Spirituality in the World's Religions*. California: New World Library

Thayer, H. J. (2015). *Thayer's Greek-Lexicon of the New Testament: Coded with Strong's Concordance with Numbers*. Peabody, Massachusetts: Henrickson Publishers.

Thornton, J.F., and Washburn, K., (Eds). (1999). *The Times: Greatest Sermons of the Last 2000 Years, Tongues of Angels, Tongues of Men*. London: Harper Collins Publishers.

Wallace, B. D. (1996). *Greek Grammar Beyond the Basics: An Exegetical Syntax of the New Testament*. Grand Rapids, MI: Zondervan.

Walsh, V. M. (2000). *A Key to Charismatic Renewal in the Catholic Church*.

Wynnewood: Key of David Publications.

Wicks, R. J. (Ed.). (1998). *Handbook of Spirituality for Ministers* Vol. 1. New York and Mahwah: Paulist Press.

Woods, R. (1996). *Christian Spirituality: God's Presence Through the Ages*. Allen, Texas: Thomas More Publishing.

Gingrich Greek Lexicon, (2006) 159, in BibleWorks 7, available from CD-rom, Norfolk, VA: BibleWorks, LLC.

Baptism in the Holy Spirit: International Catholic Charismatic Renewal Services Doctrinal Commission (2012). Vatican City: Palazzo San Calisto.

United States Catholic Bishop Conference. (1994). *Catechism of the Catholic Church*. New York: Catholic Book Publication Co.

John Paul II. (1986). *Dominum et Vivificantem. Encyclical Letter on the Holy Spirit in the Life of the Church and the World*. Rome: Pontifical Vatican Press.

C.D. Stampley Enterprises, INC. (1970). *The New World Dictionary-Concordance to the New American Bible*. World Bible Publishers.

United States Catholic Bishops Conference. (1985). *A Pastoral Statement on the Catholic Charismatic Renewal: A Statement of the Bishop's Liaison Committee with the Catholic Charismatic Renewal*. Washington, D.C.

United States Catholic Bishops Conference, confirmed by the Apostolic See. (2011). *The Roman Missal*, (2011). English Translation According to the Third Edition. (Libretrice Vaticana, Vatican City State.

The Holy Bible. (2002). *Revised Standard Version* (Kindle Edition, Second Catholic Edition). Retrieved from Amazon. San Francisco: Ignatius Press.

http://www.christusrex.org/www1/ofm/mag/TSmgenB1.html (Accessed March 28, 2016).

http://www.lloydthomas.org/3-HolySpiritStudies/OTthink.html (Accessed March 28, 2016).

http://www.catholic.sk/main.php?page=183-en-Rite_of_Baptism (Accessed March 28, 2016).

http://www.catholic.org/prayers/prayer.php?p=332 Accessed March 28, 2016.

http://catholic-resources.org/Bible/LukeActs-Spirit.htm (Accessed March 28, 2016).

http://digitalcommons.pepperdine.edu/cgi/viewcontent.cgi?article=1393&context=leaven Accessed (March 28, 2016).

http://enrichmentjournal.ag.org/top/Holy_Spirit/200611.cfm (Accessed April 1, 2016).

www.padfield.com/acrobat/history/corinth.pdf (Accessed April 1, 2016).

https://www.stthomas.edu/.../johnaryaninstitute/ (Accessed April 1, 2016).

http://totus2us.com/teaching/jpii-catechesis-on-god-the-holy-spirit/the-meaning-of-spirit-in-the-old-testament/ (Accessed April 1, 2016).

http://danwebs.com/ruah/2NaturRuah&WritingsJPII.html (Accessed April 1, 2016).

http://www.hebrew4christians.com/Names_of_G-d/Spirit_of_God/Printer_Version/printer_version.html (Accessed April 1, 2016).

http://thinktheology.org/2013/11/27/pneuma-spirit-marks-gospel/ (Accessed April 15, 2016).

http://catholic-resources.org/John/Themes-Spirit.htm (Accessed April 22, 2016).

http://www.perspectivedigest.org/article/130/archives/19-2/the-holy-spirit-in-the-general-epistles-and-the-book-of-hebrews (Accessed April 22, 2016).

https://www.adventistbiblicalresearch.org/materials/holy-spirit/holy-spirit-revelation (Accessed April 22, 2016).

http://www.catholiceducation.org/en/culture/catholic contributions/the-holy-spirit-lord-and-giver-of-life.html Accessed May 5, 2016.

http://www.biblicaltheology.com/Research/OlagunjuO02.pdf (Accessed on August 8, 2016).

http://www.theopedia.com/tertullian (Accessed September 21, 2016).

https://www.britannica.com/biography/Tertullian (Accessed September 27, 2016).

http://www.newadvent.org/cathen/12040a.htm (Accessed October 6, 2016).

https://www.britannica.com/biography/Philoxenus-of-Mabbug (Accessed October 6, 2016).

http://vatican2voice.org/91docs/convoke.htm Accessed Nov. 2, 2016.

http://www.resurrectionparish.ca/files/docs/Papal_Quotes.pdf (Accessed Nov. 3, 2016).

http://www.americamagazine.org/issue/5153/article/new-pentecost (Accessed November 12, 2016).

http://www.nsc-chariscenter.org/article/what-we-have-seen-and-heard/ (Accessed November 2, 2016.

https://w2.vatican.va/content/benedict-xvi/en/speeches/2008/october/documents/hf_ben-xvi_spe_20081031_carismatici.html (Accessed November 11, 2016).

http://w2.vatican.va/content/francesco/en/speeches/2015/july/documents/papa-francesco_20150703_movimento-rinnovamento-spirito.html (Accessed November 11, 2016).

http://www.aecrc.org/documents/aecstatement_ccr.pdf (Accessed November 15, 2016).